THE LANGUAGE OF
HISTORY
IN THE
RENAISSANCE

THE LANGUAGE OF

HISTORY

IN THE

RENAISSANCE

RHETORIC AND HISTORICAL
CONSCIOUSNESS IN
FLORENTINE
HUMANISM

BY

NANCY S. STRUEVER

PRINCETON, NEW JERSEY

PRINCETON UNIVERSITY PRESS

1970

*Publication of this book has been aided by
grants from the Whitney Darrow Publication
Reserve Fund of Princeton University Press
& Hobart and William Smith Colleges.*

This book has been composed in
Linotype Electra

Printed in the United States
of America by Princeton University Press
Princeton, New Jersey

TO

F. Edward Cranz

ACKNOWLEDGMENTS

I WISH to thank the American Association of University Women for the Fellowship which enabled me to read in Florence in 1963, and the American Philosophical Society for a grant for summer study in 1967. I should also like to thank my learned acquaintance for their conversation and criticisms; the intellectual vitality of my thesis advisers, Hayden V. White and Marvin Becker, still provides my exemplar of the essential scholarly virtue. My greatest debt, however, is to F. Edward Cranz, who was my first teacher at Connecticut College years ago, and the last patient, erudite reader of my manuscript. Both Professor Cranz and Professor Gene Wise of Case-Western Reserve have kindly allowed me to cite their unpublished papers. I wish also to thank Harvard University Press for permission to quote the Loeb Classical Editions, and the Éditions du Seuil of Paris for permission to use in my Introduction the quotation from Roland Barthes, which appears on page 45 of the 1966 edition of *Critique et Vérité*.

NANCY S. STRUEVER
Hobart & William Smith Colleges

CONTENTS

THE LANGUAGE OF
HISTORY
IN THE
RENAISSANCE

INTRODUCTION

RIEN N'EST PLUS ESSENTIEL À UNE SOCIÉTÉ QUE LE *classement*
DE SES LANGAGES. CHANGER CE CLASSEMENT, DÉPLACER LA
PAROLE, C'EST FAIRE UNE RÉVOLUTION.

Roland Barthes, *Critique et Vérité*

EVERY philosophy of history contains a philosophy of
language; every historical insight implies a notion of the
language of the protagonist or document in question as well
as of the language of the historian himself. Language theories
and techniques have great resonance in historical theory and
practice: the structure of language relates to the structure of
knowledge and thus to the definition of historical reality,
while linguistic competence may develop a psychology of
performance, a focus on the relation of ideas and action. In
the historians' training, all language disciplines have priority;
a change in discipline dictates change in historical priorities.

This study uses a recent change in fashion to illuminate
the major change in attitudes toward language and history
which Renaissance Humanism represents: the rehabilitation
of the Sophists which finds its source in Nietzsche entails a
rehabilitation of rhetoric as the historical vehicle of Sophistic
insight. The aim, however, is to present rhetoric not as a
historical constant, but as a thread of possibility, a strand of
choice which the Humanists self-consciously exploited in the
web of assumption and motive which gives shape, density,
and strength to their historical consciousness and historiographical achievement.

3

ONE

THE BACKGROUND OF HUMANIST
HISTORICAL LANGUAGE:
The Quarrel of Philosophy and Rhetoric

IN ORDER to write a history of the relations between rhetoric and history, it is necessary to grasp the triangular relationship of history, rhetoric, and philosophy, for the tension between philosophy and rhetoric dominates and gives shape to the rhetorical tradition; the quarrel of philosophy and rhetoric provides dynamic and direction in classical learning.[1] This quarrel even antedates the arrival of the first teachers of rhetoric in Athens; the deep distrust of the philosophers for the rhetors is grounded in their awareness of the connection between rhetoric and the Sophists. Socrates in the *Theaetetus* contrasts the free philosopher, liberally educated, with the rhetorically trained advocate, "a servant. . .

[1] P. Boyancé, "La rhétorique dans l'humanisme latin," *IL*, 2 (1950), p. 19. A fundamental study of rhetoric is that of W. Kroll, in Pauly-Wissowa, *Realencyclopaedie der classischen Altertumswissenschaft*, Supplementband 7, Stuttgart, 1940; see also R. Volkmann, *Die Rhetorik der Griechen und Romer*, Berlin, 1872; A. Plebe, *Breve storia della retorica antica*, Milan, 1961; H. Lausberg, *Handbuch der literarischen Rhetorik*, 2 vols., Munich, 1961. H.I. Marrou, *A History of Education in Antiquity*, trans. G. Lamb, London, 1956, and W. Jaeger, *Paideia; The Ideals of Greek Culture*, trans. G. Highet, 3 vols., Oxford, 1939-45, place rhetoric in its educational and cultural ambiance. Two modern analytic treatments are K. Burke, *A Rhetoric of Motives*, New York, 1950, and Ch. Perelman and L. Olbrechts-Tyteca, *Traité de l'argumentation; La nouvelle rhétorique*, 2 vols., Paris, 1958; but see also B. Munteano, "Des 'constantes' en litterature; Principes et structures rhétoriques," *RLC*, 31 (1957), pp. 388-420, and "Humanisme et rhétorique; La survie littéraire des rhéteurs anciens," *RHL*, 58 (1959), pp. 145-56.

5

continually disputing about a fellow-servant before his master" (172D). For Socrates the central error of both Sophists and rhetoricians is their obedience to intermediate and relative, rather than final and absolute ends. This error in turn has its source in a false ontology: the rhetors were followers of Heraclitus and Protagoras in so far as they conceived the cosmos as flux and man as the measure of all things. Socrates attacked them as part of a heterodox, a separatist movement in Greek thought. In the *Gorgias* Plato gives systematic expression to the Socratic exaltation of the philosopher over the rhetor: while the philosopher, he argues, is concerned with the sphere of the Eternally True which can be apprehended only through the operations of reason, the rhetors' only possible sphere of effectiveness is the realm of the probable (*eikos*) perceived through the senses and structured by *phantasia* and *mimesis*.

This contrast of priorities defined the debate in the history of classical philosophy long after Plato, and its radical separation of Reality and Appearance was reinforced by much of late classical and medieval theology—Neoplatonic, Gnostic, or Christian. Thus the history of rhetoric from the Socratic period to the Renaissance can be regarded as an unequal contest in which the metaphysical claims of the philosophers and theologians continually modify the rhetorical counterclaims rooted in Sophistic assumptions. The theory and structure of spoken and written discourse reflect the changing tensions between rhetorical exigencies and philosophical or theological axioms; at every crucial change in the temper of the Western intellectual tradition a new resolution of these conflicting demands alters the configurations of linguistics, literature, and pedagogy.

This quarrel of philosophy and rhetoric obviously has important repercussions in the theory and practice of history. In order to assess the effects of this tension, however, it is first necessary to establish the external analogues in the careers of rhetoric and historiography. For even on the surface the fortunes of rhetoric and history coincide: both alternate between stages where they played a vital part in a dynamic

6

political situation and those where they were relegated to the schoolroom and the study. Thus rhetoric achieved its status as a profession in the active political and juristic atmosphere of fifth century Sicily after the fall of the tyrants; and it declined as the Greek polis decayed, forensic and judicial oratory becoming increasingly irrelevant means to the realization of public alternatives. History also flourished in Greece both during the period of vitality of the polis and during its earliest period of decline when political issues were still debated with vigor and relevance; but the hardening of the political arteries afflicted history as well.

This cycle is repeated in Rome and Renaissance Italy. Polybius, Sallust, and Tacitus; the Villanis, Bruni, and Machiavelli, are all partisans of genuine debate. There is an even more exact parallel of circumstance; the onset of serious rhetorical interest coincides in all three cases with the beginning of a still hidden but genuine political decline; the concern with rhetoric is part of a destructive self-consciousness which extends to the consciousness of the past in historiography as well as to contemporaneous political and educational roles. In fulfillment of Hegel's dictum that the owl of Minerva takes its flight at dusk, the great historians—Thucydides, Tacitus, Machiavelli—all share the bitterness of describing past ideals in the crepuscular light of the declining years of once vigorous polities which had nourished these ideals.

The main theme of this survey, however, is to show internal as well as external similarities between the career of rhetoric and that of history, and to demonstrate how these similarities reflect very basic relationships between the concept of language and the concept of history. If the tension between philosophy and rhetoric is the dynamic of the history of language theory in antiquity, the history of Greek historiography can be resolved into three dialectical stages. In the first stage, broad and undifferentiated aesthetic and philosophical purposes dominate Ionic *historia*. There is a second stage of "classical" definition in the fifth and fourth centuries in which both the rhetorical and historical disciplines become distinguished by a cluster of characteristics which are *in part* the characteristics of modern "historicism": there is a commitment to confront and to extract meaning, i.e. wide and prescriptive human significance, from the flux of events of discourse and action. In the third stage, aesthetic and metaphysical ends (philosophically or theologically defined) again dominate historiography, but in a synthesis which absorbs many of the aims and techniques of the second period. In the Roman development, the three stages again appear, but in a vastly compressed or confused order.

First, then, the problem of artistic form in historiography antedates any imposition of specifically rhetorical form; the historian's preoccupation with aesthetics is rooted in the very ground of all his investigations. Next, the development of rhetoric, as a self-conscious effort at control of aesthetic means and purposes based on the recognition of the instability of the language and action with which it deals, impinges on historiography as a movement which recognizes autonomy of expression and significance. Again style is related to the order of things, but here the primary focus is on the style and order which are human creations. When in the final period the conflict between philosophy and rhetoric grows stale, and the real opportunities for political activity dwindle, the discussion of historical method and literary style exhausts itself in the confusion of philosophical and rhetorical aims, as well as in the eccentricity of Mannerist virtuosity. In a sense the last stage endures through the Middle Ages, for history does not free itself from the difficulties of the Hellenistic Age till the Renaissance, which, like the fifth century, is a ferment of self-conscious exploration of art and epistemology.[2]

To understand the first stage of this development one must

[2] There is no general survey of the relation of literary style to historiography in the classical and medieval periods, but see E. Norden, *Die Antike Kunstprosa vom VI. Jahrhundert v. Chr. bis in die Zeit der Renaissance*, 2 vols., ph. rep. Stuttgart, 1958. H. Peter, *Wahrheit und Kunst; Geschichtschreibung und Plagiat im klassischen Altertum*, Leipzig, 1911, discusses the subject from the particular angle of the changing concept of truth.

understand how the notion of form and the metaphor of unity dominate early Greek art and history: it is necessary to describe the peculiar epistemological status of form in Greek thought as well as the inextricability of the different strands of history, philosophy, fable, and poetry in the web of pre-Socratic intellectual achievement. Here all forms of verbal discourse reflect forms of mental discourse; thus most figures of speech are based on categories of antithesis and contradiction, parallelism and analogy, dichotomy and wholeness which are fundamental to the growth of dialectic as well as stylistic. Moreover, for the Greeks all investigation presupposes the existence of a covering law, the model of a single absolute order. The primary canon of all mental structuring is unity, whether it is of Being as in Parmenides, of process and paradox as in Heraclitus, or of structure itself as in Pythagoras.

To Herodotus, unity is almost arithmetically achieved; the search for meaning and form is understood as a process of compilation. Just as history is defined as a treasury of all types of knowledge, so Herodotus' style is a compendium of all significant extant styles: the early Attic oratorical eloquence of his speeches; the heightened poetic diction of the epic and the Ionic *logos* for the fables; the concise lucidity of the notes (*hypomnemata*) of the Ionian scientists for the geographical and ethnographical fabric. A nineteenth-century formulation, the Dionysian-Apollonian paradigm of Nietzsche, illumines Herodotus' dedication to stylistic concerns as well as factual completeness; according to Nietzsche, beauty is of ultimate significance to the early Greeks as the experience of the profound, and thus Herodotus' search for artistic unity becomes an expression of the "seriousness" of his investigation.[3] Yet unity of form and content is achieved in Herodotus' history by aggregation and juxtaposition; his

[3] On the early period of Greek prose see W. Aly, *Formprobleme der frühen griechischen Prosa*, *Philologus*, Supplementband 21, Heft 3, Leipzig, 1929; see also F. Jacoby, "Herodotos," in *Griechische Historiker* [a collection of his articles from P-W], Stuttgart, 1956, pp. 7-164.

historical virtues are those of inclusiveness, not of definition, his method generous, rather than autarchic.

It is the Sophists who take the crucial step in the development of the relation of what Eduard Norden calls "artistic prose" to history. The Sophistic age produced many refinements of self-awareness within rhetoric, history, tragedy, and philosophy; in part these reflect the Sophists' sharp delineation of and concentration on the sphere of the human as opposed to the metaphysical. Quite simply, the early Sophists decide to deal with the impure: to shun the ideal sphere where pure reason and perfect justice reside for the shifting and uncertain field of action and discourse. In effect, they issue a series of Self-Denying Ordinances in their axiomatic statements. These ordinances assert that only a world of flux and impurity exists, and that a mental operation cannot be divorced from this disorderly matrix. The desire for purity of thought and communication is a delusion, and even the force of logic is a form of violence (*bia*) mediated through the passions. Sophistic thought denies any stability except the stability of the relationships which it creates. The Sophists' tone can be that of relativism or humanism, subjectivism or individualism, pragmatism or expediency; their anthropocentricism sets up a tension never satisfactorily resolved in Greek thought; even in Plato and Aristotle one finds substantive dichotomies mechanically built up only to be mechanically bridged in a system which emphasizes one aspect of the dichotomy at the expense of the other.[4]

[4] C. Ramnoux, in his article "Nouvelle réhabilitation des Sophistes," *RMM*, 73 (1968), pp. 1-15, sees a book such as Mario Untersteiner's *The Sophists*, trans. K. Freeman, Oxford, 1954, as a chapter in Nietzsche's project of an Anti-Plato. On the Sophists, besides Untersteiner, see H. von Arnim, the introduction to *Leben und Werke des Dio von Prusa*, Berlin, 1898, p. 4f.; H. Gomperz, *Sophistik und Rhetorik*, Leipzig, 1912; A. Rostagni, "Un nuovo capitolo nella storia della retorica e della sofistica," *Scritti minori*; *I, Aesthetica*, Turin, 1955, pp. 1-59; E. Dupréel, *Les Sophistes*, Neuchatel, 1948; R. Mondolfo, *La comprensione del soggeto umano nell'antichità classica*, Florence, 1958, esp. pp. 131-32, 158-69, 242-66; and M. Buccellato, "Sulla retorica sofistica," in *Studi di filosofia greca in onore di R. Mondolfo*, Bari, 1951, p. 183f.

Recent classical scholarship has substantially altered the traditional view of the relation of Sophistic to historiography; the tendency had been to notice only the relative, the expedient, the subjective in the Sophists and the rhetors (those who think Sophistically about discourse), and to see in rhetorical historiography only the exaltation of personal advantage or aesthetic ends over the "truth." But an increase in sophistication about the nature of history as well as the nature of Sophism has established the relationship as positive and fruitful. Using as paradigms Gorgias, who developed Sophistic language principles into a rhetorical *techne*, and Thucydides, who transformed contemporary linguistic insights into historical insights, it is possible to demonstrate how Gorgian rhetoric and the Sophistic ideal of political *arete* are more compatible with the purpose of historical investigation than Platonic philosophy and the Socratic concept of absolute justice.

First, then, the serious content, not just the perversions, of the rhetorical tradition must be defined. Gorgias' most fundamental contribution to rhetoric is his development of the relationship of the structure of language to the structure of mind.[5] His notions of language express the Sophistic anthropocentricism which continually affirms both the creativity and the uniqueness of humanity and thus gives, in one vital respect at least, a "historicist" bent to rhetoric. This anthropocentricism has an essentially tragic tone; the "tragic" problem of knowledge—that Being itself is unknowable—underlies the development of rhetoric. A realm of pure Being can neither be known nor communicated (DK 82 B3); the operations of pure reason touch upon our opinions and wills only through the ambivalent power of discourse (*logos*), a power which can be both rational and demonic. The aesthetic

[5] I have followed closely Untersteiner's discussion of the tragic problem of knowledge in Gorgias, *Sophists*, p. 118f. Besides the articles of Buccellato and Rostagni previously cited, see C.P. Segal, "Gorgias and the Psychology of the Logos," *HSPh*, 66 (1962), pp. 99-155. The Gorgian fragments are in Diels-Kranz, *Die Fragmente der Vorsokratiker*, Vol. 2, 10th ed., Berlin, 1960; I have used the translations of K. Freeman, *Ancilla to the Pre-Socratic Philosophers*, Oxford, 1956.

nature of this mediating power is rooted in both the early Greek presupposition of the ultimate significance of beauty and in the Sophistic notion of the human condition: man lives in a world which reflects the chance patterns of play, a world which must be subjected to a human order of measure or beauty in order to be understood or at least accepted. The aesthetic-formal emphasis in Gorgias relies upon an appeal to the ear through measure and rhythm and balance transposed into grammatical, conceptual, and auditory techniques. Stylistic has its epistemological basis in the axiom that meaning in human experience can only be apprehended and communicated aesthetically.[6]

Thus Gorgias, rejecting the pretensions of pure reason, holds that only the incantatory power of words can overcome subjectivism or solipsism; through measure in rhythm and sound the artists conveys measure or proportion in meaning according to patterns of thought which are primordial— the patterns of identity and antithesis—and therefore universally appealing. According to A. Rostagni, this is a Pythagorean concept which had its foundation in Pythagorean ontology; a thing is not a single pure essence but is a unity or harmony of contraries. The harmony which assigns identity is a product of the moment, the proper and fitting circumstance (*kairos*); for the rhetor the harmony of discourse is a result of his faculty of knowing and exploiting the kairotic, of his mastery of the appropriate (*to prepon*). Excellence is the product of dynamic relationships; to make a thing beautiful or unbeautiful, just or unjust, good or bad is both a human power and a sign of the insubstantiality of these attributes. Thus rhetoric is concerned with content as well as form; the rhetorical techniques of "finding" content (*heuresis*) deals in the probable (*eikos*), which has a prob-

---

[6] Untersteiner, *Sophists*, pp. 112-13. On the domination of the appeal to the ear in speech see K. Borinski, *Die Antike in Poetik und Kunsttheorie; I, Mittelalter, Renaissance, Barock*, Leipzig, 1914, p. 124; Burke, *Rhetoric of Motives*, pp. 54-55; the contrast of aural and visual culture has become a commonplace of Marshall McLuhan and his disciples. On the mediating power of language see Segal, "Gorgias," p. 113.

lematic relationship to the truth (*aletheia*). The problematic or unstable quality of language seems exhilarating to Gorgias: he is self-consciously playful about his *Praise* of Helen of Troy (DK 82 B11.21), and Gorgian rhetoric has many of the characteristics of a "language game," with all the emphasis on epistemological suppleness and versatility which the word "game" implies. Rhetoric defines a field of activity with limited, not absolute ends, a field set aside by the rules which relate to the control of emotional forces which are fundamentally unpredictable and perverse.[7]

Yet if rhetoric trains men to speak appropriately and well (*to eu legein*), it does this because it must fit into a social framework of specific human purposes; Plato defines rhetoric as the art of persuasion (*Gorgias*, 453A). If rhetorical psychology has its roots in the philosophy of Magna Graecia, rhetoric as the persuasive manipulation of the verisimilar begins with the Sicilian litigations of Corax and Tisias; in Athens Gorgias of Leontini perceived his educational mission as to teach the use of this demonic power of words to politically committed men who must persuade others to action or decision. Discourse (*logos*) through technique penetrates opinion (*doxa*), which directs the will. Since, according to Gorgias, men are incapable of recognizing the "pure" truth (*aletheia*) when they hear it spoken, the teaching of virtue is irrelevant; Gorgias tried to teach instead the means for arousing the passion for virtue. Rhetoric is *psychagogia*, "leading of the soul" (*Phaedrus*, 271D). Gorgias compared the power of words to that of drugs which could induce either health or sickness (DK 82 B11.14); to him, rhetoric

---

[7] Rostagni claims that for Gorgias *kairos* is not only a technical term in rhetoric but a key epistemological concept derived from the Pythagoreans: "quella arcana e magnifica dote del *kairos* che permette di far parere la medesima cosa, com'egli diceva, or grande or piccola, or bella or brutta, or nuova or vecchia." "Un nuovo capitolo," p. 25. Compare Plato, 272A; Isocrates, "Against the Sophists," 12, 13; Polybius, *Histories*, XII, 26, 5. On the problematic relation of language to things see Segal, "Gorgias," p. 144; "Gorgias . . . regards *logos* as a whole, as an entity in itself, independent of and in a sense above a literal correspondence with the *aletheia* of the phenomenal world." On language games, see L. Wittgenstein, *Philosophical Investigations*, Oxford, 1963.

was not immoral but amoral; yet he felt the humanistic preoccupations with broad experience and learning should incline the rhetor to the right, the humanly appropriate, action. He praised the Athenians for preferring a mild equity (*to praon epieikes*) to a harsh justice; to Gorgias political excellence has the same inner structure as rhetorical excellence: *epieikeia* as well as literary decorum (*to prepon*) is the product of an awareness of the right moment (*kairos*), the accompanying circumstances (DK 82 B6). Paradoxically, some of the strongest evidence for the seriousness of the rhetors' commitment to the public values of persuasion is to be found in the attacks on Gorgias and his followers in Plato's dialogues. For example, Socrates' accusation of Callicles, that "the love of the Demos dwells in his soul" and blinds him to the absolutes, is based on the assumption that Gorgias' disciples feel they are responding to the real political exigencies of the period (*Gorgias*, 513C).[8]

The rhetorical aim of persuasion, of speaking for "advantage," involves analysis of will and choice as well as the classification of general lines of argument (*koinoi topoi*). Gorgias was one of the first to study the responses of the psyche to the terrible power of language (DK 82 B11.8-14), to reduce these insights to a craft, and then commit this to a handbook (*Techne*). In this now lost book he emphasized

[8] Thus Plato allows Callicles this attack on the non-engagement of the philosophers: "For, as I said just now, such a man, even if he's well endowed by nature, must necessarily become unmanly by avoiding the center of the city and the assemblies, where as the Poet (Homer, II, 9, 441) says, 'men win distinction.' Such a fellow must spend the rest of his life skulking in corners, whispering with two or three little lads, never pronouncing any large, liberal, or meaningful utterance." *Gorgias* 485D, trans. W.C. Helmbold (New York, 1962) from the OCT text. With few exceptions, however, I have used the classical texts and translations of the Loeb editions.

For Untersteiner the connection between *kairos* and equity in Gorgias' thought is strict: "*kairos* with its power of decision 'persuades' that the individual deed which is presented is ἐπιεικές," *Sophists*, p. 178. See also Dupréel, *Sophistes*, p. 110f. for Gorgias as one of the "moralistes de l'occasion." The differentiation between teaching virtue and teaching the means by which the passion for virtue can be aroused was made by G. Rensi, *Figure di filosofi*, Naples, 1921, p. 71, and quoted by Untersteiner, *Sophists*, p. 182.

the improvising power of the rhetor, the creative responses
to concrete situations. His formal values are neither pure
artifice (new creation) nor pure ornament, but imply a sense
of the vertical and horizontal, genetic and structural continuity of language. The three essential characteristics of
rhetorical prose—the figures of speech, poetic diction, and
rhythm—are rooted in a long development reaching back to
the earliest examples of Greek literature: the heightened
diction of the *epos* can also be found in the Ionic fables, and
both rhythm and the figures serve to point up antitheses
and parallels in philosophers such as Heraclitus and Protagoras. And for Gorgias there is no divorce of art from dialectic; good language is both logical—internally coherent—and
enchanting.[9]

With Gorgias, then, rhetoric achieves the identity which
has proved such a problematic heritage for the West. Rhetoric functions as aesthetics, pragmatics, and psychology. Per-
spicaciously, Roland Barthes has characterized rhetoric as the
"august forbear" of contemporary Structuralism.[10] On the
one hand, rhetoric tries to deal with language as a whole;
it grapples with the problems of a metalanguage, with discourse about discourse. On the other hand, rhetoric is not
so much systematic in the philosophical sense as a mnemo-
technical system for making fruitful connections between
disparate insights,[11] and the principle which governs its
classification and analysis is accessibility. But accessibility
here means relevance to particular human performances,
not a congruence to a familiar but rigid ontological structure.

[9] Norden, *Kunstprosa*, pp. 16-41; pp. 50-74.
[10] "Structuralism has an august forbear whose historical role has
generally been underestimated or discredited for ideological reasons—
Rhetoric, that impressive attempt by a whole culture to analyze and
classify the forms of speech, and to make the world of language intelligible." R. Barthes, "Science vs. Literature," *TLS*, Sept. 28, 1967,
p. 897. Rhetoric also anticipates structuralism in the sense which H.
Lefebvre describes, in that "signes et sens n'ont aucune valeur absolue,
mais des valeurs positives, relatives, négatives"; *Le langage et la société*,
Paris, 1966, p. 85.
[11] The phrase is rather freely drawn from F. Kermode's description
of Northrop Frye's approach, *NYRB*, October 12, 1967.

For Gorgias, rhetoric is more than a compendium, it is a directional discipline; its *topoi* are more than storage bins, they are points of departure. Rhetoric achieves heteronomy; it receives a variety of types of statements about language and sets them in a fluid structure of dynamic interrelationships.

What, then, is the relation of the rhetorical view of language to a historical view of event? In Thucydides, it appears, this new mode of regarding problems of language and behavior marks an advance in historical consciousness as well. A cluster of four Sophistic attitudes or "mental sets"—attacked, modified, transformed—appears in the *Peloponnesian War*: a definite but chaste concern for the pragmatic value of artistic form; an emphasis on will and choice in the structure and content of history; the consciousness of the creativity of the historian in attributing meaning and form to events; and the conviction that the operations of discourse can never precisely parallel phenomenal reality: that language requires the utmost self-consciousness and sophistication in its handling.[12]

The idiosyncrasy of Thucydides' relationship to Sophistical rhetoric is in itself a measure of his grasp of the concept of *kairos*. He is isolated from and antipathetic to Sophistic, yet he chooses rhetorical techniques with great skill and he

---

[12] Aly is convinced that the difference between Herodotus and Thucydides—in both content and form—is to be found largely in the intervention of the Sophistic influence; the years 450-430 B.C. are the years of "die Generation, die geistig zwischen Herodot und Thukydides vermittelt" (*Formprobleme*, p. 70). Aly emphasizes the influence of Sophistic thought rather than of Gorgian figures; of pre-rhetorical spirit, rather than of rhetorical techniques (pp. 110-11). On the relationship of Thucydides' historical expression to the linguistic ambiance of his times see J. de Romilly, *Histoire et raison chez Thucydide*, Paris, 1956; J.H. Finley, Jr., *Three Essays on Thucydides*, Cambridge, Mass., 1967; A. Momigliano, "La composizione della storia di Tucidide," *Memoria della Reale Accademia della Scienze di Torino*, ser. 2, 67 (1930), pp. 1-48; W.R.M. Lamb, *Clio Enthroned, A Study of Prose-Form in Thucydides*, Cambridge, 1914; F.M. Cornford, *Thucydides Mythistoricus*, London, 1907. For a Hellenistic appraisal of Thucydides' style see Dionysius of Halicarnassus, *Saggio su Tucidide*, Greek text and Italian translation by G. Pavano, Palermo, 1956.

explores with profound insight and sympathy the relativistic attitudes derived from the Sophists which had permeated contemporary society. One must imitate Norden and apply Cicero's dictum—that masterpieces do not follow rules, but rules come from masterpieces (*De orat.*, I, 32, 146)—to Thucydides; Norden sees his style as an extraordinary mixture of the artless and the artful, with the result as artistic unity.[13] Like Herodotus, he aims at unity because he is serious, but where Herodotus seeks to amass significance through aggregation, Thucydides creates it through analysis. He communicates a sense of control, of working from a position of intellectual independence and power; in part this is a result of the steps he has taken towards an autonomous or self-critical, a "scientific" method of gathering evidence, but in part this is a sensibility to the active and independent, the autonomous power of language itself.

Both the form and the content of the speeches in his history express his affinities with rhetorical attitudes. Faced with the impossibility of communicating "what really was," Thucydides justifies his invention of speeches in much the manner of Gorgias justifying the myths of tragedy. Gorgias claims that the dramatist has created a deception (*apate*) "in which the deceiver is more honest than the non-deceiver, and the deceived is wiser than the non-deceived" (DK 82 B23). Thucydides explains that he has designed his speeches (which of course were never delivered as he wrote them), to reflect the imperfect record of what was said but also the demands of the circumstances which had surrounded their delivery and impelled a particular reaction (I, 22.1). His speeches are thus closer to reality—the ambiance of human action and opinion—than the necessarily faulty attempts at factual reporting. They also make the reader wiser, for what Thucydides communicates in them is not the operation of ideal justice or of innocence and guilt but of political *arete* and ineptitude in response to this ambiance. The kind of justice he finds in history and which he wishes his readers to

---

[13] *Kunstprosa*, pp. 95-101.

understand is very close to the equity of the Sophists; choice must be related to the interplay of will and circumstances he organizes in the chronology of his speeches.[14]

He brilliantly delineates the importance of the appropriate choice in his sketch of Themistocles, the leader whose essential traits were the profound appreciation and apt exploitation of circumstance (I, 138.3). Thucydides' characterization of Themistocles also points to the Gorgian distinction between the gifts of fortune and one's own personal competence, what the Renaissance Humanists will call *virtù*: the implied argument is that the orator should concentrate on that which is within the protagonist's competence, not that which is merely the result of chance or fortune (DK 82 B11.4).[15] In the Melian dialogue Thucydides asserts that Athenian political excellence is exactly a devotion to that which lies within human control (V, 103).

Further, rhetorical structure can be a source of historical insight and thus political competence; on the supposition that political topics are problematic, can be debated on both sides, Sophists such as Protagoras used the *antilogiai* as "tools for discussing and manipulating man's social environment."[16] Thucydides uses paired speeches to create historical distance: to set forth two points of view permits a third point of view to be derived from the conflict of the two motives. The reader of history transcends, goes beyond, the *agon*; the historian creates a distance in the lapsed time between political debate

[14] The translation of the Gorgian aphorism is Untersteiner's, *Sophists*, p. 113; Untersteiner very briefly compares Sophistic equity with Thucydidean political realism, pp. 323-24. A.W. Gomme, *A Historical Commentary on Thucydides*, 3 vols., Oxford, 1959, furnishes background for Thucydides' explanation of his speeches (I, 21-22) in Vol. 1, pp. 138-148. See also J. de Romilly, "L'utilité de l'histoire selon Thucydide," *Histoire et historiens dans l'Antiquité, Entretiens sur l'Antiquité classique*, 4, Vandoeuvres-Genève, 1956, p. 62.

[15] Rostagni, "Un nuovo capitolo," p. 52.

[16] Segal, "Gorgias," p. 134. See C. Corbato, *Sofisti e politica ad Atene durante la guerra del Peloponneso*, Trieste, 1958, for the complex relations between politics and language, particularly in the period 430-400 B.C.

and historical judgment. Thucydidean learning is historical on two levels: it pertains to the phenomenal world of flux and it takes place in time within the development of the learner's own identity. Antithesis was a major facet of the Sophists' hermeneutic, while Thucydides saw the historian's task as to *initiate* dialogue, particularly where dialogue in historical fact was obscure or even lacking.[17] Form in Thucydides' speeches conduces to this type of historical awareness; the balance and pointed emphasis of his rhythms and syntax reinforces the parallelism and acuity of his arguments in a manner analogous to Sicilian rhetoric. Finally, his extraordinary sensitivity to vocabulary is a historical consciousness of language itself. In his description of the semantic revolution which occurred during the Corcyrean rebellion he echoes Gorgias' sentiments on the instability and relativism of language (III, 82.4).[18]

Of course, Sophistic notions of language were not the only positive influence on Thucydides' achievement; the fruitfulness of the relationship between Greek science, for instance, and historical aims and methods has been discussed elsewhere.[19] Even the quarrel of philosophy and rhetoric which began in this same period had, at first, a beneficent effect on historiography. During the prolonged crisis of the polis in the late fifth and fourth centuries philosophers and rhetors, deeply engaged in finding solutions for their political quandaries, had enough vitality to absorb elements from each other's points of view; advances in linguistic de-

---

[17] See especially de Romilly, *Histoire et Raison*, chap. 3, "Les discours antithétiques," p. 180f.; also H. Arendt, *Between Past and Future*, New York, 1961, p. 51. Compare R. Mondolfo on the temporal dimension of knowledge in Aristotle's potentiality-actuality construct in *"Veritas filia temporis* in Aristotele," *Momenti del pensiero greco e cristiano*, Naples, 1964, pp. 1-20.

[18] Peter discusses artistic form in Herodotus and Thucydides in *Wahrheit und Kunst*, chap. 4. For Norden Thucydides' vocabulary represents the crossing of at least two Sophistic attitudes—eclecticism and rectitude (*Kunstprosa*, p. 97).

[19] C.N. Cochrane, *Thucydides and the Science of History*, Oxford, 1929; see especially chapters 2 and 3.

scription, concepts and techniques of expressive form and mental discipline, psychological and anthropological *aperçus* enriched both traditions and historiography as well.

In other words, the quarrel of philosophy and rhetoric was at first both bitter and productive. In the *Gorgias* and then in the *Phaedrus* Plato sketches the basic outlines of the struggle. He discerns in the opportunities and opportunism of rhetorical wickedness and immorality; his attack is necessarily on the skeptical detachment which is the source of the rhetor's independence; he laments the freedom to make the weaker cause the stronger, and to project the untruth as well as the truth of the same cause (*The Sophist*, 267A). For Plato dialogue is properly dialectic, but in rhetoric it degenerates to eristic or duel. Over against the principle of radical contingency which governs the formal choices of the rhetoricians Plato develops systematically the equation of form with an edifice of transcendent mathematical truth— an a priori truth of clarity, translucence, symmetry.[20]

Plato concedes, however, an inferior sphere of action and efficacy to the rhetors—the realm of opinion. At the end of the *Phaedrus* he develops an approach which the philosophers and, later, the theologians will return to again and again in their quarrel with rhetoric: one must assimilate rhetoric to the structure of philosophical truth by subordinating it to dialectic. As long as dialectic provides the foundation for rhetorical method, rhetoric is acceptable (*Phaedrus*, 269C-274B, 277B-C).

Isocrates, the student of Gorgias and in some ways an even more influential figure in the history of rhetoric than

[20] On the interrelationship of philosophy and rhetoric in the late fifth and fourth centuries see Jaeger, *Paideia*, especially Vol. 3; Norden, *Kunstprosa*, pp. 104-26; Peter, *Wahrheit und Kunst*, chap. 2; Plebe, *Breve storia*, pp. 43-99. Segal states the antinomy thus: the Gorgian *logos* is "as free from the exigencies of mimetic adherence to physical reality . . . as from an instrumental function in a philosophical schematization of a metaphysical reality. The opposite of these assumptions, of course, underlies the Platonic criticism of Gorgias' rhetoric (as of all rhetoric), for the entire Platonic dialectic supposes as a working premise that the structure of *logos* corresponds or provides access to the structure of true Being" ("Gorgias," p. 110).

Gorgias, attempted to reply to this philosophical onslaught by assimilating philosophy to rhetoric, incorporating parts of dialectic in rhetoric, and assigning the by now pejorative name "Sophist" to Plato and the Socratics as well as to the teachers of eristic and the Sicilian figures. In Isocrates the concern with aesthetic form is a concern with integrity; he loads eloquence with moral content. To train men to persuade has real social value; in contrast to Plato's idea of the cultivation of the city within oneself, Isocrates' urgent commitment to the Panhellenic ideal is the driving impulse of his life. The historicist traits shared by the earlier rhetoricians and Isocrates are the prescriptive sanction placed on action as privilege and grace, the emphasis on the richness and complexity of experience, and the peculiar value attached to the faculty of intuiting and expressing *kairos*. Isocrates solidified and attempted to transmit the intellectual burden of the Sophistic Age through the organization of rhetoric as the unifying force in education; Isocrates and Aristotle are the important sources of those generative maxims of rhetoric which penetrate and modify Western literary history through the eighteenth century.[21]

Aristotle retains the philosophic position of Plato in subordinating rhetoric, which deals with the probable, to philosophy, which seeks the truth; he only modifies the Platonic connection of Appearance with particulars and Reality with universals; his aphorisms—that the whole business of rhet-

[21] Jaeger discusses Isocrates' conflation of aesthetic and moral moments: for Isocrates "the intellect possesses an aesthetic and practical faculty which, without claiming absolute knowledge, can still choose the right means and the right end (*Soph.* 17). His whole conception of culture is based on that aesthetic power" *Paideia*, Vol. 3, p. 64). On Isocrates' commitment to Panhellenism see the "Panathenaicus," "Panegyricus," and "Antidosis," especially sections 44-47, 79-80. His ideas of the civilizing power of discourse ("Antidosis," 253-57) are similar to those of Cicero, Quintilian, and the Renaissance Humanists. On *kairos* see "Against the Sophists," 12-13; like Gorgias, Isocrates believes that there is no technique for inculcating virtue but only disciplines which foster tendencies toward justice ("Against the Sophists," 21). Munteano discusses "generative maxims" at length in "Des 'constantes' en littérature." See also A. Burk, *Die Pädagogik des Isocrates als Grundlegung des humanistischen Bildungsideals,* Wurzberg, 1923.

oric is with appearance and that history is concerned with particulars where poetry is concerned with universals—are accusations. In so far as Aristotle's poetics and logic as well as his rhetoric are important in the history of language, they are formative in the history of history. Yet the unique contribution of Aristotelian rhetoric to historical consciousness lies in his extensive analysis of rhetorical invention, of the finding and tailoring of arguments to specific causes and audiences, which was a refinement of the Gorgian search for the appropriate (*to prepon*). Since the peculiar focus of both classical historiography and rhetoric was on the discourse which leads to decision, the detailed discussion in Book II of the *Rhetoric* of the psychology of decision, of the relation of the oratorical modes to the specific attitudes which are ancillary to decision, could furnish an increase in self-consciousness for the historian as well as the rhetorician. Further, the reader of history can simply reverse the rhetorical emphasis and use the recounted speeches to determine the nature of the audience. The *topoi* or places or sources of arguments have an immense popularity in Western intellectual history. But are their fortunes historically varied because their structure is dynamic? To borrow a modern vocabulary, in contemporary linguistic theory a grammar should be descriptive of the essentially creative aspect of language potential: it should demonstrate how a finite system of rules generates an infinite set of language responses.[22] The system of *topoi*, as invented by Gorgias and developed by Aristotle, is based on the premise that a finite list of arguments can generate responses to an indefinite series of demands; in this sense the *topoi* reflect the active power of language and Aristotle's rhetorical maxims are generative because they relate to the flexibility and open-endedness of language itself.[23]

[22] N. Chomsky, *Cartesian Linguistics*, New York, 1966, p. 72, 59f.
[23] F. Solmsen, "The Aristotelian Tradition in Ancient Rhetoric," *AJPh*, 62 (1941), pp. 35-50, 169-90, outlines the main contributions of Aristotle to the rhetorical tradition. While the influence of Aristotle's *Poetics* to "tragic" historiography of the Hellenistic period is obvious, that of the *Rhetoric* is difficult to assess. Aristotle's *Rhetoric* affects Renaissance historiography in great measure through the assimilation

Yet the predominance of rhetoric in pedagogy after Aristotle cannot disguise the dilution or even emasculation of the Sophistic achievement; the relation of language to history in Greek culture enters a third or decadent stage. If the age of Gorgias and Thucydides had made many positive contributions to the definition of rhetoric and history, the changes in politics, education, and style in the Hellenistic age have given most of the pejorative connotations to the term "rhetorical historiography." Isocrates had conceived of the rhetorical education as training for the life which embodies its moral commitments in action; with the shrinking of the possibilities for political action, the rhetoric dominates which is not so much immoral as something perhaps worse— a rhetoric which leads to a bookish or vulgar, an academic or commercial life, a life of dilettantism or hack-writing. With the decline of the polis the whole temper of culture changed; historians who write the history of style in terms of a Classic-Mannerist alternation see rhetorical Asianism as the first Mannerist movement. In Asianism there is a deliberate and feverish striving for effect which elevates the canons of copiousness and gravity over those of simplicity and lucidity, the abnormally heightened over the normal and natural. Elements held in suspension in Isocrates' theory crystallize out to lead autonomous formal lives of their own. Isocrates' assumption of the old claim of the poets to be the principal educators of Greece as well as of their claims to the highest spiritual currency ends with the obscuring of rhetorical purposes by specifically poetic methods and aims.[24]

---

of his tenets by Cicero; cf. Solmsen, "The Aristotelian Tradition," and "Aristotle and Cicero on the Orator's Playing upon the Feelings," *CPh*, 33 (1938), pp. 309-404.

[24] On the rhetoric of this period see the works already cited of Kroll, Norden, Volkmann, Marrou, Plebe. Phenomenological studies of Mannerism are G. Hocke, *Die Welt als Labyrinth; Manier und Manie in der europäischen Kunst*, Hamburg, 1957, and E.R. Curtius, *European Literature and the Latin Middle Ages*, trans. W. Trask, New York, 1953, p. 273f. On the relation of history to poetics see Peter, *Wahrheit und Kunst*, chaps. 5, 13; F. Jacoby, "Griechische Geschichtschreibung," *Abhandlungen zur griechischen Geschichtschreibung*, ed. H. Bloch,

At the same time, since the opportunities in political oratory were fewer, the rhetorically trained turned more frequently to historiography as their mode of expression; history is on the way to becoming Cicero's *opus oratorium maxime* (*De leg.*, I, 2, 5). In the rhetorical histories of this period there is a conscious employment of rhetorical and poetical means in the Asian manner to heighten or exaggerate the historical-aesthetic unity which had been the end of investigation since Herodotus. There is no doubt that the Sophistic rhetoric had contained the seeds of decay in the very independence of its style of thought. But while for Gorgias human nature was the norm and for Thucydides historical significance was an enduring pattern of meaning, the historians Clitarchus and Phylarchus use their powers of fancy (*phantasia*) to create deceptions (*apate*) which present a caricature of events, an unnaturally sharpened and rigidly structured view of personality.[25] In the Hellenistic period the rhetorical historians forego their historical purpose (of confronting their reconstructed reality and extracting meaning from it alone) to create a tragic or pathetic scene which would move their readers to pity or terror. The quarrel of philosophy and rhetoric is implicated in this attempt of rhetoricians to take over the purposes as well as the means of poetry, for poetry had been for Aristotle the vehicle of the universals of the cosmic order, the same universals discovered in the philosophical quest. Rhetorical history tends thus to oscillate rather violently between the task of purveying philosophic universals, a role which rhetoric had specifically renounced, and that of pandering to factional or personal advantage, a role which rhetoric by its nature was incapable of renouncing. For the original rhetorical concern with persuasion can be perverted not only by the poetic-philosophic brand of didacticism but by a cynical pragmatism which

---

Leiden, 1956, pp. 73-99; B.L. Ullman, "History and Tragedy," *Transactions of the American Philological Association*, 73 (1942), pp. 25-53.

[25] Earlier, as Norden has pointed out, it had been acknowledged that "insofern der ἱστορικός mit Hülfe seiner Phantasie die Lücken der Tradition ausfüllt, ist er auch ein ποιητής" (*Kunstprosa*, p. 91).

carries too far the connection between epideictic oratory and history and leads to a history that is either flattery or slander. The Hellenistic historian, like the epideictic orators whose speeches were set exercises in praise or blame, confined the exploration of character and causation to a rigid set of interlocking *topoi*, modifying the notion of *kairos* from the peculiarly fitting, which considers the actual circumstances, to the decorous, the "usual thing." Thus the use of invention was no longer an opportunity for creativity but the methodic intrusion of the banal.[26]

Reacting to the banal, the florid, the partisan, Felix Jacoby saw the very identity of history, its existence as a separate discipline with a unique purpose, threatened by the corrupt fashions of Hellenistic schools of history such as the Isocratean (copious) or Peripatetic (tragic).[27] However, this same era also produced the devastating attack of Polybius on this historiography. The peculiar relevance of this attack for the relation of rhetoric to history is that Polybius employs rhetorical concepts to criticize rhetorical historiography.

First, Polybius asserts positive formal values; while on the one hand he condemns Zeno of Rhodes' overconcern with the highly-structured periodic style, he also declaims against the lack of vividness (*emphasis, enargeia*) in Timaeus' narration of events—a formal excellence which proceeds only from an ability to incorporate actual experience (XII, 25^{h-i}, XVI, 17, 9).[28] He attacks Timaeus' unrealistic and prolix speeches and compares them to the school exercises de-

---

[26] U. von Wilamowitz-Mollendorf, *On Greek Historical Writing and Apollo*, trans. G. Murray, Oxford, 1908, p. 16, thus claims that the rhetorical historian Ephorus "took care that everything should run on such lines as an enlightened Philistine can at a pinch imagine."

[27] See Jacoby, "Griechische Geschichtschreibung," p. 97. In the Hellenistic period, of course, a broader view of the relation of language to history would necessarily deal with philological achievements; the organization of R. Pfeiffer, *History of Classical Scholarship*, Oxford, 1968, would provide a framework for a discussion of the relation of the history of grammar to the history of history.

[28] See P. Pedech, *La méthode historique de Polybe*, Paris, 1964, pp. 258-59, for a discussion of Polybius' use of rhetorical *emphasis* and *enargeia*.

claimed by rhetors; yet he makes clear his commitment to the use of speeches in history. If the historian indicates the psychological ambiance of the discourse, he is able to show why the speaker succeeded or failed; the discourse thus situates the event in a chain of cause and effect which is relevant to our own experience. And here the earlier rhetorical idea of creative choice appears; it is the historian who must define the crucial argument, the argument which sets forth the essential motives, and his criteria are the rhetorical ones of the harmonious (*to harmozein*) and fitting (*kairios*) (XII, 25^1, 5).

In his view of the historian's responsibility to his audience Polybius, as the historian of the new and vital political force of Rome, is concerned with matters of will and decision and his real enemy is the ivory tower, whether it is that of the philosopher or the rhetorician; the scholars of his age, he maintains, neglect the practical questions of ethics and politics. Polybius thus sees the aim of history as the inculcation of that political *arete*, the ability to foresee and exploit circumstance, which was the goal of rhetorical and sophistical training and the model of Thucydidean virtue.[29]

Finally, Polybius' concept of the language of history recalls Thucydides' in that it demands a vocabulary which eschews metahistorical grandeur, and a structure which serves relevance through flexibility and simplicity. Similarly epistemological modesty and relevance had been the virtues of Sophistic rhetoric, and, similarly, its distinctive subject matter had been the alternatives of public choice, the difficult realm of the probable. For Thucydides and Polybius, historical truth is phenomenal probability, a truth of action and word; essential historical meaning, the system of causes, is a primary network of discourse and deed. Polybius condemns the tragic or scholastic rhetorical approaches as isolating the historian from reality in a philosophers' and poets' realm of mental con-

[29] For a summary of the discussion of Polybius' "pragmatic history" see Pedech, *La méthode*, p. 21f.

structs—of myth and fable, of fictional character traits and moral homilies.[30]

In sum, the rhetorical historiography which is a corruption of the historical purpose of Thucydides or Polybius also represents a drastic modification of the rhetorical aims of the Sophistic age. The importance of form is exaggerated in a theory of artificial intensification; the goal of persuasion of will becomes translated into a narrow didacticism; the creative spontaneity of the improvisation which considers individual and peculiar circumstances is dimmed to a slavish imitation of models of decorum; the semantic self-consciousness of the earlier rhetoric is transformed into an emphasis on pure mnemonic—of rhetoric as a closed list of arguments and figures.

The debate begun in this period between the Isocratean-Peripatetic and the Thucydidean-Polybian strands of historical theory continues in Roman culture. Indeed, the debate is continued *within* the Ciceronian corpus, a fact of importance for students of Humanist historiography, since the works of Cicero are a prime source for the historiographical theory of the succeeding periods, and especially of the Renaissance. And again the essential point is that just as Polybius develops his attack on rhetorical history within a rhetorical framework, so Cicero assembles his defense of historical purpose from the point of view of the rhetorician. Cicero occupied himself with the theory rather than the practice of history, and he is a very sensitive observer of the need of Rome for historiography and the need of historiography for rhetoric.

The introduction of Greek rhetorical training into Rome

[30] See in particular the attack on Timaeus in Book XII of the *Histories*, but also his strictures on Philinus and Fabius in I, 14; Phylarchus in II, 56; on Zeno of Rhodes in XVI, 17. His insistence on the pragmatic value of history for politics is best expressed in XII; the contrast of historical truth with tragic fiction is in II, 56. J. Lohmann compares the vocabulary of causation of Thucydides and Polybius in "Das Verhältnis des abendländischen Menschen zur Sprache," *Lexis*, 3.1 (1952), p. 21f.

in the late second century B.C. seemed to some conservatives as a corruption of the pure and vigorous oratory of the forum. But in the change from the early and more mechanical treatises modeled on Hellenistic Greek handbooks (the Pseudo-Ciceronian *Ad Herrenium* and Cicero's *De inventione*), to the mature works of Cicero (the *De oratore*, the *Orator*, the *Brutus*), several of the more valuable strands of Sophistic rhetoric—as well as their Hellenistic restatements—are retrieved and added to the older Roman exaltation of eloquence as a vital component of the political life. Cicero's philosophical eclecticism both preserves and confuses these strands; the significant point remains that Latin historians looking for rhetorical guidance could find in Cicero a treasury of the vocabulary and attitudes which make up the serious content of the rhetorical tradition from the Sophistic age on.[31]

First, it is most important for the history of Renaissance Humanism that Cicero penetrates to the language theory behind rhetorical practice. His aesthetic commitment is as profound as that of the Sophistic rhetors, and, like theirs, it is rooted in human faculties and feelings. Cicero devotes a sizeable portion of the technical treatise *De partitione oratoria* to analysis of the appeal to the ear; the special province of the orator is beauty of style, and his function is to appeal through the harmonies of rhythm to the emotions of his audience in order to move them to action. Cicero regains some of the Gorgian emphasis on dynamic relationship, on the creative role of the orator in shaping this appeal to particular circumstances; *kairos*, the key concept of Gorgias' aesthetic, reappears in Cicero's decorum: *"semperque in omni parte orationis ut vitae quid deceat est considerandum"* (*Orator*, 21, 71).

---

[31] In addition to the general surveys of the history of rhetoric already mentioned see F. Leo, *Geschichte der römischen Literatur*, Berlin, 1913, Vol. 1, for the earlier period, and W. Kroll, *Studien zum Verständnis der römischen Literatur*, Stuttgart, 1924, especially the chapters on "Grammatisch-rhetorische Theorien," pp. 87-116; "Originalität und die Nachahmung," pp. 139-85; and "Historiographie," pp. 331-84.

On the other hand, the Ciceronian notion of decorum also contains a basic modification of the rhetorical tradition by the philosophical; the old rhetorical concept of language derived exclusively from analysis of linguistic performance is replaced by one which assumes a pre-existent rational armature for all phenomena. While Gorgias related the incantatory power of discourse to the impotence of "mere" reason, Cicero's Stoic training contributes to an emphasis on the congruence of the demonic power of discourse and its rational content. The idea of reason (*logos*) as both discourse and thought, rational understanding and the impulse to knowledge, is the ground of all Stoic insights; the *logos spermatikos* is the only autarchic power, the sole creative principle in Nature. Cicero discusses not only the relation of the structure of language to the structure of mind, but the congruence of the structure of the cosmos, of the mind, and of language. He emphasizes the necessity, not contingency, of beauty; the capacity for the highest form of discourse, poetry, is a purely natural, innate competence, not an arbitrary system of signs (*Pro Archia*, 8, 18). On the one hand, beauty ought not to be of the surface but of the very bone and blood of discourse (*non fuco illitus sed sanguine diffusus*; *De oratore*, III, 52, 199); on the other, the response to art is rooted deep in the structure of the psyche.[32] The Stoic equation of thinking and speaking well, the Stoic attempt to integrate rhetoric and dialectic in a single science of language offered a resolution of the quarrel of philosophy and rhetoric. But where Plato had suggested in the *Phaedrus* fitting rhetoric into a philosophical framework, Cicero inserts philosophy into the larger context of eloquence. Cicero cites the aphorism of Zeno which compares dialectic to a clenched fist and rhetoric to an open palm; he refers to rhetoric as "*dialecticam. . .dilatam*" (*Brutus*, 90, 309): oratory

---

[32] "Omnes enim tacito quodam sensu sine ulla arte aut ratione quae sint in artibus ac rationibus recta ac prava diiudicant. . . ." (*De oratore*, III, 50, 195). "Nihil est autem cognatum mentibus nostris quam numeri et voces. . . ." (*De oratore*, III, 51, 197).

is wisdom cloaked in eloquence; *"ut enim hominis decus ingenium, sic ingenii ipsius lumen est eloquentia"* (*Brutus*, 15, 59).[33]

Yet hesitations and tensions remain, however papered over with clever dichotomies; A. Michel characterizes his argument very aptly as "sinuous."[34] In the first conversation of the *De oratore* Scaevola and Antonius uphold the predominance of the rhetor's civic function, the Sophistic *bios politikos* as well as the Roman heritage of devotion to the *patria*, while Crassus defends his concern with the cultural ideal of *paideia*, the *bios theoretikos* of the Greek philosophers. The dialogue between Gorgian rhetoric and Platonic philosophy, between the usefulness of sheer linguistic virtuosity and the merits of the liberal humanistic appeal to the mind (*animi libera quaedam oblectatio*; *De oratore*, I, 26, 118), continues throughout the Ciceronian corpus.

Both terms of the debate help form Cicero's notion of history.

And as History, which bears witness to the passing of the ages, sheds light on reality, gives life to recollection and guidance to human existence, and brings tidings of ancient days, whose voice, but the orator's can entrust her to immortality?[35]

[33] On the Stoic influence consult M. Pohlenz, *Die Stoa; Geschichte einer geistigen Bewegung*, Göttingen, 1959, Vol. 1; see also E. Hoffman, *Pädagogischer Humanismus*, Zurich, 1955, where the chapter "Die Pädagogik der Stoa," pp. 162-77, is relevant; and I. Bochenski, *A History of Formal Logic*, trans. I. Thomas, Notre Dame, 1961, pp. 105-33. On the general relationship of philosophy and rhetoric see A. Michel, *Rhétorique et Philosophie chez Cicéron*, Paris, 1960, p. 300f.; also chap. 2, "Sources grecques du 'De oratore'," p. 8of.; p. 93.

[34] *Rhétorique et philosophie*, p. 84.

[35] "Historia vero testis temporum, lux veritatis, vita memoriae, magistra vitae, nuntia vetustatis, qua voce alia, nisi oratoris, immortalitati commendatur?" (*De oratore*, II, 9, 36). On the relation of rhetoric and history in Cicero see M. Rambaud, *Cicéron et l'histoire romain*, Paris, 1953; B.L. Ullman, "History and Tragedy"; V. Paladini, "Sul pensiero storiografico di Cicerone," *Rendiconti della Accademia Nazionale dei Lincei*, ser. 8, 2 (1947), pp. 511-22; and P. de Fourny, "Histoire et éloquence d'aprés Cicéron," *Études Classiques*, 21 (1953), pp. 156-66. The main references to historical theory in Cicero are to be found in the *Brutus*, *Orator*, *De oratore*, and *De legibus*.

Historians are essentially *exornatores rerum* (*De oratore*, II, 12, 54; *Orator*, 12, 39), but Cicero sees no incompatibility between the historian's commitment to rhetorical excellence and his commitment to Thucydidean-Polybian standards of historical truth.

> For who does not know history's first law to be that an author must not dare to tell anything but the truth? And its second that he must make bold to tell the whole truth? That there must be no suggestion of partiality anywhere in his writings? Nor of malice?[36]

Granting this primary allegiance to truth, Cicero distinguishes three attitudes toward rhetorical form in the three genres of history—the commentary, the monograph, and the full-scale history. Caesar's *Commentaries* excelled in limning the bare and simple narrative of events in a taut, concise style similar to that of the Ionic scientific notes (*Brutus*, 75, 262). The monograph, in concentrating upon a single major event in order to create a dramatically intense work of art which will arouse political fervor, most resembles the Isocratean-Peripatetic type of history (*Brutus*, 11, 42; *Fam.*, V, 12, 3). And history proper, the annalistic relation of the events which have created the fatherland, has as its essential characteristic the fullness and copiousness of the modified Asiatic style of which Cicero was so fond. The peculiar contribution of the historian is to add artistic form to notes of the type of Caesar's *Commentaries*; the depth of his aesthetic commitment demonstrates, rather than contradicts, his integrity as a historian (*De oratore*, II, 12, 54; 14, 58).

If Cicero transmits the quarrel of philosophy and rhetoric, Roman historiography recapitulates Greek interrelationships of rhetoric and history. Livy is the historian who came closest to achieving the Ciceronian ideal of "full" history; his annals furnish a paradigm for those who attempt the elevated style

[36] "Nam quis nescit, primam esse historiae legem, ne quid falsi dicere audeat? Deinde ne quid veri non audeat? Ne quae suspicio gratiae sit in scribendo? Ne quae simultatis?" (*De oratore*, II, 15, 62).

of history through the Renaissance.[37] And when the fifteenth-century Humanists contemplate their recovered heritage of Tacitus and Sallust as well as Thucydides they confront elaborate evidence of that linguistic sophistication which illumines historical problems. The career of Sallust alone compresses all three stages of Greek linguistic consciousness: while his early reading and training pertain to a more traditional and unsophisticated culture, his vocabulary, structure, and argument correspond to the classically defined purposes and techniques of Thucydides, and also reflect his awareness of living in a period of decadence and great historical and linguistic ambiguities. Thus, for example, Thucydidean irony transforms an intuition of ambiguity into authentic historical statement. In Sallust's and Tacitus' speeches the irony lies in the disparity between conscious purpose and unwilled result, or between facts supplied by the narrative and the protagonist's faithless reporting of the facts.[38] Historical objectivity for both is a function of linguistic detachment, not of lack of political feeling; they force the reader to accept the deceptiveness of language and to measure the distance between accepted meaning and specific distortion.

Tacitus in both the *Dialogus de oratoribus* and the histories specifically connects rhetorical and political decline (*Dialogus*, 41, 5): the practice of rhetoric is obsolete, and the task of history is the pursuit of epigoni discovering their own decadence; Tacitus possesses the same destructive self-consciousness as Thucydides.[39] Beyond Tacitus and Quin-

[37] P.G. Walsh, *Livy; His Historical Aims and Methods*, Cambridge, 1961; H. Taine, *Essai sur Tite Live*, Paris 1856; Kroll, *Studien*, pp. 351-69; R. Ullmann, "Étude sur le style des discours de Tite Live," *Skriften utgitt av Det Norske Uidenskeps-Akademie I Oslo, Hist. Filos. Klasse*, 3 (1928). For Livy as *the* authority for medieval historiographers recall Martianus Capella, *De nuptiis Philologiae et Mercurii*, 5: "Historiae est ut Livii."

[38] On irony see R. Syme, *Sallust*, Berkeley, 1964, p. 198; *Tacitus*, Oxford, 1958, Vol. 1, p. 192f.; Syme claims that in Roman historiography the Thucydidean mode "corresponds to an organic necessity," *Tacitus*, p. 197.

[39] Syme, *Tacitus*, Vol. 1, p. 107; see his chapter "From Oratory to History," p. 112f.

tilian, late classical rhetorical treatises are for the most part exhaustive but repetitive and stale discussions of both aspects of Aristotelian rhetoric—the manipulation of rational argument and of the passions. This rhetoric provides not only the framework but the rigid mold for much of late Roman and medieval thought about the relationship of language and history. Only an epistemological radicalism such as that of Protagoras can give seriousness to the role of the rhetor, and one of the chief attributes of the rhetorical cluster of insights is volatility; it is obvious from Plato's *Gorgias* that the process of formalization and "demoralization" had already started in Gorgias' lifetime. Vacillation marks the strange double heritage of promise and decadence of the rhetorical tradition.

In general, then, if Cicero and Quintilian can supply a connection between Renaissance Humanist and Sophistic attitudes through their success in restating Greek rhetorical notions of language in Latin, the history of rhetoric in late Antiquity and the Middle Ages obscures this historical connection through its enormous complexity. Besides the internal moments of decay, philosophical and theological pressures and a hostile socio-political environment contribute to diversity as well as decline. In the medieval period E. Auerbach lists at least three approaches to rhetoric—Mannerist, pre-Humanist, Scholastic—all of them oblique; the chronology of these formal periods is also confused.[40] This confusion is a result of changes in disciplines as well as world view; within the medieval *trivium* rhetoric plays a minor and dependent role; if from approximately the seventh century grammar

[40] *Literary Language and its Western Public,* trans. R. Manheim, London, 1964, p. 273f. For the history of rhetoric in the Middle Ages the standard reference work is M. Manitius, *Geschichte der lateinischen Literatur des Mittelalters,* in *Handbuch der Altertumswissenschaft,* IX. 2. 1-3, Munich, 1911f; the rhetorical texts collected in K. Halm, *Rhetores latini minores,* Leipzig, 1863, make clear the mechanical nature of the late Roman and medieval rhetorics. Consult also Norden's *Kunstprosa,* Vol. 2, and R. McKeon's "Rhetoric in the Middle Ages," *Speculum,* 17 (1942), pp. 1-32; see the work of R. Sabbadini on the fortunes of classical texts of rhetoric in the Middle Ages: *Storia e critica di testi latini,* Catania, 1914, and *Le scoperte dei codici latini e greci ne' secoli XIV e XV,* 2 vols., Florence, 1905-1914.

has hegemony, by the twelfth century the goals and forms of logic dominate both grammar and rhetoric.[41]

This Scholastic type of rhetoric is, as far as the history of Humanism is concerned, the major event in the history of medieval rhetoric, as it provides the "errors" against which the Humanists will struggle to develop their own answers. In the Scholastic view, contrary to the Sophistic presupposition of the contingent nature of language, the connection between ontology and logic was strict. The more mechanical treatises such as Cicero's *De inventione* and *Topica* (*Rhetorica vetus*), and the *Ad Herrenium* (*Rhetorica nova*), were set into a Christian metaphysical framework of truth, into a series of envelopes—God, Grace, Reason, Logic. Rhetoric as one of the Liberal Arts was a preparatory discipline for theologians, a propaedeutic to scriptural exegesis; in the higher faculties of theology, medicine, and law logical fashions prevail: a discipline must be universal, words must be univocal; the focus is on the construction of an edifice of abstractions. Where Gorgias had seen rhetorical techniques as mediating a Dionysian reality, the pre-existent reality assumed by the dialecticians is a spiritual one of absolute necessity, beyond phenomena and beyond history.

Moreover, the development of Biblical exegesis furnishes still another source of linguistic and thus historical complexity; here an elementary contrast is that between a "historicist" typology and anti-historical allegory. Auerbach has carefully defined the historical cast of the figural mode, which sees the Old Testament event as the anticipation of the New Testament event which is Christian fulfillment. The relation is thus not of phenomenal sign to noumenal exemplar, but of one historical occasion to another. But in the Greek concept of allegory also present in the patristic heritage historical

---

[41] On the hegemony of grammar in the *trivium* from approximately the seventh to the twelfth century see the references in M. Colish, *The Mirror of Language; A Study in the Medieval Theory of Knowledge*, New Haven, 1968, p. 62f.; on the dominance of logic from the twelfth century see M. Grabmann, "Die geschichtliche Entwicklung der mittelalterlichen Sprachphilosophie und Sprachlogik—ein Überblick," *Mittelalterliches Geistesleben*, Vol. 3, Munich, 1956, pp. 243-53.

events are shadows or prefigurations of occult events, masks of spiritual realities; in the late classical Neoplatonic ontology which underwrote this point of view history is necessarily of a lesser order of reality as an image or likeness of the intelligible cosmos. Thus the strong historicist moment of the doctrine of the Incarnation, which provides for the intrusion of the divine into history, does not counteract entirely the pejorative change in the status of rhetoric; since the direction of thought is assumed always to be from the sensible to the divine both history and rhetoric no longer deal primarily with the relative and ambiguous texture of life as in the Sophistic period.[42]

In the final development of medieval rhetoric a new tone of engagement and vitality characterizes the *ars dictaminis* of the Italian communes; this stems from the political ferment in the new city-states and represents a fusion of secular ideology and almost sacramental purpose. The continuity between Brunetto Latini's fresh and concrete restatement of the Ciceronian tenets of "civic eloquence" and the political rhetoric of the late fourteenth- and fifteenth-century Humanist Chancellors is obvious. Still, to read a popular thirteenth-century text such as Guido Fava's *Parlementi e epistole* or even Coluccio Salutati's notarial protocol is disenchanting; in great measure the communal rhetoric merely exchanges subordination to dialectic for a subordination to the narrow political, juristic, or notarial aims of its practitioners.[43]

[42] Auerbach has discussed the figural mode in several studies; see, for example, his essay "Figura," in *Scenes from the Drama of European Literature*, New York, 1959; on typology see A.P. Charity, *Events and their Afterlife; The Dialectic of Christian Typology in the Bible and Dante*, Cambridge, 1966; on allegory see the unpublished paper of F. Edward Cranz, "Some Changing Contexts of Allegory from the Greeks through the Renaissance," [read at the New England Renaissance Conference, 1966]. H. de Lubac, *Exégèse médiévale; Les quatre sens de l'Écriture*, 4 vols., Paris, 1959-64, is essential.

[43] See Latini, *Rettorica*, ed. F. Maggini, Florence, 1968; G. Fava, *Parlamenti ed epistole*, ed. A. Gaudenzi, in *I suoni, le forme, e le parole dell'odierno dialetto di Bologna*, Turin, 1889, pp. 127-60; *Il Protocollo Notarile di Coluccio Salutati (1372-73)*, ed. A. Petrucci, Milan, 1963. On the developments in rhetoric in Italy from the twelfth through the fourteenth centuries see A. Galletti, *L'eloquenza dalle orig-*

In the Middle Ages, then, rhetoric continues to influence historiography, but it is a different rhetoric; the quarrel of philosophy and rhetoric has faded into the domination of philosophy by theology. The extraordinary proliferation of manuals of the thirteenth century—on inditing official letters and composing public discourses, on preaching and on poetry —in many ways marked an attenuated existence of the rhetorical tradition. In Christian dualistic theology rhetoric is not only relative and limited but secular and impure; paradox and tension characterize the discussion of language by the church fathers such as Augustine and Gregory; the feeling for language as masterful combines with a hesitation about the roots of this power. And Augustinian rhetoric as "redeemed" has necessarily been drained of the radical semantic assumptions which informed Gorgian rhetoric.[44] The historiography of the entire medieval period exploited rhetoric as a source of rules for the arrangement of material, the structure of narration, the ornamentation and artificial elevation of discourse.[45] But as long as the contingent nature of language

---

ini al XVI secolo, in *Storia dei generi letterari italiani; II, Eloquenza politica e politica-accademica,* Milan, 1938; R. Weiss, *Il primo secolo dell'Umanesimo; Studi e testi,* Rome, 1953; A. Schiaffini, "Avviamenti della prosa del secolo XIII," in *Momenti di storia della lingua latina,* Rome, 1949, pp. 71-89, and *Tradizione e poesia nella prosa d'arte italiana dalla latinità medievale a G. Boccaccio,* Rome, 1943; and the articles of H. Wieruszowski, especially "*Ars dictaminis* in the Time of Dante," *M&H,* 1 (1943), pp. 95-108. Two more recent studies of communal eloquence in the late medieval period, M. Becker, "Dante and his Literary Contemporaries as Political Men," *Speculum,* 41 (1966), pp. 665-80, and J.E. Seigel, *Rhetoric and Philosophy in Renaissance Humanism,* Princeton, 1968, chap. 7, "From the *Dictatores* to the Humanists," pp. 200-25, emphasize both continuity and change between the late medieval and Renaissance eloquence.

[44] Colish, *The Mirror of Language,* p. 8f. describes the "redemption" of human speech by St. Augustine.

[45] A survey of medieval historiography is F. Cognasso, "Storiografia medievale," in *Questioni di storia medioevale,* ed. E. Rota, Milan, n.d., pp. 785-836; see also A. Dempf, *Sacrum Imperium; Geschichts-und Staatsphilosophie des Mittelalters und der politischen Renaissance,* Darmstadt, 1954; J. Spörl, *Grundformen hochmittelalterlicher Geschichtsanschauung; Studien zum Weltbild der Geschichtschreiber des 12 Jahrhunderts,* Munich, 1935. More specifically on the relation of rhetoric

and the creative independence of the orator-historian were denied, the use of rhetorical techniques did not foster insights into the attribution of continuity and the definition of discontinuity, the two primary historical tasks. In the Renaissance the persistence of philosophical and theological notions which impose these denials guaranteed the prolongation of the pejorative effects. On the other hand, in so far as the Renaissance re-created the original Sophistic concepts and made them a possession of the modern Western intellectual tradition it liberated historical consciousness from some major liabilities.

To summarize: the strand in the rhetorical tradition which had as its core the Protagorean metaphor of "man the measure" contains some essentially historicist insights. First, rhetors choose to attempt attributing structure to material—the flux of human event and character—which is extremely resistant to the imposition of form and the discovery of meaning. At the same time they cling to their assumption that form and meaning cannot exist apart from the particular event or person. Here there is a clear antinomy between rhetoric and the dominant strand of classical philosophy: philosophy aims to find the truth beyond events, to discover occult relations between the visible happening and an invisible purpose, while rhetoric deals only with the truth *of* events, the manifest (*phenomena*). Rhetorical concepts of discourse emphasize change, not permanence, the many, not the one, the particular, not the universal—emphases which are essential in a serious commitment to historical understanding, i.e., historicism.

While any study of language which penetrates to the level of psychology and structure would be of value to the his-

---

to historiography see H. Wolter, "Geschichtliche Bildung im Rahmen der Artes Liberales," in *Artes Liberales; Von der antiken Bildung zur Wissenschaft des Mittelalters*, Leiden, 1959, pp. 50-83; and M. Schulz, *Die Lehre von der historischer Methode*, Berlin, 1909, especially chap. 5, "Der Einfluss literarischer Quellen, insbesondere der Rhetorik," pp. 120-34.

torian, the rhetorical discipline has the peculiar value of its lack of system. Rhetorical and historical investigation share a constellation of characteristics; since the individual identity of any single characteristic is determined by reciprocal relations with other characteristics, there is no overall architectonic order. A list of rhetorical descriptions generates not a philosophy of history but a list of insights into authentic historical experience. Rhetorical modes are historicist possibilities: language as "social" or pragmatic permits history as anthropocentric; language as perverse and irrational allows history as irreverent and inclusive. From a view of language as kairotic, one moves to a grasp of authentic historical time, of cultural pattern or *Gestalt*; from language as illusory and masterful, to history as sensitivity to human artifice and free creation; from a rhetorical emphasis on language as mediating, not reflecting, reality, to historiography as the analysis of motive and fashion. History as a tissue of arguments and figures makes heavy demands on the reader: language structure as antilogic engenders historical explanation, as antithetical, historical detachment; in the metaphors the reader must find relevance by analogy; through irony, he must engage in comparison of intention and effect. Rhetorical techniques can be as useful to history as those of classical logic to classical philosophy; in a sense to choose one of the two types of discourse is to anticipate the content of which the discourse is the vehicle.

Both rhetors and historians boldly take possession of the sphere of flux rather than try to escape or transcend it. They tend to minimize the interference of either the divine or the purely rational in the realm of mutability. For both there is still the possibility and necessity of rational decision, but mind can not operate as a totally free entity in an ideal world; its effects are continually modified by circumstance and mediated by language. The theory of knowledge implicit in both the rhetorical and historical disciplines is pessimistic in tone; in contrast to Platonic philosophy the epistemology of Sophistic rhetoric is modest in its claims; the shameless calculation of effects of the rhetorical *techne* is an archetype of the statistical nominalism of historical descriptions of cause.

The Sophists' only model is man; the basic metaphors are all anthropocentric. But autarchy can be eccentricity, and the price of autonomy alienation. In the Hellenistic age two things marred the union of rhetorical discourse and historical intent: a Mannerism which distorted the human scale of a Classicist norm, and a philosophical didacticism which predicated one absolute order as the only burden of any type of discourse. Further, the Stoic-Ciceronian attempt to circumvent alienation by reintegrating cosmic and human *logos* can be the basis for a philosophical withdrawal from the phenomenal world to a mental realm of stability. And when Christian theology equates *logos* with the divine will, this withdrawal can become a flight to a supernatural realm; human life has then transcendental meaning or none at all.

The next task, then, is to show how a change of language habits forces change in historical attitudes; how the Humanists' re-creation of the self-conscious purpose and public role of the rhetorician both militates against philosophical or religious withdrawal and helps make possible a methodic "saving of the phenomena" and thus a saving of history.

 ❧ TWO ❧

Rhetoric, Poetics, and History—
COLUCCIO SALUTATI

1. POETRY AND RHETORIC

THE PRUDENCE OF THE FLORENTINES IS TO BE COMMENDED IN
MANY THINGS, BUT MOST OF ALL IN THEIR SELECTION OF
CHANCELLORS, FOR THEY DO NOT SEEK OUT LAWYERS, AS MOST
STATES DO, BUT THOSE SKILLED IN ORATORY AND WHAT IS CALLED
THE *studia humanitatis*. FOR THEY ARE AWARE THAT NOT
BARTOLUS OR INNOCENTIUS BUT CICERO AND QUINTILIAN TEACH
THE ART OF SPEAKING AND WRITING WELL. WE HAVE KNOWN
THREE IN THAT CITY, ILLUSTRIOUS IN GREEK AND LATIN
LEARNING AND IN THE REPUTATION OF THEIR OWN WORKS, WHO
HAVE HELD THE POST OF CHANCELLOR IN SUCCESSION: LEONARDO
AND CARLO OF AREZZO AND POGGIO OF THE SAME CITY-STATE,
WHO AS APOSTOLIC SECRETARY WROTE LETTERS FOR THREE
POPES. PRECEDING THEM WAS COLUCCIO, WHOSE ELOQUENCE
WAS SUCH THAT GALEAZZO, THE RULER OF MILAN WHO WAGED
A TERRIBLE WAR AGAINST FLORENCE WITHIN THE MEMORY OF
OUR FATHERS, WAS OFTEN HEARD TO SAY THAT A THOUSAND
FLORENTINE KNIGHTS DID HIM LESS HARM THAN COLUCCIO'S PEN.

Pius II, *Historia de Europa*; chap. 54,
"De Florentinis, et diversis apud eos rebus gestis"[1]

AENEAS SYLVIUS' *Cosmographia* serves very well as a
fifteenth-century Humanist world-view. It is indicative of the
special Humanist self-consciousness, then, that in his very

---

[1] "Commendanda est multis in rebus Florentinorum prudentia, tum
maxime quod in legendis Cancellariis non juris scientiam, ut plerae-

brief account of Florence he devotes as much space as he does to the Humanist Chancellors, and that his devotion specifically relates to their rhetorical virtuosity.[2] In the history

que civitates, sed oratoriam spectant, et quae vocant humanitatis studia. Norunt enim recte scribendi dicendique artem non Bartholum aut Innocentium, sed Tullium, Quintilianumque tradere. Nos tres in ea urbe cognovimus, Graecis et Latinis et conditorum operum fama illustres, qui Cancellarium alius post alium tenuere, Leonardum et Carolum Aretinos, et Pogium eiusdem reipublicae civem, qui secretarius apostolicus tribus quondam Romanis pontificibus dictarat epistolas. Illos praecesserat Colucius, cuius ea dicendi vis fuit, ut Galeacius Mediolanensium princeps, qui patrum nostrorum memoria gravissimum Florentinis bellum intulit, crebro auditus est dicere, non tam sibi mille Florentinorum equites quam Colucii scripta nocere." A.S. Piccolomini, *Opera omnia*, Basel, 1571, p. 454. The part of the quotation which refers to Poggio and Bruni was used as a preface to *Poggii Florentini, Dialogus, et Leonardi Aretini, Oratio adversus hypocrisim*, London, 1679. Coluccio Salutati (1331-1406) was Chancellor from 1375 to 1406; Leonardo Bruni (c.1370-1444) was Chancellor briefly in 1410-1411 and from 1427 to 1444; Poggio Bracciolini (1380-1459) was Chancellor from 1453 to 1458. On the Humanist Chancellery see E. Garin, "I cancellieri umanisti della Repubblica fiorentina da Coluccio Salutati a Bartolomeo Scala," *La cultura filosofica del Rinascimento italiano*, Florence, 1961, pp. 3-37; D. Marzi, *La Cancelleria della Repubblica Fiorentina*, Rocca S. Casciano, 1910; F.P. Luiso, "Riforma della Cancelleria fiorentina nel 1437," *ASI*, ser. 5, 21 (1897), pp. 132-142.

2 On the rhetorical nature of Humanism see G. Voigt, *Die Wiederbelebung des classischen Altertums*, Berlin, 1893; P.O. Kristeller, "Humanism and Scholasticism in the Italian Renaissance," *Studies in Renaissance Thought and Letters*, Rome, 1956, pp. 556-83; C. Trinkaus, "A Humanist's Image of Humanism; The Inaugural Orations of Bartolomeo della Fonte," *SRen*, 7 (1960), pp. 90-125; H. Gray, "Renaissance Humanism; The Pursuit of Eloquence," *JHI*, 24 (1963), pp. 497-514. On the place of rhetoric in the general culture of the Humanists see J. Seigel, *Rhetoric and Philosophy*; E. Garin, *Medioevo e Rinascimento*, Bari, 1961, especially "La prosa latina del Quattrocento," pp. 119-23, and "Discussioni sulla retorica," pp. 124-29; F. Flora, "Umanesimo," *Lett. mod.*, 1 (1950), pp. 19-29; W. Rüegg, "Die scholastische und die humanistische Bildung im Trecento," in *Das Trecento*, Zurich, 1960, pp. 141-81; R. Sabbadini, *Il metodo degli umanisti*, Florence, 1920; C. Trabalza, *La critica letteraria nel Rinascimento; Secoli XV-XVI-XVII*, Milan, 1915; and in the *Storia letteraria d'Italia*, N. Sapegno, *Il Trecento*, Milan, 1948, and V. Rossi, *Il Quattrocento*, Milan, 1964. Also important is the Humanists' attitude toward Cicero; see T. Zielinski, *Cicero im Wandel des Jahrhunderts*, Leipzig, 1912; W. Rüegg, *Cicero und der Humanismus*, Zurich, 1946. On the relation of medieval to Humanist rhetoric see, besides the works

of Humanist rhetoric Coluccio Salutati is a Janus: he both summarizes the achievements of fourteenth-century Humanists and transmits them to his fifteenth-century successors. He underlines rather than obliterates the complex relationships between the rhetorical functions of the Florentine Chancellery which were medieval in origin and the innovations of Italian Humanism in the philosophy of language. While Salutati did not write a formal history of Florence, he remains a very important figure in the history of Humanist historiography, as he makes clear how linguistic change informs changes in historical, ethical, and political consciousness in the Italian Renaissance.[3]

---

cited in note 43 of chapter 1, F. Tateo, *"Retorica" e "Poetica" fra Medioevo e Rinascimento*, Bari, 1960; and G. Vallese, "Retorica medioevale o retorica umanistica," *Da Dante ad Erasmo; Studi di letteratura umanistica*, Naples, 1962, pp. 39-75.

[3] E. Walser, in his "Coluccio Salutati, der Typus eines Humanisten der altesten Schule," in his *Gesammelte Studien zur Geistesgeschichte der Renaissance*, Basel, 1932, pp. 22-37, discusses the ambiguity of Salutati's position as a Janus, facing in the direction of the Middle Ages as well as the Renaissance. A. von Martin, in *Coluccio Salutati und das humanistische Lebensideal*, Leipzig, 1916, and his *Mittelalterliche Welt-und-Lebensanschauung im Spiegel der Schriften C.S.*, Munich, 1913, emphasizes the medieval aspects of S.'s thought; the study by B.L. Ullman, *The Humanism of C.S.*, Padua, 1963, on the other hand, tends to stress Renaissance tendencies in S.'s work. The ambiguities and tensions in Salutati are stressed in R. Fubini's "La coscienza del latino negli umanisti," *Studi medievali*, ser. 3, 2^2 (1961), pp. 520-29; see also A. Petrucci's introduction to *Il Protocollo Notarile di C.S.*, p. 16. See also F. Novati, *La giovinezza di C.S.*, Turin, 1888; L. Borghi, "La dottrina morale di C.S.," *"Annali della R. scuole normale superiore di Pisa; Lett., stor., e filos.,* ser. 2, 3, Bologna, 1934, pp. 76-102; G. Sciacca, *La visione della vita nell'Umanesimo di C.S.*, Palermo, 1954, and "Il valore della storia nel pensiero di Coluccio Salutati," *Annali della facolta di lettere, Palermo*, 1 (1950), pp. 351-66. The notes as well as the texts of F. Novati's edition of Salutati's *Epistolario*, 4 vols., Rome 1891-1911, are necessary to an understanding of S.'s achievement. [Henceforth cited as E., with volume and page number] Other editions of Salutati's work used are *De laboribus Herculis*, ed. B.L. Ullman, 2 vols. Zurich, 1951; *Il trattato "De tyranno" e lettere scelte*, ed. F. Ercole, Bologna, 1942; *De nobilitate legum et medicinae*; *De verecundia*, ed. E. Garin, Florence, 1947; *Invectiva in Antonium Luschium Vicentium*, in *Prosatori latini del Quattrocento*, ed. E. Garin, Milan, [1952], pp. 8-36.

Renaissance changes in language are so great, in fact, that the Trecento "rhetorical revolution" of G. Billanovich describes only one facet of a general "linguistic revolution."[4] To define this linguistic revolution is to dwell upon the shared insights of Northern European logicians and Italian Humanists. Certainly by the early fourteenth century in the North as well as in Italy an atmosphere of ferment and change is noticeable in the discussions of language as well as of political theory. Especially in the period 1270-1340 the access of new groups and territorial units to power, coupled with the difficulties of the older forms of lay and ecclesiastical government, gave rise to wide-ranging speculation on the nature of authority.[5] At roughly the same time the political developments in the Italian city-states and courts fostered certain possibilities in discourse—aesthetic form as value and power, public debate as political nutriment, speech as expression of personality, and ordinary language as exploration of reality—which gave a new coherence and prestige to the rhetorical function.[6] On one level, the ferment seems a simple professional rebellion; while the predominantly Northern

[4] G. Billanovich, *I primi umanisti e le tradizioni dei classici latini*, Freiburg, 1953, p. 37. For recent studies on the important changes in linguistic theory see the bibliography in J. Pinborg, *Die Entwicklung der Sprachtheorie im Mittelalter, Beiträge zur Geschichte der Philosophie und Theologie des Mittelalters; Texte und Untersuchung*, 42, Heft 2 (1967), pp. 345-52. The "revolutionary" aspect of fourteenth-century language changes has been underlined by the analogous radical changes in twentieth-century *Sprachphilosophie*, grammar, and the "new rhetoric" of Structuralism. Where Pinborg concentrates on changes in grammar and logic in the North, and where Lohmann sees Nominalism as the turning point in the history of the theory of language ("Verhältnis des abendländischen Menschen zur Sprache," pp. 6, 10), Karl Apel, in *Die Idee der Sprache in der Tradition des Humanismus von Dante bis Vico, Archiv für Begriffsgeschichte*, 8 (1953), sees three concurrent movements in the period 1300-1700—Occamism, *Logosmystik*, and humanism—(p. 160); the Renaissance for Apel is primarily a new relation of the West to language (p. 130).

[5] G. de Lagarde, *La naissance de l'esprit laïque; II, Secteur social de la scolastique*, Louvain, 1958, p. 302f.

[6] See Seigel, *Rhetoric and Philosophy*, Part II, "Some Contexts of Petrarchian Humanism," p. 173f. for a good survey and full references for this development.

43

modistae assert the independence of grammar from logic,[7] the Italian pre-Humanists demonstrate the autonomy of rhetoric. Here Humanism seems merely to replace one imbalance with another: the logicized rhetoric of the thirteenth century gives way finally to a rhetoricized logic in the sixteenth century.[8] On a deeper level, however, both the mature literary practice and theory of the Humanist Petrarch and the developed idea of language of the Nominalist William of Occam represent a profound change of front in the history of the philosophy of language.

First, language for both Humanists and Nominalists has become problematic: the congruence of the structure of language and the structure of being strikes them as a desideratum, not a fact; their concern with the relation of symbol to reality in contemporary usage is critical or even self-critical in tone. In both approaches there is a shift in what Gilbert Ryle calls the logical tone of voice; both are engaged in forming more descriptive languages about language, metalanguages, in short.

Further, like other pairs of enemies, the Nominalists and Humanists share a common enemy: what the Scholastics call "Realism" the Humanist sees as intellectual narrowness and the Nominalist immodest epistemology; what the Realists call "real" was to both Nominalists and Humanists unrelated to the phenomenal reality accessible only to experience. And, like other pairs of antagonists, the Humanists and Nominalists share basic assumptions on which they build strikingly different edifices. Both concentrate on the sphere of sign and symbol, and both concern themselves with a "middle ground" of communication and perception, expression and sensibility.[9]

---

[7] Pinborg, *Die Entwicklung*, pp. 55-56.

[8] On the rhetorical "imperialism" of the Humanists and the development of a logic dominated by rhetoric see C. Vasoli, *La dialettica e la retorica dell'Umanesimo; "Invenzione" e "Metodo" nella cultura del XV e XVI secolo*, Milan, 1968 [a collection of revised articles]; W.J. Ong, *Ramus: Method, and the Decay of Dialogue*, Cambridge, Mass., 1958; W. Risse, *Die Logik der Neuzeit; 1. Band, 1500-1650*, Stuttgart—Bad Cannstatt, 1964.

[9] The preoccupation with a sphere of meaning, not being, F.E. Cranz sees as a major change in the twelfth, rather than the fourteenth,

Finally, they see language as *mediating* reality, and this leads them to recognize the active, independent power of language.[10] For the Nominalists, according to J. Pinborg, language is not simply a system of signs; it is not so much the case that concepts use language, as that language uses concepts.[11] The Humanist emphasis is the traditional rhetorical one on language as an educational force: thus Dante anticipates this emphasis when he explains his epithet "illustrious" attached to the ideal vernacular as signifying not merely "illuminated" but "illuminating" (*De vulgari eloquentia*, I, 17, 2). Both Nominalists and Humanists base their new position of intellectual power on their understanding and control of language; they derive their *virtù* from the fact that language has its own *virtus*.[12] An analogy of Nicholas of Cusa, a Northern philosopher with strong Humanist ties, makes explicit their basic premise that not only is the realm of symbols peculiarly man's, but that within this sphere man is peculiarly free and powerful:

> For as God is creator of real entities and natural forms, so man is creator of rational entities and artificial forms, which are nothing except similitudes of his intellect, as creatures are similitudes of the divine Intellect.[13]

---

century; "New Dimensions of Thought in the Early Middle Ages: Anselm and Abailard as against Augustine and Boethius" [paper read at the Columbia Medieval Seminar, Nov., 1968]. Tateo, in *"Retorica" e "Poetica,"* p. 152, cites Dante's *De vulgari eloquentia*, I, 3 as exhibiting this concentration on a middle range, *medietas*, of experience, which is characteristic also of Boccaccio. [I have used A.G.F. Howell's edition of the *D.v.e.*, London, 1934]

[10] A Maierù, "Il problema della verità nelle opere di Guglielmo Heytesbury," *Studi medievali*, ser. 3, 7^1 (1966), p. 43.

[11] Pinborg, *Die Entwicklung*, p. 185.

[12] M. dal Pra, "Linguaggio e conoscenza assertiva nel pensiero di Robert Holcot," *RCSF*, 11 (1956), p. 15; quoted by Pinborg, *Die Entwicklung*, p. 198; cf. Pinborg on the power of language for the Humanists, pp. 210-12.

[13] "Nam sicut Deus est creator entium realium et naturalium formarum, ita homo rationalium entium et formarum artificialium, quae non sunt nisi sui intellectus similitudines, sicut creaturae Dei divini intellectus similitudines." Nicolaus Cusanus, *De beryllo, Opera omnia*, ed. L. Baur, Vol. 11^1, Leipzig, 1940, chap. 6, p. 7.

The analogy is a potent one; the demonstration of man's similitude to God lies precisely in his *creative* use of symbol. In effect, the Renaissance language theorists repeat some of the basic moments of Sophistic thought in their attempt to reassess the relation of language to being, their emphasis on the mediating power of language, and their sense of role as derived from their language skill.[14] Is it possible to proceed one step further and claim that the key tenets of Humanist rhetoric are analogous to those of Gorgias? For while the linguistic revolution for the Nominalists is related to a change of attitude toward perception and takes the form of a search for epistemological elegance and economy in stating theological truths, the innovations of the Humanists relate to problems of sensibility and artistic expression.

The distinctive contribution of fourteenth-century Humanism to the linguistic revolution is the defense of poetry. Thus Roberto Weiss points out that Dante is intellectually oriented to medieval patterns in every sense but one, and this the most important one—the recreation of classical poetry.[15] Here the relation of rhetoric to poetry has a very nourishing circularity. Francesco Tateo has demonstrated that in the twelfth and thirteenth centuries it is the use of the rhetorical *impalcatura* which begins to turn the discussion of poetry away from metaphysics and towards art.[16] On the other hand, the growth of poetry contributed to a rhetoric functioning as a broadly conceived aesthetic, which supplants the medie-

---

[14] Another "Sophistic" trait of the Humanists, perhaps, is their hostility to pretensions to exact or "pure" knowledge; Apel (*Die Idee*, p. 14) considers the archetype of the Renaissance tension between "exakter (mathematischen) Naturwissenschaft und hermeneutischen (an die geschichtliche Umgangssprache gebundener) Geisteswissenschaft" to be the confrontation of Plato and the Sophists. Vasoli finds Salutati useful in bringing out both antagonisms and agreement of the Humanists and logicians (" 'Antichi' contro 'moderni'," *La dialettica*, p. 9f.).

[15] "Dante e l'umanesimo del suo tempo," *Lett. ital.*, 19 (1967), pp. 279-90; cf. C. Trabalza, *Storia della grammatica italiana*, Bologna, 1963, pp. 11-12, who insists on the priority of poetry in the history of grammar.

[16] Tateo, *"Retorica" e "Poetica,"* p. 7; cf. Salutati, *De lab.*, I, 3, 13.

val rhetorical handbooks of lists of *figurae* and *colores* mugged up from the more decadent late classical treatises.

In both the early stages of Humanist rhetoric and in Gorgias' establishment of rhetoric as an independent art, then, the discipline benefits from the application to prose of the poetic discoveries of the previous decades; the rhetorical revolution of the fourteenth century reflects, among other things, what Mario Praz would call a "revolution in sensibility."[17] Fritz Saxl claimed that the men of the Renaissance returned to the pagans because they discovered types in their literature and art which expressed feeling similar to those which they wished to express.[18] Thus it is the feelings first discovered in poetic experience which gave new meaning to classical rhetoric. The discovery of new texts is not innovating but symptomatic; it is not the finding of new texts so much as the fresh reading of them—of Cicero's *De inventione* by Brunetto Latini, of Cicero's letters by Petrarch—that matters; most of the major discoveries of the mature oratorical works of Rome come only later with Poggio's discoveries in France and Germany and Bishop Landriani's at Lodi (1416-1420).[19]

Just as Gorgias emphasized the incantatory value of sound, and the affective pleasures of fictional imagery, of deception (*apate*), so the major figures of Trecento Humanism engage in a defense of the sensual and imaginative pleasures of discourse as both functional and meaningful. The prototype here as in other aspects of Humanism is Petrarch. Since the

[17] *The Romantic Agony*, London, 1933, p. 5.
[18] H. Frankfort, in "Three Lectures," *JWI*, 21 (1958), p. 141f., discusses Saxl's Theory in the first essay, "The Dying God"; cf. J. Seznec, *The Survival of the Pagan Gods; The Mythological Tradition and its Place in Renaissance Humanism and Art*, New York, 1953, p. 320.
[19] A. Buck makes the point that the decisive factor is not the broadening of the knowledge of antiquity, in *Italienische Dichtungslehre; Vom Mittelalter bis zum Ausgang der Renaissance, Beihefte zur Zeitschrift für romanische Philologie*, 94 Heft (1952), p. 54. On the discovery of texts see Sabbadini, "Due questioni storico-critiche su Quintiliano," *Rivista di filol. class.*, 20 (1891), pp. 307-22, as well as his *Le scoperte dei codici latini*, and *Storia e critica di testi latini*.

chief sensual pleasure of language is sound, it is significant that this is precisely Petrarch's special injunction to readers: "*non modo corde concepte, sed etiam ore prolate*" (*Fam.*, I, 9, 11).[20] In Petrarch's case the imitation of the classics is no longer a matter of following a handbook, but, as Professor Gmelin puts it, a kind of acoustical meditation upon the text itself.

Das Ausschlaggebende aber war, dass in jenem Lande der Trobadors sein Ohr an den Weisen ihrer Lieder geschult ward, und dass er nun daraus verfiel, die lateinischen Autoren zum erstenmal auch mit jenem musikalischen Sinn der Trobadors zu lesen und sich an der klanglichen Schönheit der ciceronianischen Sprache zu berauschen. Wie dies als eine Art musikalischer Rausch ihn schon als Knaben erfasste, hat er in einem seiner Altersbriefe selbst berichtet: '*et illa quidem aetate nihil intellegere poteram, sola me verborum dulcedo quaedam et sonoritas detinebat, ut quicquid dissonum rideretur.*' (*Sen.*, 15, 1) Diese musikalische Einfühlung und Feinhörigkeit hat sein ganzes Verhältnis zur antiken Literatur und, wie wir sehen werden, auch den Charakter seiner Imitatio bestimmt.[21]

For Petrarch the classics have authority as experience; he follows the classical authors in so far as their sensibility is identified with his own; it is his own sensitivity which provides the touchstone for imitating antique models in his eloquence (*Fam.*, XXII, 2, 20; I, 8, 4).

Like Petrarch, Salutati resents the domination of the

---

[20] The edition cited of Petrarch's *Le familiari* is that of V. Rossi and U. Bosco in the *Edizione Nazionale*, Vols. 10-13, Florence, 1938-42, cited henceforth as *Fam.* with the book, number, and section of the letter.

[21] H. Gmelin, *Das Prinzip der Imitatio in den romanischen Literaturen der Renaissance*, RF, 46 (1932), pp. 98-99; Gmelin claims "So ist ihm [Petrarch] die Imitatio eine Art akustischer Meditation" (p. 173). See also M. Seidlmayer, "Petrarca, das Urbild des Humanisten," AKG, 40 (1958), pp. 141-93, reprinted in *Wege und Wandlungen des Humanismus*, Göttingen, 1965, pp. 125-173; E. Cassirer, *The Individual and the Cosmos in Renaissance Philosophy*, trans. M. Domandi, New York, 1963, pp. 128-29.

mechanistic, unspontaneous *cursus*, or set rhythmic ending, rigidly prescribed by the medieval *ars dictaminis*. The ears of the public which applauds this jangling ornament rather than the pure elegance of classic style, than a *"solido . . . prisco more dicendi,"* are truly asses' ears, *Mideiæ auriculæ.*[22] He specifically approves of the style of Iacopo da Teramo because

> Here is not that equality of syllables, which never happens without careful counting; here are not the *clausulae* which end or close monotonously: things which our Cicero reprehends as a kind of puerility, by no means appropriate to serious subjects or to use by people of dignity.[23]

The mechanical is boring; he condemns also the *lubricatio* of the "moderns," i.e. the followers of medieval precept, and the *rhythmica sonoritas* of the friars (*E.*, I, 77; cf. IV, 234; II, 78). Salutati connects the defective ear of the moderns with defective experience; there is no natural response but a deliberate choice of meretricious display, where

> the picture not better, but more ornate is commended; not manners, but splendid clothes signify: few elect to be good rather than to seem good.[24]

On the other hand, Salutati deplores the false asceticism displayed by the religious orders in their attacks on the literature of the Gentiles; he emphasizes the use, not abuse, of

---

[22] *E.*, I, 133. For the change in the appreciation of sound from Middle Ages to Renaissance see E. De Bruyne, *L'esthétique du moyen âge*, Louvain, 1947; U. Eco, "Sviluppo dell'estetica medievale," and C. Vasoli, "L'estetica dell'umanesimo e del Rinascimento," in *Momenti e problemi di storia dell'estetica*, Vol. 1, Milan, 1959, pp. 114-229, 325-433.

[23] "non est ibi syllabarum equalitas, que sine dinumeratione fieri non solet; non sunt ibi clausule, que similiter desinant aut cadant, quod a Cicerone nostro non aliter reprehenditur quam puerile quiddam, quod minime deceat rebus seriis vel ab hominibus qui graves sint adhiberi." *E.*, III, 631-32. Cf. *Ad Herr.*, 4, 20; *De orat.*, III, 54; Quintilian, *I.O.*, IX, 3, 79; IX, 4, 42.

[24] "pictura non melior, sed ornatior commendatur, non moribus, sed vestium splendori defertur; pauci se fore bonos magis eligunt quam videri." *E.*, I, 133.

form and the senses it affects, "for indeed divine Providence has granted these instruments for the edification, not the ruin, of the soul" (*E.*, I, 265).

Think how much enters the mind through these channels of the ears; it is scarcely credible how much they profit the health of the soul,—if you hear correctly, and if you harvest the good and reject the bad, as if separating the wheat from the tares.[25]

The capacity of music to heal a sick man proves the natural power of sound; the tremendous power of rhetoric to sway large assemblies of men lies in part in the rational control of this potential.[26] The regaining of the lost balance of the classics which was the goal of Renaissance Humanism involved the recognition of the importance of natural sensitivity as well as rational control in the orator:

In nothing, however, is doctrine less efficacious than in that faculty of speaking. . . . Nature indeed lays the foundation of discourse, art merely builds from there.[27]

Crucial for the Humanist ideal of form in discourse is this necessary relationship between artificiality and naturalness; it fills with concrete content the old classical dictum, prescriptive in poetic through the eighteenth century, that art imitates nature. Humanist aesthetic is a revaluation of

[25] "adde quot per has aurium fistulas penetrent, quibus, si recte accipiantur, si quasi lolium a frumento secernens, bona recondas et eligas, mala vero devites, vix cogitari queat quantum animi proficiant ad salutem." *E.*, I, 267.

[26] "Non ergo putem graves cum facundo sermone sententias, qui sine quadam harmonia non enuntiatur, que placidis auribus admisse descendunt ad animum, hoc etiam posse quod effecisse soni seu modi referuntur. Ego vero cum quamlibet artem potentiam esse sciam, rhetoricam arbitror potentissimam esse, que non solum specialiter unum afficiat, sed magnos exercitus maximasque civitatum conciones impellat et regat." *De verecundia*, 286-88.

[27] "in nulla tamen minus operatur doctrina, quam in ista facultate dicendi. . . . Natura quidem dicendi fundamenta iacit, ars edificat." *De verecundia*, 280-82; cf. *E.*, III, 606.

aesthesis, in the original meaning of "feeling," a return of art to its foundation in modes of sensibility.[28]

Further, since poetry consists of metaphor as well as meter, Salutati has a fresh and direct approach to the mass of traditional material on figure as well as sound.[29] Just as the appreciation of melody is inborn so the delight in images is natural: "*Hac autem similitudine mentes nostras naturaliter delectari et habere cum melodiis ingenitam familiaritatem.* . . ." (*De lab.,* I, 3, 15). The soul of poetry is invention, and invention is nothing more than a subtle and acute perception and distinction of natural operations,—"*naturalium operationum quedam subtilis et acuta perceptio atque distinctio*" (*De lab.,* I, 3, 4). But the distinctive feature of a poem is that it says one thing and means another; poetry is a "bilingual faculty, exhibiting one sense externally, signifying another by an internal process; always speaking in a figure" (*E.,* IV, 235). The extreme simplicity of his definition of poetry, "*per unam rem aliud designare,*" is liberating; the poetic task is dynamic, open-ended; the poet effects a delicate and continuous balance between a series of intentions and a series of figures. If Cusanus posits an infinite world of creative meanings as the only possible explication of the infinite creativity of God, Salutati sees the realm of poetic fancy as a "secularized world of free intentions or meanings" with unlimited possibilities for exploration and discovery.[30]

If the Humanists' fascination with the natural affect of

[28] See H. Marcuse's chapter on "The Aesthetic Dimension" in *Eros and Civilization,* New York, 1962, p. 157f.; E. Panofsky discusses the tendency in the Middle Ages to neglect the associative and emotional values in the classical heritage, *Renaissance and Renascences in Western Art,* Stockholm, 1965, p. 71. In a wide-ranging and brilliant article on Renaissance aesthetic G. Argan also emphasizes that the Renaissance artist in his determination to know himself in nature focuses his first interest on his sensory capacity, for nature is conceived of as full and lucid sensory experience; see "The Architecture of Brunelleschi and the Origins of Perspective Theory in the Fifteenth Century," *JWI,* 9 (1946), p. 98.

[29] See particularly *De lab.,* I, 1.

[30] Cranz, "Some Changing Contexts of Allegory"; the definition of poetry is in *De lab.,* I, 3, 10.

discourse seems to give them an insight into thought-as-experience, then their attribution of value to figure might be interpreted as a recognition of dealing with experience-as-expressed; both recall the Sophistic preoccupation with the sphere of *logos*—with discourse as selected forms which not only express but order our insights into reality. The three Trecento Humanists attribute a very high epistemological status to the figures of poets: Petrarch in his defense of the obscurities of invention, Boccaccio in his concept of the fourfold sense of secular fable, Salutati by maintaining that only the indirections of figure can express divine things; it is as if "only in this world which he creates and orders by his own act can man be fully himself."[31] Their emphasis on the transcendental ends of poetry results, paradoxically, in a eulogy of the variety and richness of human artifice.

Further, all three Humanists stress the self-containedness of the poetic faculty when they utilize the passage from Cicero's *Pro Archia poeta*:

> . . . while other arts are matters of science and formula and technique, poetry depends solely on an inborn faculty, is evoked by a purely mental activity, and is infused with a strange supernal inspiration.[32]

Salutati manages to intimate the autonomy, even while re-iterating the Platonic-Hermetic convention of the divine inspiration of the poet: his words recall the humanistic insight

[31] Petrarch's defense of poetic figure is in the *Invective contra medicum, III,* in *Francesco Petrarca; Prose,* ed. G. Martellotti et al., Milan, [1955]; Boccaccio's defense in Book XIV of *Genealogia deorum,* ed. V. Romano, in *Scrittori d'Italia,* X, Bari, 1951; Salutati's in Book I of *De laboribus Herculis,* as well as the letters to Benvenuto da Imola and Giovanni Dominici in the *Epistolario,* Vol. 4. The quotation is from Argan, "Brunelleschi," p. 121.

[32] . . . ceterarum rerum studia et doctrina et preceptis et arte constare, poetam natura ipsa valere et mentis viribus excitari et quasi divino quodam spiritu inflari" 8, 18. Salutati, *De lab.,* I, 3, 1; Petrarch, *Invectivarum contra medicum quendam libri quatuor, I, Opera,* Basel, 1581, p. 1091; Boccaccio, *Gen. deo.,* XIV, 7, p. 701. See Tateo, "La crisi della tradizione medievale," "*Retorica*" e "*Poetica,*" chap. 2, p. 82f.; Apel, *Die Idee,* p. 174f.

of the pre-Socratics who made Fate Character when he calls it a *"divinitatis donum, quod poete fatum vocant,"* for by making the divine act a human potential he "internalizes" the gift (*E.,* III, 601).[33]

Paradoxically, this reassertion of the independent and superior value of poetics and poetry benefits rhetoric and prose. Gorgias had made poetic techniques the foundation of the new rhetorical discipline, and Salutati is careful to repeat the traditional emphasis on the debt of rhetoric to poetic figure and rhythm (*De lab.,* I, 13, 10-12; *E.,* IV, 177).[34] Poetics and rhetoric together furnish the techniques for eloquence, and, according to Salutati, it is the combined pursuit of wisdom and eloquence which distinguishes the *studia humanitatis,* the etymological source as well as the intellectual core of the movement called Renaissance Humanism.[35]

Wisdom and eloquence are the peculiar endowment of man, by which he is distinguished from other living creatures. And how excellent, how glorious, how appropriate it is to excel in those gifts of nature which make man preeminent above other animals. The wise and the eloquent seem to me to have achieved for themselves that step of excellence above other men, which God and nature have decreed between men and creatures devoid of reason; and

[33] Salutati speaks of poetry as a natural, spontaneous power in Petrarch, *E.,* I, 341; as an inborn capacity, II, 399. Poetry as a divine gift is a Humanist commonplace: cf. Guarino Veronese's Preface to his *Vita Platonis* where he characterizes eloquence as not human but oracular,—"ut non hominis ingenio sed quodam delphico: ut poeta diceret, videatur oraculo dei instinctus" (Bibl. Laur. Gadd. 189, f.3). But G.M. Filelfo, in his etymological discussion of poetry as stemming from the verb "to make" emphasizes poetry as an autonomous activity, "De clarissimi poetae Dantis Florentini vita et moribus," in *Vite di Dante,* ed. A. Solerti, Milan, n.d., pp. 177-78.
[34] Aristotle discusses the borrowing of metaphor from poetry in the *Rhetoric,* III, 7; *Poetics,* 19; Quintilian in the *I.O.,* I, 8, 13.
[35] See Gray, "The Pursuit of Eloquence," and Seigel, *Rhetoric and Philosophy;* on the *studia humanitatis* see Kristeller, *The Classics in Renaissance Thought,* Cambridge, Mass., 1955; A. Campana, "The Origin of the Word 'Humanist'," *JWI,* 9 (1946), pp. 60-73; A. Buck, "*Studia humanitatis* und ihre Methode," *BHR,* 21 (1959), pp. 273-90.

a step so much higher as benign fortune has added to this gift prominence in power, dignity, and family.[36]

According to convention, as *scientia* is the *materia* of all discourse, *eloquentia* is the *forma* (*E.*, III, 70). But occasionally eloquence for Salutati seems to be learning-expressed-in-form; the fullest definition is *"scientie copia cum elegantia facultateque dicendi"* (*E.*, III, 506). Eloquence tends, in fact, to become the final and distinctive element in Humanist learning:

> This is that faculty which adorns, cherishes and honors all other types of knowledge, whether speculative or practical, and all aspects of life; the faculty for whose perfection the knowledge of all, even the greatest things, both divine and human, is necessary: indeed, to attempt to praise this faculty after Cicero is an act of temerity.[37]

Eloquence is both rarer and more difficult than *sapientia* (*E.*, III, 602). Later, Lorenzo Valla will call eloquence *"regina rerum . . . et perfecta sapientia."*[38]

Within the larger category of eloquence as in poetry the Humanists emphasize autonomy and freedom. Francesco

---

[36] "sapientia quidem et eloquentia proprie dotes hominis sunt, quibus a ceteris animantibus separatur. et quam excellens, quam gloriosum quamque decorum est illis nature donis hominibus antecellere, quibus constat hominem animantibus aliis eminere: fecisse michi videntur sapientes et eloquentes sibi super alios homines illum excellentie gradum, quem Deus et natura constituit inter homines et animalia rationis expertia; tantoque excelsiorem, quanto fortune benignitas donum hoc potentia, dignitate vel sanguine supereminentius collocavit." *E.*, III, 599-600. Cf. *E.*, I, 70, 77, 229-30; 248-49. One source of the *topos* is Cicero, *De inv.*, I, 4, 5; see also, in *Reden und Briefe italienischen Humanisten*, ed. K. Müllner, Vienna, 1899, Antonio da Rho, "Oratio ad scolares," pp. 167-68; and F. Filelfo, "Oratio de laudibus eloquentiae," p. 153.

[37] "hec est illa facultas, que cunctas alias scientias, sive speculative sive practice sint, et omnes vite nostre partes exornat, colit celebratque et ad cuius perfectionem omnium etiam maximarum rerum scientia, sive divine sive humane sint, necessaria est, de cuius laudibus post Ciceronem dicere temerarium est." *E.*, III, 411.

[38] *Elegantiae, Praefatio IV, Opera omnia*, Vol. 1, ph. rep. Turin, 1962, p. 120; cf. Cicero, *De orat.*, II, 44, 187.

Filelfo maintains that while the powers of eloquence are great, they are not superhuman:

> Nor should the immense magnitude of eloquence deter us. Nothing is to be attempted beyond nature; she orders nothing which human ingenuity is not able both to undertake and to finish.[39]

And Roberto de' Rossi returns to a rhetorical commonplace when he contrasts the uncertainty of riches and the instability of fortune with the inalienability of the sciences,—of which rhetoric is an illustrious example—which have the virtue of being permanently attached to one's person.[40]

But if rhetoric is a highly portable it is also a highly ambivalent discipline; Salutati acknowledges that there is another dimension to rhetorical freedom or lack of circumscription, i.e. rhetoric is amoral.[41] Where Salutati insists on the strict necessity of not only moral goodness but moral excellence on the part of the poet, he admits the orator is very often not even good.[42] Yet one must separate virtuosity in the art of rhetoric from the use to which it is put, and not condemn it for the fault of some of its users (*De lab.*, I, 12, 22; *E.*, IV, 204, 224). Salutati has no lesser authority than St. Augustine for the traditionally Sophistic argument that there is no point in letting the wrong side take advantage of you:

[39] "neque nos id deterreat, quod immensa sit eloquentiae magnitudo. nihil enim supra naturam nitendum est. nihil praecipit, quod humana non possint et aggredi et perficere ingenia." From "De laudibus eloquentiae," in *Reden und Briefe*, p. 154; cf. Dante, *De vulgari eloquentia*, I, 2; Salutati paraphrases Cicero, *De orat.*, I, 3, 12, in pointing out that oratory is a "facultas non abstrusa, sed in medio sita est," *E.*, IV, 137, 142.

[40] "Sermo factus . . . sub supradicto Cino Dominici Francisci super detractione rhetorice," ed. A. Manetti, *Rinascimento*, 2 (1951), pp. 49-50.

[41] "infinitum et intranabile mare fit eloquentiae si dimiseris veritatem. vera quidem fixa sunt, determinata sunt, que qui sequitur in solido semper est." *E.*, III, 424.

[42] Where Quintilian had defined an orator as "vir bonus dicendi peritus" (*I.O.*, XII, 1, 1), Salutati maintained that some of the greatest orators were not even decent, *De lab.* I, 12, 5; a poet should be a "vir optimus . . . et long magis ad hanc excellentiam quam oratores ad viri boni statum et formulam accessise." *De lab.*, I, 12, 22.

For since the faculty of eloquence is neutral, very competent to persuade either evil or good, why do not good men study it, in order to advance the truth, if evil people usurp it to obtain perverse and worthless ends in the service of iniquity and error?[43]

At the same time, Salutati conceives of this lack of circumscription in a more positive sense, as copiousness in all aspects of aesthetic pleasure becomes an article of faith for the Humanists. In this respect, it is greater to be an orator than a poet:

In my opinion it is fine to be able to write poetry, but the greatest talent, I assure you, is to be able to overflow with ripe *sententiae* and praises in prose. For in the proportion that a river differs from the sea, so is poetry lesser than prose. The greatest achievement is eloquence because as Cicero says, no one can ever speak so fully as to completely satisfy his audience; always we feel some deficiency, when we either hear or read our own or others' discourse; nor can so great a potential be confined within the narrow boundaries of meter, when it exceeds even the infinite spaces of prose.[44]

Salutati uses frequently the contrast of the sweet and domesticated rivers of verse with the great sea of eloquence: "a great ocean not constricted by banks, but bounded by the almost immeasurable span of the curved shores" (*E.*, III, 424, 607; cf. I, 338-40; IV, 143, 148). Cicero specifically attributes to

[43] "cum ergo sit in medio posita facultas eloquii, que ad persuadendum seu prava seu recta plurimum valet, cur non bonorum studio comparatur, ut militet veritati, si eam mali ad obtinendas perversas vanasque causas in usus iniquitatis et erroris usurpant?" *E.*, IV, 204. Quoted from *De doctrina christiana*, IV, 2, 2.

[44] "magnum, fateor, versibus scribere, sed maximum, crede michi, prosaico stilo cum laudibus plenisque sententiis exundare. quantum flumen a pelago differt, tantum carmina prosis credito fore minora. maxima res est eloquentia, adeo quod, ut refert Cicero, adhuc nemo tam pleno resonaverit ore qui audientium aures impleverit; semper enim aliquid deficere perpendimus, cum nostra vel aliena legimus vel audimus; nec ex toto potest tanta res metrorum angustiis coarctari, que etiam infinitis prosarum spaciis non valet implecti." *E.*, I, 338.

Gorgias the affirmation of the infinite range of prose (*De inv.*, I, 5, 7); the Humanists reaffirm the Gorgian presupposition of rhetorical freedom. Again Dante anticipates Humanist linguistic attitudes; with many concrete examples from his own experience of the Italian vernacular he claims that the extreme variety of language, the absolute arbitrariness of signs, stems from the freedom of human reason as opposed to the necessitarian structure of the animal passions (*De vulgari eloquentia*, I, 3, 1-3).

An essential characteristic of eloquence (*facundia*) is richness, and richness is not only copiousness, but a fluidity, a flexibility of form to correspond to the infinite variety of human nature to which one must appeal (*E.*, III, 62).[45] Moreover, both Humanists and Sophists justify richness as a manifestation of high human potential rather than as necessarily immoral or voluptuous. The attack of Giovanni Dominici on poetry which Salutati attempted to repel is one aspect of a conservative reaction to the growth of a lay culture which emphasizes sheer activity; a similar reaction had taken place in the Sophistic age against the *polypragmosyne*, the political vitality and aggressiveness which had upset the political balance of Greece and which the Sophists had tried to justify. The audience has changed; in the Middle Ages the use of affective techniques was justified by citing the necessity of working on the feelings of the vulgar who were unable to function in the rare atmosphere of intellectual vision of Scholastic dialectic, by the need of talking down to an audience.[46] Now the audience is rich and busy itself, and

[45] Cf. *E.*, IV, 142. On *facundia* see also G. Vico, *La filosofia di G. Vico; I, Gnoseologia ed estetica*, ed. F. Nicolini, Florence, n.d., pp. 122-23, where the etymology is *facilitas*, the Italian meaning *naturalezza*.

[46] On *polypragmosyne* see Finley, "Euripides and Thucydides," *Three Essays*, p. 13f.; an excellent short study on the Humanists' audience is F. Schalk's *Das Publikum in italienischen Humanismus*, Krefeld, 1955; contrast this with the projection of H. Welter of the medieval audience, *L'exemplum dans la littérature religieuse et didactique du Moyen Âge*, Paris, 1927, p. 66f., where the use of *exempla* is justified by descriptions of the rude and unpolished audience; cf. Boccaccio, "Trattatello in laude di Dante," in *Vite di Dante*, p. 44. Schalk most usefully reminds us that the Humanists' Latin had a large audience,

rejoices in similar success and virtuosity; Burckhardt mentions that eloquence became "the indispensable element and ornament of all elevated lives," with "listening" among the chief pleasures of life.[47] Richness is not meretricious ornament; nudity in discourse as well as dress is a false choice, unnecessary self-sacrifice. Thus Trapezuntius asks

> For how can a person show himself to be wealthy, if he doesn't possess ample funds and magnificent dwellings? Besides, if his toes protrude from his shoes, and he is dressed in a filthy garment full of holes, the man is ridiculed as not only poor, but poverty-stricken and necessitous. Thus whoever professes to know the extent of the world, the nature of the heavens, their origins and destiny, unless he also adorns and illumines his learning with copiousness of speech, as with so much gold or gems, will seem destitute of any knowledge.[48]

For the Humanists the natural affective potential of eloquence—its infinite range, its copiousness, its amorality—all contribute to the great and unique power of eloquence. Thus a further parallel with the Sophistic rhetors is that the Humanist emphasis on "artistic prose" is part of an emphasis on the will rather than the intellect. Both Humanist and

---

p. 19; while Hans Baron points out that in early Quattrocento Florence the supposed clash of a popular Volgare culture with a learned Latin one is not founded in fact (*The Crisis of the Early Italian Renaissance*, Princeton, 1966, chap. 15, p. 332f.). The tidiest expression of the Humanist attitude toward the audience is that of Guarino Veronese: in history "Dictio sit . . . ut cum omnes intelligant, tum periti laudent et admirentur. . . . ," *Epistolario*, ed. R. Sabbadini, Venice, 1916, Vol. 2, pp. 464-65.

[47] J. Burckhardt, *Civilization of the Renaissance in Italy*, London, 1945, p. 138.

[48] "nam ut qui se divitem ostentat, si neque fundos amplissimos, nec magnificos aedes habeat. praeterea si e calceis digiti erumpant, totumque corpus sordida, a fenestrata veste contectum sit, is non modo pauper, sed egenus omnino, atque inops deridetur. sic, qui mundi se ambitum, caelestium naturam, unde quaelibet fiant, quo ruant, scire profitetur, nisi orationis quoque copia, tanto quam auro, aut gemma, exornet et illustret doctrinam, omni scientia inops videri debet." *Rhetoricorum Libri V*, Venice, 1523, f. 60r.

Sophistic culture have a strong voluntarist cast; the pre-eminence of the will over the intellect is fundamental to many of Salutati's discussions of learning (*De nobilitate*, chap. 23; *E.*, II, 479; III, 447).[49] Salutati agrees with Cicero that of the three sections of philosophy—physical, logical, moral—eloquence and rhetoric are connected with moral rather than logical science (*E.*, III, 605; cf. Cicero, *De orat.*, I, 25, 68-69). Learning as well as good intentions is necessary for virtue (*E.*, I, 106; III, 535-36); the end of learning must be virtue, not mere erudition (*E.*, I, 248-49; II, 274, 430; III, 330, 604; IV, 203). But "*omnis . . . virtus in actione consistit*" (*E.*, I, 65). Eloquence is essential to the *studia humanitatis* because of the necessity of moving the will to action (*E.*, IV, 216); for action is the product of the soul, not just the intellect, and the only way to transform an idea into action is through affecting the senses, the imagination as well as the reason; form is the only recourse.[50] One facet of the Humanist justification of rhetoric is a kind of anti-Stoicism; Salutati distrusts any hypothesis of perfect rational control; to ignore the feelings is impossible, only the Saviour could be a Stoic: "Indeed, I know not if any mortal ever attained to such perfection, besides Christ" (*E.*, II, 310).[51] But for the Humanists Christ is not primarily an exemplar of a perfect constancy and control which is "inhuman" but of charity; a positive aspect of their justification is surely their assumption of the preeminence of Christian *caritas* over intellect. The foundation of a Christian rhetoric is

---

[49] On the primacy of the will in Salutati see Garin, *Italian Humanism*, trans. P. Munz, Oxford, 1965, p. 29f.; Sciacca, "La valore," p. 359f.; Galletti, *L'eloquenza*, p. 543. A facet of the emphasis on the will is the high valuation of *caritas*: ". . . hec denique sola virtutes vivificat, hominem supra hominem statuit, prospera feliciori felicitate felicitat. . . ." *E.*, I, 247; cf. III, 44.

[50] "affuit enim vehementie verborum lenocinium et sententiarum profundissima gravitas, quorum illud iocunditate quadam animum movit, istud potenter impulit iam commotum." *E.*, I, 219; cf. 115, 179; III, 377, 451, 454, 601.

[51] "illam remotam a sensibus nostris fortitudinem seu constantiam sive, ut verius loquor, inhumanitatem et duriciam semper exhorrui." *E.*, II, 55. See L. Borghi's discussion of Salutati's progressive liberation from Stoicism, "La dottrina morale di C.S.," p. 84f.

Augustine's emphasis on the role of speech in the redeem-
ing work of love; the origins of pre-Humanist rhetoric are in
part Augustinian attitudes. Thus Brunetto Latini in his
Rettorica paraphrases Cicero's completely naturalistic explanation of the origins and end of rhetoric but adds that
rhetoric's final and highest purpose is *"per amare Idio e 'l
proximo."*[52]

If eloquence without wisdom is amoral, wisdom without
eloquence is impotent in either divine or human affairs;
eloquence, not knowledge, is power. Hence it is here that the
tie between eloquence and rhetoric is most strict, for rhetoric
teaches the art of persuasion of the will. Erik Erikson has
suggested that the Renaissance represents the regaining of the
executive power of the will; similarly, Renaissance rhetoric
illustrates the regaining of the executive power of language.[53]
One cannot learn eloquence through the study of dialectic,
an intellectual exercise the moderns have developed for
subtlety, not use (*E.*, III, 604). For Petrarch and Salutati,
the "modern" dialecticians, not the rhetors, are the Sophists
in the pejorative sense; with them the bare structure of
dialectic, denuded of human purpose, has become an end
in itself, rather than a means to an end (Petrarch, *Fam.*, I,
7; I, 12; Salutati, *De lab.*, I, 1, 5). Where the Terminist
logicians, the "Britannici," are interested in mere *verba*, the
Humanists are interested in *res*, in whatever conduces to the
"beatam atque excultam et ornatam vitam" (*Fam.*, I, 12, 4).[54]

There is a decisive shift in attitude in the fourteenth-
century revolution of sensibility; the Humanists come to
regard *only* the beautiful as useful.[55] The Humanists thus
come close to saying that the thought unexpressed is not

[52] *Rettorica*, p. 19. See Colish, *Mirror of Language*, p. 8f.
[53] Erikson, *Young Man Luther*, New York, 1958, p. 193.
[54] Vasoli, " 'Antichi' contro 'Moderni'," *La dialettica*, 9f.; Garin,
"La cultura fiorentina nella seconda metà del 300 e i 'barbari britanni',"
La Rassegna d. lett. ital., 64 (1960), pp. 181-95.
[55] "Der ethische Nützlichkeitsbegriff aus Platos *Republik* begegnet
hier in rein ästhetischer Fassung. Nur das Schöne is nützlich, d.h. im
sinnlich-geistigen Verstande der *convenientia*: zweckmässig, bequem,
(*commodum*)." Borinski, *Die Antike in Poetik*, Vol. 1, p. 163.

worth having; their central metaphor of the relationship of
thought and form is that of Trapezuntius:

> For indeed, reason itself lies hidden in the obscure proc-
> esses of the intellect before it has been drawn forth by
> speech; it has just so much light or brilliance as the fire
> hidden in the flint, before the iron strikes it: indeed, while
> it is hidden no one would think to call it a "fire."[56]

This concept of knowledge as a spark brought to visibility
and efficacy by eloquence is a Humanist commonplace; con-
ventionally, they describe eloquence as capable of "firing" the
spirit to action. Further, rhetoric is the most powerful of the
arts because it is capable of swaying not just a single reader
but a multitude (*De verecundia*, 288; cf. Cicero, *De orat.*, I,
24, 79). They characterize eloquence as essential, not accidental; to add form radically transforms the content; eloquence can make "the transitory seem eternal, the absent
present, it causes the dead to seem alive, the mute to speak,
and finally, the blind to see."[57] The rhetor is preeminently a
mediator, i.e. the vital link between exemplary action and
action imitative of the exemplar.[58] The original deed must be
expressed in artistic prose in order both to live on and to move
the will of others.

And it is exactly these two purposes which link eloquence
and history in Humanist theory. The conventional rhetorical
program for historiography appears succinctly in Guarino

[56] "nam ratio quidem ipsa, quae in mentis intellectusque abditis re-
condita est, nisi oratione fuerit elicita, tantum splendoris habet, quantum ignis abstrusus in silice, quem, nisi ferro provocetur, nec ignem
quidem aliquis unquam appellabit." *Rhetoricorum libri* V, f. 59v.
M. Merleau-Ponty demonstrates the continuous life of this maxim: "A
thought limited to existing for itself, independently of the constraints
of speech and communication, would no sooner appear than it would
sink into the unconscious, which means that it would not exist even
for itself." *Phenomenology of Perception*, tr. C. Smith, London, 1962,
p. 177.
[57] Lapo da Castiglionchio, "Oratio Bononiae habita in suo legendi
initio ad scolares . . . ," *Reden und Briefe*, p. 135.
[58] Valla, ". . . sine qua [elegance] caeca omnis doctrina est et illiber-
alis. . . ." *Elegantiae, Praefatio III, Opera*, Vol. 1, p. 80.

Veronese's "*De historiae conscribendae praeceptis libellus.*"[59] In most of the Humanists' discussions of history the peculiar function of the historian is to add form to the raw materials of historical narrative; history is still Cicero's *opus oratorium maxime.* Indeed, their explicit theories of history contain a surfeit of convention; as D. R. Kelley has pointed out, if they omitted to quote Ciceronian injunctions about form and content—that full history is formal history, that history is *lux veritatis*—it is an oversight; they repeat all the shibboleths of the classical rhetorical theory of history ad nauseam.[60] This description of the formal contribution of the historian merely adds the category of time to the concept of rhetoric as mediating experience; the essential capacity of the historian is his power to endow human endeavor with glory and perpetual fame, to "immortalize" (*E.*, I, 227; III, 86; IV, 70-71). Where other methods of commemoration such as pictures or statues are fragile, words are imperishable monuments.[61] Moreover, statues and pictures are "mute," conveying impressions of the body only, where eloquence is the vehicle of the spirit.[62] In an even more encomiastic vein, Andrea Juliano claims that eloquence can lend a certain immortality even to bodies: witness the reverent awe which surrounded the discovery of the body of Livy at Padua.[63]

For the Humanists the connection of glory and fame with history is almost an identity:

> The first of the muses is obviously Clio. And first because the first impulse to learn stems from the desire for the celebrity of fame which is glory. Whence Clio is said to come from "*cleos,*" which is glory. For as glory is the end which the studious pursue to the last, so it is first in the

[59] *Epistolario*, II, pp. 458-65; the letter is addressed to Tobia Borghi in 1446; Guarino's source is Lucian.

[60] "Historia Integra; François Baudouin and His Conception of History," *JHI*, 25 (1964), pp. 38-57.

[61] Ognibene da Lonigo, "Oratio in Valerium Maximum," *Reden und Briefe*, p. 144; cf. Guarino, *Epistolario*, II, p. 459.

[62] Guarino, *Epistolario*, II, p. 311.

[63] "Oratio super principio orationum M. Tullii Ciceronis . . . ," *Reden und Briefe*, p. 117.

intention of the student, the reason why he begins to work.[64]

Thus eloquence, and therefore rhetoric, is an essential, not accidental, part of history; to Petrarch eloquence is the sum of the virtues of Livy's work, *"opus . . . ut ab arce eloquentiae non multum abesse videantur."*[65]

2. ELOQUENCE AND HISTORY

If, then, eloquence was the distinctive concern of the Humanists, the next task is to show that since their rhetorical interests had such priority, and their rhetorical judgments functioned at such a basic level, rhetoric sponsored the productive as well as the difficult aspects of Humanism, and more specifically, that it fostered, not disguised, the innovative and liberating historicist insights which the Humanists attained. Yet from Jacob Burckhardt to Hans Baron, Renaissance scholars have stressed the pejorative influence of rhetoric on history; Burckhardt states their case when he deplores the fact that

> Livy was taken as a pattern just where he is least worthy of imitation—namely, because he "turned a dry and naked tradition into grace and richness." We find the suspicious declaration that it is the function of the historian to excite, charm, or overwhelm the reader—as if he were a poet.[66]

[64] "Prima quidem Musarum est Clyo. Prima namque cogitationi discere cupientium primum occurrit fame celebritas que gloria est. Unde Clyo a 'cleos', quod est 'gloria', dicta est. Sicut enim gloria finis est quem studiosi assequuntur in ultimis post laborem, ita primum est in intentione studentis propter quam subicit se labori." *De lab.*, I, 8, 10. Cf. *E.*, I, 70, 219, 336; Cicero, *Tusc.*, I, 24.

[65] *Rerum memorandum libri*, ed. G. Billanovich, Florence, 1937, p. 18.

[66] *Civilization of the Renaissance*, p. 187; cf. Voigt, *Wiederbelebung*, 488. The standard view of the pejorative effect of rhetoric on historiography is expressed in E. Fueter, *Geschichte der neueren Historiographie*, Munich, 1911, Part 1, "Die humanistische Geschichtsschreibung in Italien," pp. 1-136, esp. 10-11; also B. Croce, *History, Its Theory and Practice*, trans. D. Ainslie, New York, 1923, pp. 224-42; F. Schevill, *Medieval and Renaissance Florence*, New York, 1961, Vol. 1, p. xvii. E. Santini, *Leonardo Bruni Aretino e i suoi "Historiarum*

The general tendency has been to view the Humanist historian as a philologist *manqué*: a philologist too concerned with his own language. Yet the Humanist's general interest in language precedes and stimulates his specific interest in establishing texts; it is in the area of philosophy of language, not philology, that the important Humanist achievement lies. In a large proportion of the debates and dialogues of the fourteenth and fifteenth centuries—debates on law, medicine, theology, religious hypocrisy; on the Ancients and the Moderns, the active and contemplative modes; on the nature of philosophy, fortune and the moral life—the argument hinges on questions of language. The rhetorical revolution which

---

Florentini populi Libri XII", Pisa, 1910; B.L. Ullman, "L.B. and Humanistic Historiography," *Studies in the Italian Renaissance*, Rome, 1955, pp. 320-44; Garin, "I cancellieri," and "La storia nel pensiero del Rinascimento," *Med. e Rin.*, pp. 192-210; Baron, "Das Erwachen des historischen Denkens im Humanismus des Quattrocento," *HZ*, 147 (1933), pp. 5-20, and *Crisis*, esp. chap. 3, p. 47f.—all have rehabilitated the Humanist historiographers, such as Bruni; yet the "new rehabilitation of the Sophists" has not impinged on their notions of the bad effects of rhetorical language on historical insight; cf. Baron, *Crisis*, p. 199.

On the other hand, C. Varese, *Storia e politica nella prosa del Quattrocento*, Turin, 1961, stresses the fine values and historical insights shared by Humanist rhetoricians and Volgare memorialists in the fifteenth century. Two other scholars deal with the positive contributions of rhetoric to historiography: in *Caesar: Geschichte seines Ruhms*, Leipzig, 1924, F. Gundolf emphasizes the interrelationship of the growth of critical and formal insight in Petrarch; Hanna Gray concentrates on Pontano's dialogue *Actius* in her unpublished doctoral dissertation, "History and Rhetoric in Quattrocento Humanism," Radcliffe, 1956. Some other studies which bear upon the relation of Humanist language to Humanist history are A. Buck, *Geschichtsdenken der Renaissance*, Krefeld, 1957; Sabbadini, *Il Metodo*, chap. 7; P. Joachimsen, *Geschichtsauffassung und Geschichtsschreibung in Deutschland unter dem Einfluss des Humanismus*, Leipzig, 1910; H. Gmelin, *Personendarstellung bei den florentinischen Geschichtsschreibern der Renaissance*, Leipzig, 1927; F. Lamprecht, *Zur Theorie der humanistischen Geschichtsschreibung: Mensch und Geschichte bei F. Patrizi*, Zurich, 1950; G. Spini, "I trattatisti dell'arte storica nella controriforma italiana," *Contributi alla storia del Concilio di Trento*, Florence, 1948, pp. 109-36; D.R. Kelley, "Guillaume Budé and the First Historical School of Law," *AHR*, 72 (1967), pp. 807-34. I regret that D.J. Wilcox's *Development of Florentine Humanist Historiography*, Cambridge, Mass., 1969, appeared too late for me to make use of it.

begins in the fourteenth century underwrites the highly sophisticated discussions of the nature of language and the relation of language and meaning which begin in the sixteenth century and culminate in the eccentric philology of Vico's *New Science*. In truth there is much in rhetoric which is antipathetic to modern concepts of philology; yet it is not always the case that the anti-philological is anti-historical.

In short, there is a logical as well as chronological priority to the aesthetic and specifically poetic interests of the Humanists; the impetus for the revival of a rhetoric which is in many ways an analogue of Sophistic rhetoric came from without, from the changes in sensibility expressed in the new tone of the defense of poetry by Petrarch, Boccaccio, and Salutati; *"nessuna forma di eloquenza può essere infatti estranea alla poesia, nessun modo di espressione può avere altra origine o nascita."*[67] Humanist rhetoric is the mediator of the effect of this sensibility on the specifically historical consciousness of the Humanists. The new rhetoric is a preperceptive set, a *facultas praeformandi*, that allows a valuation of experience which could be considered historicist; it is a cluster of not only aesthetic but pragmatic and psychological attitudes which permit contemplation of significance within the flux of phenomena. That there is a shift from logic to rhetoric as the dominant linguistic discipline implies palingenesis rather than retrogression in historical consciousness, for rhetorical principles provided an objective framework for the definition and criticism of historical events, and rhetorical functions provided an authentic role for the historian.

To consider first the aesthetic canons, functions, and principles of rhetoric in their relation to the historical consciousness of the Humanist, it is obvious that the major, almost exclusive, source of knowledge of literary form through the eighteenth century was the classical rhetorical tradition; without rhetorical discipline the program of the revival of classical form would have been empty ideology, devoid of application

65

and drained of existential meaning.[68] Classical rhetoric was a compendium of the generative maxims which regulated a wide range of value judgments as well as of lists of figures and rhythms of discourse. By long habit the Humanists turned to rhetoric to settle the connection between expression and mood, gesture and tone, form and purpose in painting and sculpture as well as in literature: "Die Kunstlehre ist von Anbeginn eine Schöpfung der Renaissance und zwar speziell, ihrer Schuldoktrin: der antiken Rhetorik."[69]

The parallel which will illuminate the hypothesis that rhetoric is the objective framework for Humanist historical consciousness is the one between Humanist rhetoric and Renaissance perspective. K. Borinski maintained that the whole corpus of Greek science was useless to the development of an illusionist art till a practical science of optics came into being.[70] In the same way it was necessary for the Humanists to grasp rhetoric not as a pedantic rule book but as the source of what knowledge they possessed of the structure of language. The development of perspective proved a breakthrough in the fine arts:

> Like every process of historical understanding, or, which is the same, of critical reflection, the idea of perspective, the more it is clarified and developed in the mind of the artist, the more it enlarges that mind to take in new experience.[71]

And just as perspective in Renaissance art enlarged experience, so Humanist rhetoric gave a more comprehensive view

[68] E. Bonora, *Stile e tradizione; Studi sulla letteratura italiana dal tre al cinquecento*, Milan, 1960, p. 10.
[69] Borinski, *Die Antike in Poetik*, Vol. 1, p. 176, cf. p. 125. For the use of rhetorical categories in the theory and practice of fine arts see J.R. Spencer, "*Ut rhetorica pictura*: A Study in Quattrocento Theory of Painting," *JWI*, 20 (1957), pp. 26-44; E.H. Gombrich, "Vasari's *Lives* and Cicero's *Brutus*," *JWI*, 23 (1960), pp. 309-11; S. Alpers, "*Ekphrasis* and Aesthetic Attitudes in Vasari's *Lives*," *JWI*, 23 (1960), pp. 190-215.
[70] *Die Antike in Poetik*, Vol. 1, p. 149.
[71] Argan, "The Architecture of Brunelleschi," p. 115.

of reality to historical consciousness. The selection and assimilation of strands of the classical rhetorical tradition,
particularly the mature Roman contribution, helped establish
that sense of "fixed distance" which characterized their critical posture in respect to the classical past, and by analogy,
to the recent past.[72] The dimensions added to the understanding of the classical experience are a list of rhetorical virtues—
*harmonia, concinnitas, decorum, convenientia, gravitas,
magnitudo.* A series of judgments on aesthetic worth become
a series of matrices imposed on material to reveal or conceal
historical patterns. The humanist availed himself of rhetorical
analysis to determine his priorities in historical narration; at
the same time purely formal motives of rhetoric appear as
historical moments in his pursuit of the meaning of classical
antiquity. Rhetoric mediates on two levels: to make judgments on the past as well as to transmit these values to
posterity.

First, rhetorical analysis made the Humanists sensitive to
the affective aspects of language; the concern with figure and
sound is conducive to the inclusion of irrational as well as
rational aspects of thought in the reconstruction of the past,
of thought-as-experience. Of all the rhetorical canons, the
principle of decorum is probably the most crucial,[73] since it
predicates the synthesis of the other criteria of expression.

[72] That the major innovation of the Renaissance historical consciousness was the ability to look at antiquity from a fixed unalterable distance as in the focused perspective of Renaissance painting is a theory
of E. Panofsky; see his "Renaissance or Renascences?" *KR*, 6 (1944),
p. 225, as well as his *Renaissance and Renascences in Western Art.*
R. Barthes, *On Racine,* trans. R. Howard, New York, 1964, pp. 160-61,
discusses rhetoric as another "perspective"; ". . .[In Racine] there is a
whole interpretation of the world that language imposes, through these
figures of rhetoric. Does this interpretation have to do with style? With
language? With neither one nor the other; what is involved is actually
an institution, a *form* of the world, as important as the historical representation of space among painters: unfortunately, literature is still
waiting for its Francastel."

[73] K. Vossler, *Poetische Theorien in der italienischen Renaissance,*
Berlin, 1900, p. 80: "Das Passende is die grosse ästhetische Norm der
damaligen Kunstlehre. . . ."

Chief of all, however, which pertains to the precepts of elocution, is that everything, as I have said, must be accommodated to the dignity of time, place, and person of the subject we treat.[74]

Since the Humanists' critical apparatus was rhetorical analysis, the concept of decorum became the framework of their attempts to establish internal coherence in their texts. The criterion of decorum tends to shift the attention to a network of existential relationships; the Humanists' discussions of the style of the ancients is also of the ancients' appreciation of style, habits and attitudes of mind, habitual judgments of audience as well as author. Humanists realize that classical authors not only sound better, but that they meant to sound better and this intention is part of their character and style. By juxtaposing classical models to medieval precepts and classical precepts to medieval models they arrive at two distinct cultural structures, defining differences which would be unintelligible in the terms of the logico-metaphysical axioms of Scholastic notions of language.

The Humanists can also use the fact that the principle of decorum can be consciously chosen or passively ignored to characterize a historical period. Salutati points out that the mark of modernity is the lack of feeling for decorum in his strictures on the sermons of the friars; similarly, the central intuition of Leon Battista Alberti's classicism is that *convenientia* is the mark of beauty.[75] Therefore in their historiographical roles the Humanists feel that to present the classical authors as wise but not eloquent is a distortion. The gist of Bruni's letter to Niccolò Niccoli on the translation of Plato is that since Plato chose to be eloquent not to translate him as eloquent would be unethical, would do him an injustice as well as distort the truth; for

---

[74] "Caput autem omnium, quae ad elocutionis praecepta attinent, illud visum est, ut omnia, sicut dixi, ad rerum, de quibus loquimur, dignitatem, temporum, locorum, et personarum accommodata sint." Gasparino Barzizza, "De compositione," *Opera*, ed. J. Furietti, Rome, 1723, p. 6.
[75] Borinski, *Die Antike in Poetik*, Vol. 1, pp. 148-49.

. . . here Plato himself seems to command me, who, since he was one of the most elegant speakers of the Greeks, certainly would not wish to appear inept to the Latins.[76]

Since Plato's wisdom had come through beauty in the first place, to read his teachings in halting Latin would cut the reader off from this experience; history becomes a matter not so much of authority as of individual confrontation, since the reader is assumed to make judgments on the basis of his own literary expertise. The foundation of historical reconstruction is literary sensitivity and rhetorical technique; according to Bruni's *"De interpretatione recta"* it is necessary that the translator read "widely and eclectically in all types of authors," and that he possess an "acute ear"—*"auris severum judicium."*

> Thus the best translator devotes himself in his translations with his whole mind and soul and will to the original author, and consciously tries to duplicate his figures, colors, mood, rhythm, to express all the features of his speech.[77]

The reason why the medieval translations of Aristotle are so deplorable is that the translators had skipped over most of their grammatical and all of their rhetorical training to study dialectic.[78]

---

[76] "Hoc enim ipse Plato praesens me facere jubet, qui cum elegantissimi oris apud Graecos sit, non vult certe apud Latinos ineptus videri." *Epistolarum Libri VIII*, I, 8. The edition of Bruni's letters is that of L. Mehus, Florence, 1741; the citation is of the book and number of the letter, found in Vol. 1, p. 17.

[77] "sic in traductionibus interpres quidem optimus sese in primum scribendi auctorem tota mente et animo et voluntate convertet et quodammodo transformabit eiusque orationis figuram, statum, ingressum coloremque et liniamenta cuncta exprimere meditabitur," *L.B. Aretino, Humanistisch-philosophische Schriften*, ed. H. Baron, Leipzig, 1928, p. 86; cf. pp. 85, 104, 126. [This will be cited henceforth as *Schriften*.] See Apel, *Die Idee*, p. 181f., where he speaks of Bruni combining the "artistic" identity with "einer gewissen asketischen Selbstverleugnung" in his notion of the translator. See also Fubini, "La coscienza," pp. 529-31; Seigel, *Rhetoric and Philosophy*, chap. 4, "Leonardo Bruni and the New Aristotle," pp. 99-136.

[78] ". . . Rapti de grammaticis immaturi et rudes et pleni adhuc puerilium tenebrarum ad ea properant audienda, quorum nec verba nec sig-

The list of stylistic virtues Bruni attributes to Plato, and which must appear in a translation of Plato are the phenomenal attributes with which the Humanist defines the Greek experience:

> . . . urbanity, the highest order of disputation, and a subtlety of the most fruitful and divine *sententiae* joined with a marvelous charm in the protagonists and an incredible copiousness of speech. . . . In discourse truly there appears the greatest fluency and much of the most admirable quality which the Greeks call χάρις.[79]

The unity of a language is its unique value; Bruni argues that each language has its own perfection because each has its own perspective.[80] And the unity first plotted through rhetorical analysis becomes a unified culture; Poggio Bracciolini fits literary remains and physical ruins into one symbolic whole;[81] the total symbolic heritage of forms, designs, words becomes historical evidence. There is a case for some kind of continuity beginning with Humanist rhetorical history, developing in Voltaire's *Essai sur les Moeurs*, and culminating in the Collingwoodian idea of history as reliving past experience from the inside. Further, as decorum is not only a synthesis of other values but a value in itself, the pattern, the *Gestalt* is liable to judgment on an aesthetic scale; the interrelationships

---

nificata intelligunt, ac rerum ipsarum vix umbram quamdam intuentur." "Vita Aristotelis," *Schriften*, p. 47.

[79] ". . . urbanitas, summaque disputandi ratio, ac subtilitas uberrimae divinaeque sententiae disputantium mirifica jocunditate, & incredibili dicendi copia. . . . In oratione vero summa facilitas, et multa, atque admiranda, ut Graeci dicunt χάρις." *Epistolarum Libri VIII*, I, 8; Vol. I, p. 16.

[80] "La vita di Dante," *Schriften*, p. 60; Fubini, "La coscienza," p. 539.

[81] *Historiae de varietate fortunae*, in *Opera omnia*, ed. R. Fubini, Vol. 2, *Opera miscellanea edita et inedita*, Turin, 1966, p. 511; further, there is a feeling that unless men can read these symbols of the past and can fit them into a meaningful whole, they can make only an inferior, a barbarized use of the past, as, for example, the Romans ransack the ruins for materials for ignoble buildings, *De varietate*, p. 507f.

themselves are seen as possessing value and force. The idea that each age has a pattern of its own has a remarkable development in Humanist historical method, beginning with Valla's treatment of the Donation of Constantine and finding full expression in Vico's notion of the congruence of language, character, literary achievement, and "age." There is a world of difference between the philologist's chaste purpose of establishing a particular text, and the Humanists' program, their concern with why a text should be established.

Thus the clearest manifestation of their acknowledgment of thought as experience, of the inseparability of rational doctrine and irrational matrix is in the Humanists' concept of translation. Without its penumbra of affective form the doctrine is not fully intelligible; Plato was a personality as well as a mind.[82] Of course, if rhetoric is influential here it is because it both influences and transmits the impetus of the new seriousness of poetry. The defense of poetry in Salutati's *De laboribus Herculis* rests on the implicit argument that it is not advantageous to deal with experience compartmentally (*De lab.*, I, 4, 8). Salutati contends that literature is an *opus*, not an *instrumentum*, a total performance, not a tool to be grasped opportunistically. Here there is a clear break with the medieval aesthetic that had placed the affective elements of eloquence on an inferior plane of the theologically determined hierarchies.[83] Now Renaissance Humanism replaces condescension with acceptance; the whole of the Old and New Testaments whether prose or poetry is a work of art; a theologian cannot use poetry, only a poet can make poems. The result is neither the ambiguous enjoyment of

[82] See, besides the works of Seigel, Apel, and Fubini cited above (note 77) Sabbadini's chapter on translation in his *Il metodo*; E. Garin, "Ricerche sulla tradizioni di Platone nella prima metà del secolo XV," *Medioevo e Rinascimento; Studi in onore di Bruno Nardi*, Florence, n.d., Vol. 1, pp. 339-74; and his "La fortuna dell'etica Aristotelica nel Quattrocento," *La cultura filosofica*, pp. 60-71. See Bruni's preface to his translation of Aristotle's *Ethics, Schriften*, p. 77; cf. Salutati, E., IV, 356-57.

[83] E., IV, 199. See De Bruyne, *L'esthétique*; Eco, "Sviluppo dell' estetica medievale"; Vasoli, "L'estetica," on the comparative intellectualism of medieval aesthetic.

Panofsky's twelfth-century "proto-humanism" nor Scholastic defense, but the realization of the autonomy and validity of the literary experience (*E.*, IV, 198-99). The Humanists found their experience of poetry, their profession of rhetoric gave them daily, concrete, immediate admonitions and strictures to take the affects seriously, to pay meticulous attention to "*omnes vitae partes*" (*E.*, II, 296). Petrarch had contended that contemporary logical forms were empty; that rational concepts cannot exhaust the possibilities of life.[84] It is the breadth and depth of the task which makes Salutati claim not only that eloquence is the most rare of faculties, but that history is "*difficilimum genus dicendi*" (*E.*, III, 602; IV, 140).

The concern with experience rather than idea involved in rhetorical assumptions has another ramification. One of the pejorative remarks that even the Humanists made about Humanists was that they were overly bemused by fame and glory, especially by their ability to attribute fame through style. Salutati himself takes contradictory positions: at times denouncing it as not conducive to eternal glory, at other times calling fame the ornament of virtue (*E.*, II, 404f., 422f.; III, 62f.; I, 76); he is ambiguous even in his ambiguity, explaining after a long denunciation of praise that his argument is only against intentionally misplaced praise (*E.*, II, 425). But the ubiquitous concern with fame which is part of the rhetorical personality also promotes a wider consciousness of ideas as active power rather than merely contemplative exercise. The purpose of rhetoric is to persuade its audience through form; the rhetor is occupied with the phenomenal reality of the idea for the audience, not the "pure" idea. Eloquence, not knowledge, is power, and the Humanists' involvement with power is a gain in sophistication in so far as it is an interest in what we call ideology rather than idea. As far as their historical sense is affected, their position is an analogue of the Hegelian dictum that the force of mind is

[84] *Invective contra medicum Liber III, Prose*, pp. 656-58, 670-72, 690-92; Bruni's definition of *eruditio* is "litterarum peritiam cum rerum scientia," *Schriften*, p. 6; cf. 84-85.

only as great as its expression.[85] This formal interest is not only one more facet of their interest in pattern as a whole, but it leads to an analytic dissection of rationalization and program. The Florentines, Machiavelli said, were subtle interpreters of appearances, and the speeches of the Florentine rhetorical histories, since they were created by the Humanists and thus were products of rhetorical analysis, reveal a rhetorical but also historical concern with the appearance and trappings of power.[86] Salutati is aware that both the historian and his protagonists play before an audience (*E.*, I, 89f.). In his *Invectiva* addressed to Antonio Loschi of Milan there is no political event which is not weighed in the balance of political use; his consideration of formal history is tied to a consideration of the reverberation in public opinion.[87] Thus while Valla's cynical analysis of the Donation of Constantine is the mature product of this interest, the state correspondence of either Salutati or Bruni is an earlier manifestation of a lack of naïveté which is also a gain in historical sensitivity.

The professional concern with fame which makes the Humanists dissectors as well as masters of the programmatic statement contributes, then, to a growth in historical sophistication if not in moral stature. Similarly, the formal concern with figure, with invention, with artifice, that is part of the aesthetic change which marks Humanism, lends itself to the analysis of intention, for to use a figure, as Salutati pointed out, is to say one thing, and mean another (*De lab.*, I, 3, 10). This provides an impetus for the long career of what the twentieth-century scholastic criticism calls the "intentional fallacy," which was, however, a prime instrument in the critical control of texts in the intervening centuries. Funda-

---

[85] *Phenomenology of the Mind*, tr. J.B. Baillie, London, 1961, p. 74.
[86] *History of Florence*, New York, 1960, p. 383.
[87] Also, no event of contemporary history can escape being weighed in the balance of rhetorical sophistication: see P. Herde, "Politik und Rhetorik in Florenz am Vorabend der Renaissance," *AKG*, 47 (1965), pp. 201-02, on Salutati's letter to his Milanese friend P. Capelli on the idiocy of the Florentine-Milanese hostilities just concluded (*E.*, II, 337).

mental to the fruitful connection of historical and philological method in the new Biblical criticism of Valla's *Adnotationes* and Erasmus' edition of the New Testament is the distinction which Salutati makes between conventional and intentional meaning in the Bible—"not by appropriation, which stems from custom, but by intention; a sense not etymologically derived . . . but of the mind of the author" (. . . *non illa que sumitur ex origine proprietate * * * sed mente, E.,* IV, 239).[88] There is an important assumption about the past involved in this hermeneutic: i.e. that there is a coherence and integrity about the intention, about the experience of either sacred or secular author behind the literary work which goes beyond, which transcends, literal or conventional meaning. By means of his grammatical and rhetorical erudition the Humanist critic establishes the text as an integral, concrete experience in the past. Thus the intention, the hidden saying is neither occult prophecy nor pagan wickedness; by recovering the intention one recovers a completely comparable psychological experience of objective historical value.

But objectivity is not substantialism; the voluntarist, rather than intellectualist, cast of rhetorical attitudes not only reinforces this preoccupation with intention which is so obvious in Petrarch and Salutati, but, as in other phases of rhetorical activity, makes it a focus on attributed rather than hypostatized virtue or vice—on good and evil as relatives, as products of human motives: "For there is nothing, no matter how sincere, in human behavior which a man may not pervert, if he feels contrary, and desires to malign" (*E.,* IV, 198).[89] Thus Humanist rhetoric is not only an important stage in the history of sensibility or psychology, but it once again makes possible, because it makes conscious, a historical psychology. Rhetorical texts were the psychology books of the Humanists; Renaissance rhetorical and poetical theories of figurative speech describe the connection of form with will,

[88] Fubini, "La coscienza," p. 525f.
[89] Petrarch, *Fam.,* XX, 4, 27f.

of language with intent. Rhetorical attitudes encourage analysis of character through analysis of language, of conscious and unconscious usage. On the one hand, names in themselves are not offensive or evil, Salutati insists (*E.,* IV, 194); behind the scurrilities of Biblical examples lies an ethical purpose. On the other hand, vulgar taste in language can be the mark of specific vulgarities of character (*E.,* I, 77).[90]

There is still a deeper level of the complex relationship between rhetorical historiography and rhetorical ideals of figure. History itself is similar to both poetic figure and the parables of Christ, according to Boccaccio (*Gen. deo.,* XIV, 707). One must contrast Roman Ingarden's sharp differentiation between historical narrative and poetic imitation which represents a modern consensus with the impression Salutati gives that the distinction between *fabula* and *historia* is a simple intention, that both are figurative language, but history has the additional advantage of truth (*E.,* I, 196).[91] Or note the resonance of the language with which Salutati defines poetry: the poet's function is to transfer meaning, "to take what has happened or could happen and give it another signification,"—"*et si qua gesta fuerint vel quasi gesta narraverint ad significandum aliud ordinare*" (*De lab.,* I, 13, 9). Illusionism is the essence of historical method, for the subject of history as of art is the invisible action of the mind only in so far as it is manifested in the visible behavior of the person, in the *res gestae aut gerendae.* For illusionism is the source of historical and artistic efficacy and value since abstractions, *rationes,* are such that "after they are assimilated, they neither make a man better nor more prudent in his affairs" (*E.,* II, 295). Verisimilitude is the route to verity. If even the artists of the Renaissance turned to rhetoric for

---

[90] Borinski, *Die Antike in Poetik,* Vol. 1, p. 125.
[91] R. Ingarden, "A Marginal Commentary on Aristotle's Poetics," *JAAC,* 20 (1961-62), pp. 163-73, 273-85, see esp. p. 275f. See also Boccaccio, *Gen. deo.,* p. 722, for a purely formal distinction between history and poetry.

formal injunctions on how to achieve the illusion of the real, the historians were bound to avail themselves of the rhetorical tools for verisimilitude.[92]

The centrality of illusionism in Humanist historiography is a product of poetic consciousness of figure and rhetorical ideas of argument by *exemplum*.[93] By means of rhetorical *enargeia* or *illustratio* the vision of man is focused on behavior. Just as Guarino Veronese repeats the classical formula which distinguishes history from annals as that which deals with the part of experience which one sees or could see, could be an eyewitness to, as opposed to the narrative of the remote past,[94] so Salutati in his praise of history in his letter to Juan Fernandez de Heredia points out the insufficiency of precept without image: Frontinus

> was not content to impart his science by means of precepts and rules but placed it before the eye, as it were, by means of infinite examples, which they call *stratagemata*, and thus proved his arguments as if by the most valid reasoning.[95]

The connection of image and example, narrative and illusion is an essential one in Humanist aesthetic; for Leon Battista Alberti the *istoria* is the greatest work of the painter.[96] Further, Professor E. H. Gombrich has pointed out that the impulse to a "convincing" rather than a magically efficacious narrative is the starting point of the art which constructs its own world of illusion in which the "How?" as

---

[92] See Spencer, *"Ut rhetorica pictura."* Quintilian, I.O., II, 17, 39, speaks of verisimilitude, not truth, as the field of the rhetor. De Nolhac has a brilliant passage on the innovating aspects of Petrarch's use of verisimilitude in his history in Le *"De viris illustribus"* de *Pétrarque; Notices sur les manuscrits originaux*, Paris, 1890, pp. 50-51; cf. Borinski, *Die Antik in Poetik*, Vol. 1, p. 104.

[93] In this sense poetics and rhetoric mediate the Greek illusionist "revolution" described by Gombrich, *Art and Illusion*, London, 1960, p. 116f.

[94] *Epistolario*, II, p. 460.

[95] ". . . scientiam non contentis preceptis et regulis tradidisse, infinitis exemplis, que *strategemata* vocant, ante oculis posuit et, veluti ratione validissima, confirmavit." E., II, 292.

[96] Alberti, *On Painting*, trans. J. Spencer, London, 1956, p. 72.

well as the "What?" of human behavior is explored.[97] Once again, then, stylistic emancipation relates to historical explanation; when the Humanists focus on the aesthetically convincing they raise the argument to a plane where only the reader's judgment and the author's insight count. The Humanist's critical point of view is strongly affected by his mimetic impulse, his imaginative involvement with the narrative—precisely the elements the positivist historian would subtract from Humanist historical texts.

Further, the Humanists respect the temporal dimension of narrative. Alberti admonished the painter that one of his primary tasks was to create movement in his *istoria* by means of the atemporal medium of paint; he must confront the viewer with a story to "follow."[98] In Salutati's letter to de Heredia the praise of history centers on the value of narrative. But "following" a narrative is generically different from following an explicit argument, according to W. B. Gallie, and the difference accounts for the peculiar efficacy of historical knowledge.[99] Anecdote demands mobility, a willingness to pursue lines of continuity and relevance and to find the implicit argument. For Salutati the narrative of deeds stimulates, leads the reader on, where static repetition of received truths puts him to sleep.[100] Following the "movement" of the narrative engenders movement, moral change in the reader, for who, with such exemplary deeds before his eyes, "*titillante quasi quodam pruritu, ad idem audendum non animetur?*" (*E.*, I, 105).

Thus the Humanists are convinced that the use of rhetorically instead of logically oriented discourse leads one to reality through illusion. Guarino reiterates that history de-

[97] *Art and Illusion*, p. 129.
[98] *On Painting*, p. 78.
[99] *Philosophy and the Historical Understanding*, London, 1964, p. 67, 84-85.
[100] "sint que scribuntur subtilia, sint ex moralibus documentis, sint etiam ex fidei preceptis instituentia vitam nostram, generant tamen aliquando fastidium mentibusque legentium tedium ingerunt; ut nulla sit tam vehemens applicatio mentis, que non quasi defatigata retundatur atque torpescat." *E.*, II, 295.

77

rives its utility from transmitting not only the words, the doctrines, the precepts of men but their deeds:

> Thus it is that great thanks are due to the writers of histories, since through their labors they give birth to things of great utility to the affairs mortals have in common, and the utility is so much greater because they praise deeds, where other teachers are content with praising words in their writings.[101]

The Humanists consider the movement of culture no longer as the progress from pre-existent system to unlived doctrine, but as recurrence of types of ethical problems and behavior. It is the concrete reality of the force of justice, the strength of truth, the value of modesty which history purveys (*E.*, II, 294).

But there is another aspect to the rhetorical nature of their concern with things, not words; the canons of unity and simplicity which saved Italian Renaissance historiography from the chaos of detail, from the "magic" realism which characterized the aesthetic of the Northern Renaissance, are much more probably rhetorical than ascetic injunctions. It is exactly this mass of detail, this faith in multiplicity that approaches modern positivist faith in statistical profiles which distinguishes even the great Trecento chroniclers such as the Villanis from the Humanist rhetorical historiographers. Any one book of the *Chronicle* of Giovanni Villani shows the utter lack of *harmonia*, the jumbling together of a number of levels of interests and importance—foreign politics, domestic politics, didactic excursuses, trivial anecdotes, tales of crusades, tales of miracles, lengthy descriptions of civic insignia—which is also characteristic of the late medieval

---

[101] "Quae cum ita sunt, ingentes historiarum scriptoribus habendae sunt gratiae, quod eorum labore tantas communi mortalium vitae utilitates pepererunt, et eo maiores quo ceterorum vivendi magistrorum scriptis [hominum] dicta, horum autem facta laudantur. . . ." *Epistolario*, II, 310. Cf. Petrarch, who stresses in his preface to the *De viris* that he is interested in bringing back the deeds themselves, not just particular versions of them; quoted in De Nolhac, *Le "De viris,"* p. 55.

culture of the North described by Johan Huizinga.[102] Admittedly, partly because of a precocious Humanistic illusionism, these anecdotes are intensely descriptive, with a marvelous evocative power that is almost "magical."

But, as Borinski pointed out, one of the first discoveries of the Renaissance was of the magnitude and solidity of antique art.[103] Humanist historiography is not only constrained by the rhetorical principle of decorum but marked by a devotion to the rhetorical values of *gravitas* and *magnitudo*. When the fragments are not related the meaning of the whole is inaccessible; the inconsistent and ahistorical criteria of the chronicles—religious, antiquarian, partisan—serve to provide the materials for history, not history. The philosophical principle of *to prepon* and the rhetorical principle of decorum which it underwrites saved Humanist history from the mere piling up of facts, from the kind of history Collingwood characterizes as "scissors-and-paste." Here rhetorical historiography is comparable with the painting of the Florentine Quattrocento, where the background does not dominate but is integrated with the protagonist.[104] The purpose of the historian is to form an armature for important personalities, events, struggles; the possibility of ethical seriousness accompanies the formal concern with "high" seriousness and the question of genre.

Petrarch had regarded one of the more important tasks of the historian as a formal, organizational one. In his case the principle of unity underwrites his rhetorical-voluntarist taste for *res gestae* as opposed to *res naturales* and requires the limitation of subject in his collection *De viris illustribus* to the truly illustrious rather than the merely lucky action; the

---

[102] *The Waning of the Middle Ages*, New York, 1956, p. 274, 317; see also Panofsky, *Renaissance and Renascences*, p. 207, and G. Weise, *L'ideale eroico del Rinascimento e le sue premesse umanistiche*, Naples, 1961, Vol. 1, p. 1f.

[103] *Die Antike in Poetik*, Vol. 1, p. 143; see Salutati, E., II, 259.

[104] Vasoli suggests an analogy between Villani's abstract but real style with contemporaneous paintings which have realistically depicted bodies on gold backgrounds, in "Storia e politica nel primo umanesimo fiorentino," *Itinerari*, (August, 1955), p. 124.

supineness, the lack of *virtù* of contemporary princes have saved Petrarch a world of bother.

I thank our princes who have saved me,—feeble and desirous of quiet—, from such effort, for they furnish material not for history but for satire. And if I know some who of late have been remarkably successful, all their victories were gained either through good luck or the inertia of their enemies, and there was no glory or virtue involved at all.[105]

Petrarch had made the point that the historian must seek formal unity in the materials of history and Salutati repeats this theme. He refers frequently to historians as *concinnatores*: Petrarch as historian *"concordat discrepantes hystorias"*; Boccaccio had noticed the *"ambiguitas historiarum"* in order to resolve it (cf. *E.*, I, 184; I, 227; III, 81). This predilection for unity is manifest in the use they make of Livy's annalistic style; where the medieval chroniclers produce a scrapbook approach with contemporaneity as the only criterion, the Humanists employ the annalistic form to juxtapose and coordinate domestic and foreign affairs of the political unit they had chosen as subject.[106]

Stylistic canons become critical exactions; aesthetic values force them to select the experiences of history. The Hu-

[105] "Gratiam habeo principibus nostris qui michi fesso et quietis avido hunc preripiunt laborem; neque enim historie, sed satyre materiam stillo tribuunt. Nam, etsi quosdam nuper victoriis satis insignes noverim, ita tamen fortune aut hostium inertie cuncta cedunt, ut nullus ibi vel virtuti victoris aut vere glorie locus sit," from the preface to the *De viris*, in de Nolhac, *Le "De viris,"* p. 55. Gorgias makes a similar distinction in the *Encomium of Helen* (DK 82 B11.4) between men with inherited or personal assets such as wealth, nobility and health, and those with wisdom which is the product of free will; as Rostagni points out ("Un nuovo capitolo," pp. 50-52), this distinction between virtues dependent on fortune and those on man himself is common in the Sophists, and is related to Gorgias' "historicist" practice of discussing always specific virtues rather than the universal "virtue."

[106] See M. Dazzi, *Il Mussato preumanista*, Venice, 1964, p. 81, who regards Mussato's unity of style as evidence of his modernity; contrast J.K. Hyde, *Padua in the Age of Dante*, Manchester, 1966, p. 288f., who sees Mussato as essentially medieval, since he lacks the unity and coherence of Rolandino of Padua.

manists relate *brevitas,* a criterion which could be used pedantically to constrict narrative, to *gravitas;* Salutati advises the student of affairs to spare himself, for he will find greatness only in the great events of history: *"maxima quidem virtus in minimis apparere non potest"* (*E.,* II, 259).[107] And in yet another way the purely formal considerations of scale affect the Humanist concept of what constitutes history. Between medieval and Humanist rhetoric there is a shift in the size of the prose unit considered from small to large, from a concern with the superficial and limited regularities of the *cursus* and *colores* to the balance and antithesis of the long and complex periodic sentence.[108] In other words, the execution of a good periodic style with its complex syntax involving rigid parallelism in condition and result, and with the necessary contrasts of the pointed and abrupt sentence of wit and paradox, demands a sensitivity to the complexities, paradoxes, and parallelisms of the subject expressed. If every sentence is a statement of syntactical relationships, every rhetorically organized sentence is a self-conscious acknowledgment of a macro-structure of relationships between orator and protagonist, audience and ambiance. Thus in the brilliant practitioners of historiography in the Humanist tradition such as Machiavelli and Gibbon the balance and antithesis which contribute so much to the force with which their historical insights strike the reader seem not so much externally imposed as internally generated; they have found the analogues for the formal structures in the events themselves. A question of genre, of the stated intention of writing full or formal history in the classical manner, becomes a question of the degree of significance of purely human events; high seriousness becomes an attribute not so

[107] On *brevitas* see Norden, *Kunstprosa,* II, p. 740; Bruni discusses it as a historical criterion in "Ad Johannem Franciscum Gonzagam principem Mantuanorum de origine urbis Mantue," Laur. Plut. LII, 5, 89v.
[108] See L. Malagoli, "Forme dello stile mediolatino e forme dello stile volgare," *Studi letterari; Miscellanea in onore di E. Santini,* Palermo, 1956, pp. 57-86.

much of cosmic forces and providential history as of political and even social struggle.[109]

As a result of these choices, it is the congruence of aesthetic and ethical value which distinguishes Petrarch's history for Salutati in his rhetorical question

> For in discourse what is there to be observed beyond dignity of person, magnitude of event, propriety of speech, elegance in official affairs, solidity of style, sobriety and decorum?[110]

The organization of particulars around the great classical ethical antitheses, which of course were also rhetorical *topoi*, finds its consummation in the coherent structure of insight in Machiavelli's politico-historical treatises. Every age is anthropocentric to a degree, but perspective when clarified enlarges experience; the gain or loss in historical perspective is relative to the breadth and depth of human experience admitted within the field of vision or system.[111]

3. Eloquence and the Historian

A change in grammatical voice is required, an exchange of the assumption of substance passively sacrificed to form, to a hypothesis that form contributed actively to both process and result in Renaissance Humanism; rhetorical perspective, besides enlarging experience, also increased the historian's self-consciousness of role. But while it is precisely this self-

---

[109] On magnitude as a historical criterion see Bruni, *Historiarum Florentini populi libri XII, RIS*, 19³, ed. E. Santini, 1914-20, p. 247. F. Mehmel states that "Was Bruni und Poggio in der Florentinischen und italienischen Geschichte suchen und finden, sind grosse Männer, die grosse Dinge getan haben und die darum wert und würdig sind als historische Gestalten . . . ," "Machiavelli und die Antike," *Antike und Abendland*, 3 (1954), p. 179.

[110] "in dicendo quidem nonne servata est personarum dignitas, magnitudo rerum verborum proprietas, negociorum elegantia, stili soliditas, sobrietas atque decus?" *E.*, IV, 140.

[111] "For it is true that all thought begins with remembrance; it is also true that no remembrance remains secure unless it is condensed and distilled into a framework of conceptual notions within which it can further exercise itself." H. Arendt, *On Revolution*, New York, 1963, p. 222.

consciousness, and the critical insights which stem from it, which distinguish the Humanist historiographers from the Trecento chroniclers, nineteenth-century historians of history tended to reject these traits and to see Humanist histories as a regression from the Trecento chronicles whose quantitative categories are more analogous to those of their own inductive historical method, a method in turn patterned on nineteenth-century scientific method. One may isolate the naïveté of this judgment and more correctly define the successful insights of Renaissance Humanism by turning instead to the categories of Martin Heidegger.[112]

Heidegger differentiates between an era characterized by authentic historical consciousness—one in which history is grasped as the recurrence of the possible, of a genuine possibility of existence—and a historiographically oriented era such as the nineteenth century—one preoccupied with expressions, and the theory or methodology of expression, of the past. He maintains that "such historical consciousness does not necessarily require histories. It is not the case that unhistoriographical eras as such are unhistorical also."[113] Thus there are two problems to discuss: the possibility of the authentic historical consciousness of Humanism, as well as of an *authentic* historiography—a confrontation with the entities of the past in their "primordial wholeness"—which can spring only from such a consciousness. But the paradigmatic instance of the authentic historical consciousness of the Humanists is their repetition of the classical role of historian, their revival of the rhetorical history of antiquity.[114] The

112 This section is based on Heidegger's *Being and Time*, trans. J. MacQuarrie and E. Robinson, London, 1962, Part II.5.

113 *Being and Time*, p. 448; I have changed some terms: "Geschichtlichkeit," which was translated "historicality," is now "historical consciousness"; "Historie," which was translated as "historiology," is now "historiography"; "Historismus" remains as "historicism," however. The notion of historicism which I employ in this book, of course, has only a "family resemblance" to nineteenth-century Historismus, or "historicism."

114 Compare Argan, "The Architecture of Brunelleschi," p. 97: "The Renaissance begins, so far as the figurative arts are concerned, when to artistic activity is added the idea of art as a consciousness of its own act. . . ."

Humanists identify with Cicero, who had brought the wisdom of the Greeks to Rome through the golden river of his eloquence.[115] In repeating the terms of the classical rhetorical notion of history, Salutati emphasizes that the source of fame is the author of the history, not the author of the deed:

> The second last muse is called Clio, from *"cleos"* of the Greek, *"gloria"* in Latin, and it is not inappositely associated with the lunar sphere, the lowest, since it is itself ordered in a lunar fashion. For the lustre of the famous originates not in themselves but in the witness of their celebrants, just as the moon glows not by its own but by an alien light. For no one, no matter how brilliant, is famous except as he is celebrated.[116]

Bruni employs another popular figure to describe the active rather than passive role of the historian: just as Camillus had acted as the second founder of Rome, so Poggio became the second author of the books he restored.[117] Obversely, Salutati berates the scholar who hides classical texts as a robber of those to whom the reading of the text is thus barred (*E.*, II, 259). And the Humanist is to lend fame to the recent as well as to the classical past; where Petrarch rejected contemporary events as a subject worthy only of satire, Salutati claims, in an extremely "rhetorical" passage, that the deeds of present-day are as worthy of immortalization as those of antiquity (*E.*, I, 89; I, 191). Since Bruni later undertakes this task in his history of Florence, here again Salutati acts as a transitional figure in his sensitivity to the possibilities of Italian experience. He grasps the classical connection between the role of historian and of the man of action; he

[115] Bruni, *Ad Petrum Paulum Histrum Dialogus*, in *Prosatori latini*, p. 54.
[116] "Penultima vero Musarum, que dicitur Clyo, a 'cleos', videlicet Grece, Latine 'gloria', non inapposite cum lunari circulo, qui quidem infimus est, ipsi lune huius dispensationis ordine sociatur. Fama namque non famosi sed famam exhibentium attestatione relucet; et ipsa luna non suo sed alieno splendet a lumine. Nullus enim, quantacunque scientia eluceat, famosus est nisi quatenus celebratur." *De lab.*, I, 10, 20.
[117] *Epistolarum Libri VIII*, IV, 5; Vol. 1, p. 113.

assumes that the choice of writing a full history of contemporary events is dependent upon a recurrence of political *virtù*; that there is a moral imperative inherent in the capability of attributing value through form.

> If the Luccan affair proceeded according to the Roman pattern, it certainly is no less worthy to be celebrated in history than Roman politics. . . .
> As much as I hesitate over these deeds, however, so much am I impelled to write; although they are so far beyond the ordinary measure of human affairs, they nevertheless imperiously demand to be fitly commemorated. . . .[118]

In other words, both in its view of history and its historiography Humanism is "authentically" historical in Heidegger's terms; it makes choices revering the existential possibilities which the classical past holds; it does not have the "inauthentic" historical consciousness of the characteristic medieval attitude to antiquity which "only retains and receives the 'actual' that is left over, the world-historical that has been, the leavings and the information about them that is present at hand."[119]

Heidegger is also very suggestive when he defines authentic historiography by the three Nietzschean terms: monumental —openness to the "monumental" possibilities of existence of the past—; antiquarian—reverent preservation of the existence whose possibilities have been seized—; critical—the critique of the present from the point of view achieved by the previous two attitudes. For Humanist rhetorical historians accept the magnitude and solidity of classical form as a contemporary possibility of existence; they acknowledge their

---

[118] ". . . si Romanorum auspiciis res Lucana procederet, non minus quam eorum aliquem monumentis hystorie celebrandum. . . ." *E.*, I, 192.
". . . inter hec tamen quantum illa me retrahunt, tantum ista manum ad scribendum impellit, ut, quanvis hec transeant omnem humane condicionis terminum et mensuram, irrecusabiliter tamen exigant ut stili memoria celebrentur. . . ." *E.*, II, 147.
[119] *Being and Time*, p. 443.

vocation to preserve by repetition; and from their experience of recurrence reject the concept of the impermeability and uniqueness of the present.

Authentic historiography can have its ground only in authentic historical consciousness; the ability to confront an audience with the entities of past existence so that they "strike home" is based here on the discovery by the historian of the classical spirit within himself. The Humanist's rhetorical-analytical method, used as objective framework, allows him both to delimit the past more sharply and understand its limitations more deeply. It also, as a cast of mind, makes him more free and open to this experience in making him conscious of his critical powers, his powers of choice and rejection, as they are based on consciousness itself, experience of Self—in this case, his aesthetic or literary potential. The Humanist is *"homo literatus"* above all;[120] the "communication problem" of historiography is in the Renaissance more complex and more complexly understood; the Humanists posit a direct relation between the transcendence of historical consciousness and the validity of historical formal expression. They assume the necessity of eloquence for immortality, but they also see this transcendence as grounded in the facts of the historian's life, in the potential of the historian for understanding formal experience of the classical period in the sense of repeating classical form himself. "Good" history is dependent on lack of hypocrisy in aesthetic, in the response of feeling to form. In sum, formal interests have dictated a shift in the intellectual *locus* of the historian, in the place from which he addresses his audience.

The place of the rhetorical discipline and function in the Humanists' historical experience is obvious; it not only purveys the classical norms but it fosters their devotion to form as the preoccupation of their official duties as well as of their leisure. In their daily rhetorical activity the Hu-

[120] M. Seidlmayer, "Nikolaus von Cues und der Humanismus," *Humanismus, Mystik und Kunst in der Welt des Mittelalters*, ed. J. Koch, Leiden, 1959; reprinted in *Wege und Wandlungen des Humanismus*, p. 77.

manists filled with concrete content not only the classical commonplaces of the relation of art to nature but also those of the classical ideas of renewal; rhetorical imitation was experienced as a revitalization of personal powers.

If the classical revival, according to Burckhardt, is the mode of the new Italian spirit, so classical rhetoric modifies the new historical epistemology. The rhetorical attitude is a peculiar combination of congruence and paradox. It presumes the congruence of the eloquent, the historical, and the humane. It is paradoxical in its insistence on reciprocity —of liberty as existent only within limitation, continuity as the basis for discontinuity, tradition as the ground of innovation.[121]

Reciprocity as the form of the rhetorical attitude anticipates the reciprocity which is the essence of a modern historical approach. The central paradox of rhetoric is its dual dependence on the rational and irrational, the demonstrable and the enchanting; while the efficacy of logic and poetry as disciplines rests on their exclusiveness, rhetoric deliberately mixes and confuses their techniques in utilizing both.[122] In rhetorical historiography aesthetic delight reinforces the rhetorical critique, but rhetorical analysis in turn transcends the "merely" aesthetic experience of the past and underwrites enduring historic worth.

Mme. de Romilly calls Thucydides' technique rhetorical exactly in so far as it regards *logos* as an entity, as "it does not dissociate foundation and form, reflection and persuasion."[123] In Humanist rhetoric, the Trecento revolution in sensibility had been the admission of new evidence for the real—figure and sound. At the same time, its acknowledg-

---

[121] There are two general discussions which emphasize the paradoxical character of Humanism: V. Benetti-Brunelli's chapter "I caratteri della cultura umanistica," *Le origini italiane della scuola umanistica,* Milan, 1919, pp. 325-41; and Seidlmayer's "Petrarca, das Urbild des Humanisten."

[122] When Cicero insists on reason and experience as the dual source of rhetorical excellence he underwrites a reciprocity or oscillation between modes of learning; *De orat.,* III, 22, 92; 24, 93.

[123] *Histoire et raison chez Thucydide,* p. 216.

ment of aesthetic experience as epistemological limitation, i.e. that the mechanical ease and simplicity of "pure" contemplative activity is a chimera, has a kind of Occamist elegance to it. The acceptance of complexity and imperfection obviates a resort to an elaborate structure of abstractions which would prove the simplicity and perfection of knowledge. The Humanists, like the Sophists, embrace the distortive power of language; they accept the complexity of discourse as an attempt to reflect the complexity of phenomena.

The central metaphor of Christian epistemology since Augustine had been the Paulinian "now we see in an enigma, then, face to face." The Humanists still accept the religious implications of this metaphor as referring to a confrontation outside of space and time, but their rhetorical vocation offers a new vantage point on the whole problem of phenomenal communication thus implied. Instead of laying stress on the phenomenal as merely the shadow of the real, now they emphasize the realities of created experience, the manifest or the phenomenal, as the only access to the noumenal; artifice is all we have to express truth:

> And although men are not able to apprehend God directly, they are able to notice many of his effects, and thus have been able to know him solely by effects, that is, indirectly. So they began to speak of the divine numen, as if it could be any man, since they have nothing more sublime than man which they have understood, or have learned from the senses, whence comes all our knowledge.[124]

As in expression, so in hermeneutic: Humanist exegesis reflects a development from the use of allegory as a mechanical exercise of a rigidly pious mind to a notion of figure as a primary mode of discovery. When Salutati claims that "one

[124] "et quia non poterant homines Deum ante videre, multos tamen eius videbant effectus, cognoscere potuerunt eum solum ab effectibus, hoc est retro, ceperuntque de numine divinitatis loqui, velut aliquis foret homo, nichil habentes homine sublimius quod intelligerent et sensibus, unde movetur nostra cognitio, comprehendissent." *E.*, IV, 176.

cannot possibly draw any meaning congruent to the letter of the Bible which God in his infinite wisdom had not intended from the beginning," interpretation of Biblical figure is no longer a matter of conforming to a single primordial truth but an exercise of linguistic responsibility.[125] Truth is a pattern within the symbolic sphere. The change in emphasis becomes striking when Bruni employs the very strong Pauline metaphor with all its heavy ontological implications to describe the recovery of Greek literature by the Humanist translators—now *"non per aenigmata interpretationum ineptarum, sed de facie ad faciem intuere."*[126] To make the understanding of a text dependent upon the stylistic capacity, the purely formal values of the translator is to place knowledge and control of total experience, wisdom as felt and imagined, at the center of historiographical activity (cf. *E.,* II, 480f.). The radical change in aesthetic which makes the objective standard of this control coherence not with a metaphysical system which has been logically constructed but with a phenomenal armature aesthetically perceived changes the position from which the historian views the past as well as the type of experience considered as historical.

Essential both to the rhetorical ideal of reciprocal method and to the new stance of the rhetor-historian is the easy movement between surface and depth, aesthetic expression and intended meaning. Guarino employs one of the best figures to express this necessary link in his description of the pleasure which accompanies, even if unintentionally, the instruction of historical narrative as similar to the "pleasing blush which often arises on the great athlete when he is competing" (*Epistolario,* II, 462; cf. Cicero, *De orat.,* III,

---

[125] "Nec potest excogitari veritas littere congruens quam illa infinita sapientia de cuius throno processit ab initio non intenderit." *De lab.,* II, 2, 16. Dante had contributed to this movement in reversing the direction of the image-exemplar relationship; the purpose of the superterrestrial journey is to understand and change terrestrial life. See Cranz, "Some Changing Contexts of Allegory" on the quotation from Salutati; Charity, *Events and Their Afterlife,* p. 185f., on new directions in Dante.

[126] "Oratio in funere Nannis Strozzae equitis Florentini," *Stephani Baluzii Miscellanea,* Lucca, 1764, Vol. 4, p. 4.

53, 199). As Vossler observed, while the Germans took over only the grammar of Humanism and became pedantic school-masters, the Italian Humanist is "a dilettante in the best sense of the word," i.e. in the sense that the root of *dilettare* means "to take delight in."[127] The point of the Humanist is merely that when accidents are inseparable from essence, when delight is inseparable from act, delight is inseparable from utility. Illusionism, as we have noted above, is one of the connections between rhetorical aesthetic and Humanist historical purpose (*E.*, II, 294-95). Since a beholder is necessary for illusion, the rhetorician never forgets his audience, and the rhetorical historian includes his audience in his effort to make history. The reciprocity affects the reception as well as the creation of images; as Alberti points out the *istoria*, the pictorial narrative, "will move the soul of the beholder when each man painted there clearly shows the movement of his own soul."[128] To associate this aesthetic insight with subjectivism or solipsism is to associate it with the difficulties, not the creativity, with the isolation rather than the fluidity, mobility, *disponibilità* which is characteristic of the Renaissance.[129] The proper analogues are the insights into the nature of the universal of Augustine when he maintains in the *De Trinitate* that each man possesses faith as he possesses a countenance—it is the same yet different in all—, or of Cusanus when he uses in the *De visione Dei* the superb metaphor of the Icon of God whose eyes seem to follow every person in the room whether they stand or move.[130] The omnipresent rhetorical consciousness of audience in Humanist historiography anticipates the modern sentiment that every man is his own historian.

Reciprocity is the historical mode, reciprocity is mutual influence, and rhetoric is the model for historical reciprocity.

[127] *Poetische Theorien*, p. 73.

[128] *On Painting*, p. 77.

[129] Sir Kenneth Clark discusses the sense of *disponibilità*, of "lively repose" in *The Nude*, New York, 1956, p. 180f.

[130] Augustine, *De trinitate*, XIII, 2, 5; Cusanus, *De visione Dei*, "Prefatio," *Nicolai Cusae Cardinalis Opera*, Vol. 1, Paris, 1514, ph. rep. Frankfurt, 1962, p. 99r.

The mediate position of rhetoric, its interposition between poetry and philosophy, poetry and history, is the paradigm for the movement from illusion to insight, figure to critical analysis which characterizes the Humanist historical consciousness. Reciprocity is also realism, since criticism is the intent to know the real: for Salutati the essential trait of the *studia humanitatis* is that instead of pursuing abstract essences they lead us back to solid existence,—*"vere realitatis solidam existentiam attingebat"* (*E.*, I, 106; IV, 197). Thus the artistic failures of Humanist rhetoricians are irrelevant to this inquiry; even when aesthetic values remain conventional, remain tied to the old Platonic-Neoplatonic ontology, the critical consciousness of these values as historical models increases. The commitment to realism in Humanism tended to modify rhetoric to critical rather than artistic achievement and gave rhetoric the same kind of cutting edge, the same critical potential, as Sophistic rhetoric.

Alberti rationalizes this Humanistic criticism when he makes the statement that all judgment is measurement, is *per comparatione*. In Humanist rhetoric comparison is based on the possibility of objectively valuing a personal experience of form, of apprehending significance and meaning, not as imposed from outside but as "felt," and enabling the historian to see history as attributed rather than ordained meaning and significance.

The Humanist thus can proceed from concrete to categorical, from empirical to systematic thought without a break; the foundation of form is in nature conceived as "full and lucid sensory experience."[131] It is significant that Alberti, the most self-conscious of the Humanist theorists of art, specifically refers to the great Sophist:

> Perhaps Protagoras, by saying that man is the mode and measure of all things, meant that all the accidents of things are known through comparison to the accidents of man. . . .

[131] Argan, "The Architecture of Brunelleschi," p. 99; see Merleau-Ponty's chapter on "The Body as Expression and Speech," *Phenomenology of Perception*, p. 174f.

All knowledge of large, small; long, short; high, low; broad, narrow; clear, dark; light and shadow and every similar attribute is obtained by comparison. Because they can be, but are not necessarily, conjoined with objects, philosophers are accustomed to call them accidents. . . . Thus all things are known by comparison, for comparison contains within itself a power which immediately demonstrates in objects which is more, less, or equal.[132]

The method is truly self-critical and self-verifying. The rhetorical criteria are extracted from experience itself; unity and proportion are based on harmony and *concinnitas* in human nature, in the body and senses.

Renaissance sensuality tried to make the body an intuitive and disciplined tool of reality. . . . it insisted on a full interplay between man's senses and intuitions and the world of appearances, facts, and laws.[133]

Their criteria were found or "invented" by poets, systematized in rhetoric, and confirmed by historical-critical comparison of their expressions in culture. Moreover, Humanism is critical in tone simply through its preoccupation with *res*, with experience as expressed, with tradition as accumulation of the records of experience. The rhetoric, like the architecture of the Trecento, partakes of

quella rigorosa e logica revisione della cultura artistica, quella precisa ricerca delle fonti ideali nel grande ambito della tradizione, che segna l'inizio del Rinascimento.[134]

Meaning is the central problem of historiography; the rhetorical tenet which reinforces this insight is that the formless is insignificant. Rhetorical habits freed the historian to cor-

---

[132] *On Painting*, pp. 54-55; cf. Cusanus, *De beryllo, Opera omnia*, Vol. 11¹, chap. 5, pp. 6-7; chap. 36-37, pp. 48-51.

[133] Erikson, *Young Man Luther*, p. 192; cf. Argan, "The Architecture of Brunelleschi," p. 98; see also Santini, "La produzione volgare di L. Bruni," *GSLI*, 60 (1912), p. 289f., on Bruni's insistence on self-criticism, internal assurance, *tacitum iudicium animi*, in method.

[134] Argan, *L'architettura protocristiana, preromantica, e romantica de '200 e del '300*, Florence, 1936, p. 7.

relate the attribution of meaning and the creation of form; the act of giving form is an act of *virtù* of the protagonist and a responsibility of the historian.

The analogy of Cusa—that as God created realities so man creates images; that artistic activity is related to divine creativity as the artistic forms are related to the creatures of the divine—casts a special light on Humanist historical consciousness. Rhetorical historiography has two basic assumptions: 1) that we confront the past as expressed in symbols or language, as mediated, rather than as naively or notionally handed down; 2) that the historian is a mediator, and, in so far as he adds form, he is a creator. The richness of the Renaissance metaphors indicate the seriousness of their preoccupation with image and creativity. Cusa repeatedly describes the mind with the metaphor of a curved mirror, as in a spoon, or as a "living" mirror. Alberti claims that Narcissus was the inventor of painting, for "what else can you call painting but a similar embracing with art of what is presented on the surface of the water in the fountain?"[135] For both, consciousness is self-reflecting; images and symbols are products of self-consciousness, not a passive reception of an a priori reality. The concentration on a separate sphere of symbol and meaning is also an assertion of the autonomous nature of the mental powers of measurement. Thus the "distance" from antiquity is "fixed," to use Panofsky's expression, because the re-presentations of the classical past are internally generated, the point of stability is egocentric. Further, from the metaphor of Narcissus it is obvious that the subject of art is man himself, and the only image of an autonomous mind is liberty. History is the story of liberty. Humanist theory of history is a version of the Cusan metaphor of creating and created: there is no sense of freedom of action and thus no historically worthy subject, unless consideration is limited to phenomenal behavior. Again, history is the narrative of the *virtù* of the illustrious; liberty is defined by the critical establishment of limitation.

[135] *On Painting*, p. 64.

History is limited to the control of phenomenal behavior and historiography to the control of discourse. The function of the historian is circumscribed by the congruence of aesthetic and critical parameters, the facts of affective life. In the logical as well as chronological priority of aesthetic interests rhetorical historiography anticipates not nineteenth-century philology but that twentieth-century cultural history which asserts the logical as well as chronological priority of literary criticism to historical criticism. Certainly Lucien Goldmann's model of historical method as an oscillation between aesthetic absorption of particulars and the contemplation of universal criteria echoes the Humanist reciprocity. Further, oscillation obviates a fixed direction either of the inductive or deductive type; perhaps there is no privileged direction in rhetorical method because there is no clearly privileged direction in the hopelessly complex rhetorical notion of language.[136]

The hypothesis of aesthetic priority is demonstrated on still another level of dependence of historical on rhetorical insight: the Humanists appreciate the employment of form in discourse as a kind of reciprocity which is an interaction with the past itself. Again to turn to Heidegger—

> The authentic repetition of a possibility of existence that has been—the possibility that Dasein may choose its hero—. . . makes a reciprocative rejoinder to the possibility of that existence which has-been-there.[137]

History, as the understanding of past experience in terms of future choices, is a form of knowledge which asserts the mutual concession of reality by polar opposites—tradition and innovation, discontinuity and continuity; the aim is not elimination of one but synthesis of both.[138] But the rhetorical

---

[136] Goldmann, *The Hidden God*, trans. P. Thody, London, 1964, chap. 1; cf. Merleau-Ponty, *Les aventures de la dialectique*, Paris, 1955, p. 31; P. Ricoeur, *Histoire et Vérité*; *La condition humaine*, Paris, 1964, pp. 168-74.

[137] *Being and Time*, pp. 437-38.

[138] For Panofsky, then, the Renaissance differed from the medieval Renascences in that it made a permanent acquisition of the classical past ("Renaissance or Renascences?" p. 222f.).

attitude towards language is also synthetic: rhetoric transcends the *nomos-physis* controversy about language by accepting both terms; on the one hand tradition, and particularly Cicero, places great emphasis on the natural impulses which are the sources of figure and structure; on the other hand, it acknowledges conventions established in response to specific demands. The historical dimension of the rhetorical nature-convention duality is the notion of continuity in discontinuity. Further, the rhetorically trained focus not so much on words as opaque and invariant entities as on the precisely historical evidence of language structures and relationships; the concerns of the Humanist rhetoricians anticipate the Vichian thesis of the priority of language structure.

Thus the two most fundamental categories of the historian, continuity and discontinuity, took on new meaning for the Humanists. The first affirmation of a radical break with the classical past as a purely phenomenal break lies in the Humanist notion of the Middle Ages as a change in linguistic structure—a failure in form, a loss of eloquence.[139] The first self-conscious notice of the break of their own era with the Middle Ages is specifically in the regaining of form in discourse; beauty is the first aspect of the classical experience to be revived.

The "Moderns" thus become those who still cling to the recent barbaric past; the "Ancients" are the party of renewal and illumination. Salutati points out that the Moderns trained in the *ars dictaminis* regard rhetoric as merely "a congeries of splendid words, terminating in lubricious *clausulae* and in trisyllabic or even quadrisyllabic rhythms" (*E.,* IV, 234). One of the obvious features of modernity is its lack of eloquence (*E.,* IV, 216); Valla scorns the rhetors of the recent past as teaching only "*gothice.*"[140] Salutati returns to that sophisticate Augustine to pick up his censures of Chris-

---

[139] Dante, *De vulgari eloquentia,* I, 9. For a Humanist such as Salutati in secular studies "la decadenza non può configurarsi altrimenti che come storia, appunto, di approssimazioni retoriche. . . ," Fubini, "La coscienza," p. 523.

[140] *Elegantiae, Praefatio III, Opera omnia,* Vol. 1, p. 80.

tian culture for the tedium of its theology, the boredom of its doctrine (*E.*, IV, 204, 224; cf. *De doctrina christiana*, IV, 2, 2).

Salutati's historical hero is Petrarch, who restored eloquence; the implication is that in restoring eloquence he makes men more humane, he restores a lost potential to human existence (*E.*, I, 183, 249, 337f.; III, 80, 83, 320). Good structures and sound relationships or styles have an independent value and thus a history of their own (*E.*, I, 301; IV, 136, 188); Valla will take the premise of the innocence of beauty and develop the argument that it is the eloquence of the ancients which is to be retrieved, not their philosophy, which had led the theologians of the past into grievous error.[141]

The question of just how much of classical form can or ought to be revived, however, not only gave birth to the famous quarrel of the Ancients and the Moderns but stimulated fresh speculation on general historical premises. The argument of the Ancients is that it is exactly in form that the classics can't be surpassed (*E.*, III, 80); that is, one must accept discontinuity as true and comprehend time as a limitation of personal choice. Filelfo invokes the rhetorical principle of decorum to admonish his contemporaries not to try to surpass the classics, but to attempt in elegant discourse only what the times and customs, and the audience, permit, "... *simus ea contenti, quae cum nobis tum ipsis auditoribus pro rerum temporumque natura non indigna prorsus iudicetur.*"[142] Yet, at the same time in so far as the *principle* of decorum and the *concept* of harmony are rational, the apprehension of form provides a continuity from which discontinuity can be defined; here is a transcendence which is not imposed from the outside as a dispensation but is genuine historical choice. Rational form, formal relationships, can be indefinitely repeated and accepted: "*rursus quod rationabile fuerit, semper in omnibus et ubique a sue rationis convenien-*

---

[141] *Elegantiae, Praefatio IV, Opera omnia*, Vol. 1, p. 119.
[142] "Oratio de laudibus eloquentiae," *Reden und Briefe*, p. 154; cf. Petrarch, *Fam.*, I, 8, 5; XXII, 2, 17.

tia non discedit" (*E.*, II, 472). The Humanist advocates the *riproponibilità* of form as a self-conscious and fruitful repetition of the past.[143] But it is not precept but experience which they "repropose"; they have "the objective assurance that the patterns of experience are the same," at the same time as they apprehend the standards by which individual choice can be judged; form is not a pre-existent entity but a historical challenge.[144]

In discourse, Salutati maintains that while we are free to make certain choices, the ingredients, the principles of form remain the same:

> Believe me we create nothing new, but like tailors we refashion garments from the oldest and richest fragments, which we give out as new.[145]

Salutati distinguishes mutations of form within the classical periods as well as between the classical and Christian eras (*E.*, IV, 144). He sets up a question of relative merit in the history of form—if it is difficult or almost impossible to transcend the excellence of the greatest of ancients, does that mean that there is no glory left? (*E.*, IV, 40). Salutati and his successors assume the possibility of endless permutations of basic forms dependent both on stable rational harmony and the changing exigencies of decorum. From their literary historical consciousness the Humanists derive a notion of time as permitting an open-ended series of comparable but different experiences.[146]

While form is the first aspect of culture to be attributed a

[143] On *riproponibilità* as characterizing an achievement such as the Renaissance, see P. Rossi, "La fallacia del 'superamento' come categoria storiografica," *RCSF*, 12 (1957), p. 466; the category of "fresh restatement" has the advantage over "supercession" of not presuming a privileged direction to history.

[144] P. Wheelwright, *Metaphor and Reality*, Bloomington, Ind., 1962, p. 162.

[145] "crede michi, nichil novum fingimus, sed quasi sarcinatores de ditissime vetustatis fragmentis vestes, quas ut novas edimus, resarcimus." *E.*, II, 45.

[146] See Fubini's discussion of Salutati's "relativismo storico," "La coscienza," pp. 525-27.

purely secular or phenomenal history, the Humanist notion of the coincidence of the eloquent and the humane, and of their recurrence as phenomena of choice represents a shift in emphasis which is a significant change from both the medieval concept of ages of exclusive dispensations of the spirit and the classical cyclical-substantial theory. There is nothing new under the sun; there is nothing that does not have a history (*E.*, II, 295). Salutati's discussion of Virgil's cyclical theory excludes the noumenal from historical recurrence, "not placing the numen, which pertains to God, in the revolution of the times, but rather attaching to it the epithet 'stable,'" but develops a pattern of alternation of prophecy and reaction in the history of religion (*E.*, I, 327-28). This is not the return of cosmic force as substance but of created image, artifice, behavior:

> If one should diligently search through history, he would plainly see the same cyclical course in human affairs, where although nothing exactly the same ever recurs, still, every day we see a sort of image of past events renewed.[147]

Moreover, the Humanists experience image, likeness, or similitude as a kind of personal opportunity; thus Petrarch avers that *"sum quem similitudo delectet, non identitas. . . ."* (*Fam.*, XXII, 2, 20). Renaissance notions of renewal are not identical with classical cyclicism; since their experience of their discontinuity with the Middle Ages was the experience of the recurrence of form as an act of will rather than as the result of cosmic necessity, they are able to strip recurrence of its substantial, metaphysical causation. Just as the Reformation divested religion of its theological envelope, so early rhetorical Humanism divested form of its metaphysical envelope.[148]

---

[147] ". . . si quis diligenter revolvat historias, in rerum humanarum cursu plane videbit, ut quanvis non eadem redeant, videamus tamen quotidie quandam preteritorum imaginem renovari." *E.*, I, 326. Cf. *E.*, III, 80: "mansit tamen in proximis successoribus similitudo quedam et aliquale vestigium antiquitatis. . . ."

[148] P. Vignaux, *Luther, Commentateur des Sentences*, Paris, 1935, p. 24.

The essential trait of the Humanist category of continuity is phenomenalism; their formal preoccupations dictate the setting aside of supernatural for phenomenal recurrence. Historical recurrence is phenomenal transcendence. What they have attained is the idea of form as achievement, as *res gestae*, and as neither substance nor accident; an achievement which not only survives discontinuity, but is enriched by it in the case of a Modern such as Luigi de Marsili who practices a Christian eloquence (*E.*, IV, 138f.). Their own contribution is the connection of the repetition of past experience of form and of value; the ideas of reform, renewal, rebirth, renovation of the fifteenth and sixteenth centuries cluster around the central idea of the enduring value of form—creative human order—and the paradigmatic value of classical ideas of form. Thus Argan points out that the artist of the Renaissance is a historian in so far as he criticizes tradition in order to break with it:

> The mental process which, in the same act eliminates matter and chronicle (tradition) by judging them as values, is, as we have said, perspective.[149]

The Humanists' "paradigm shift," to use T. S. Kuhn's phrase, is the transvaluation of their paradigms as of depth, not surface value. And, just as the humanists avoid our aesthetic dilemma of content vs. form by making eloquence content-in-form, so in their historical consciousness they avoid the medieval dilemma of noumenal intuition impeded by crass earthly abilities by the economy and elegance, the modest resolution of their rhetorical realism—human artifice is all we have, phenomenal transcendence is all we are able to achieve.[150]

The Humanists in their rhetorical pursuits had found a strand of meaning which survives flux without supernatural intervention; within the area of form the activity of the

---

[149] Argan, "The Architecture of Brunelleschi," p. 102.
[150] See E. Grassi's discussion of the Humanist experience of transcendence in their use of language, *Verteidigung des individuellen Lebens*, Berne, 1946, pp. 64-65.

will is transcendent, i.e. it achieves a new relation to reality underwritten but not dictated by theology and metaphysics.[151] Moreover, form is not timeless; their idea of decorum is significant change. Form is deliberate choice where a belief in a timeless, authoritative art would rob Humanism of the vital element of historical reciprocity. The rhetorical concept of *kairos* or *opportunitas* saves the Humanists from the further implications of poetic universality; rhetorical intuitions of discontinuity give a sense of life to the different expressions of form of the past; the rhetorical sense of continuity in form gives a stable, unitary point of view from which to know comparable values. Their rhetorical experience provided a model for their participation in and consciousness of the general renewal of the Renaissance, not as the return of identical events through the intervention of cosmic forces such as Fate—a classical attitude reiterated in the medieval figure of Fortune's wheel—but as historical renewal, i.e. the creation of similitude, the attribution of analogous meaning.

[151] "Der im vorherigen Abschnitt entwickelte Zusammenhang einer menschlich sinnvollen Wirklichkeitsdarstellung mit der geschichtlichen Dimensionierung der Sprache wird mit Salutatis auf der Rhetorik fussenden Erörterungen bestätigt, das Gewicht der Aussage soll erreicht werden nicht durch den Schwulst der Rede, sondern durch Sätze, die den Erfahrungem des Lebens und den Werken der grössten Autoren entnommen sein könnten"; from W. Rüegg, "Die scholastische und die humanistische Bildung," p. 175.

❊ THREE ❊

Rhetoric, Politics, and History—
LEONARDO BRUNI

1. RHETORIC AND POLITICS[1]

THE second facet of the rhetorical attitude is the commitment to what Hannah Arendt calls public happiness.[2] The rewards and values of rhetorical excellence are in large meas-

[1] On the relation of politics to rhetoric in Renaissance Italy, besides the article cited above of Herde, "Politik und Rhetorik in Florenz," and Baron's *Crisis*, see also Baron's "La rinascita dell'etica statale romana nell'Umanesimo fiorentino del Quattrocento," *Civiltà moderna*, 7 (1935), pp. 3-31, and his *Humanistic and Political Literature in Florence and Venice*, Cambridge, Mass., 1955; Part 3 of Galletti's *L'eloquenza dalle origini al XVI secolo*, "L'eloquenza politica dagli inizi del Quattrocento alla caduta della repubblica fiorentina"; C. Curcio, *La politica italiana del '400; Contributo alla storia delle origini del pensiero borghese*, Florence, 1932; E. Santini, *Firenze e i suoi "oratori" nel Quattrocento*, Milan, 1922; D. Cantimori, "Rhetoric and Politics in Italian Humanism," *JWI*, 1 (1937), pp. 83-102; Garin, *Italian Humanism*, chap. 2; F. Adorno, "La crisi dell'Umanesimo civile fiorentino da Alamanno Rinuccini al Machiavelli," *RCSF*, 7 (1952), pp. 19-40; G. Radetti, "Le origini dell'Umanesimo civile fiorentino nel '400," *GCFI*, 38 (1959), pp. 98-122; L. Martines, *The Social World of the Florentine Humanists, 1390-1460*, Princeton, 1963; M. Becker, *Florence in Transition*, Vol. 2, Baltimore, 1968, esp. chaps. 1 and 4; Buck, "Matteo Palmieri," *AKG*, 47 (1965), pp. 77-95.
A discussion of the relation of politics and rhetoric since 1955 almost inevitably must confront Baron's thesis of "civic Humanism"; on Baron see particularly Seidlmayer, "Die Entwicklung der italienischen Früh-Renaissance. Politische Anlässe und geistige Elemente," rep. in *Wege und Wandlungen des Humanismus*, pp. 47-74; Seigel, " 'Civic Humanism' or Ciceronian Rhetoric? The Culture of Petrarch and Bruni," *Past and Present*, 34 (1966), pp. 3-48; and Baron, "Leonardo Bruni: 'Professional Rhetorician' or 'Civic Humanist'?" *Past and Present*, 36 (1967), pp. 21-37.
[2] This is a general theme in both *Between Past and Future* and *On Revolution*.

ure public rewards and values; rhetorical functions are archetypally and also ideally political functions. If Salutati starts,
Bruni continues the notion of the logical priority of aesthetic
interest; the Humanist's command of form justifies his
assumption of a political role. Central still is the emphasis on
the mediated experience; the Humanist opens the way to
political persuasion through his technical knowledge of the
ground of the will and his mastery of the methods derived
from poetry of controlling aesthetic effect.

But while in the discussion of rhetoric and poetics it was
necessary to posit a radical break between the medieval and
the Renaissance attitudes, in political rhetoric it is equally
necessary to understand the continuity between late medieval
and early Renaissance practice in Italy. Rhetoric is claimed
as the political instrument *par excellence* by Brunetto Latini
and the masters of the *ars dictaminis* as well as the great
Humanist chancellors singled out by Pius II—Salutati, Bruni,
Marsuppini, Poggio.[3] This continuity, moreover, is historically significant; H. Wieruszowski has hypothesized that the
activity of the notaries, jurists, and rhetors of the early
communes represents a beginning stage of an important
Renaissance political development, the laicization of politics,
which found its most complete statement in the works of
Machiavelli.[4]

[3] See the passage quoted above, chap. 2, note 1, from the *Historia
de Europa, Opera*, p. 454.
[4] Wieruszowski, "*Ars dictaminis* in the Time of Dante," p. 103;
see also Kristeller, "Humanism and Scholasticism," and Seigel, *Rhetoric
and Philosophy*, Part 2. But there are refinements of the notion of
continuity: where R. Morghen sees Florentine *volgare* as unique in
the continuity of the political passions which inspire and inform it
("La storiografia fiorentina del Trecento," *Secoli vari* ('300-'400-'500),
Florence, 1958, pp. 72-73), C. Segre emphasizes the rhetorical discipline
as guiding and inspiring a continuous Italian literary development
(*Lingua, stile e società; Studi sulla storia della prosa italiana*, Milan,
1963, p. 177). A. Pagliaro, on the other hand, in listing the "modern"
traits of Dante's *De vulgari eloquentia*, hypothesizes a profound change
in linguistic consciousness which could serve as the basis of a "modern"
political consciousness ("La dottrina linguistica di Dante," *Nuovi
saggi di critica semantica*, Messina, 1956, p. 238).

If Brunetto Latini used a wide variety of concrete examples from Florentine affairs to suggest the relevance of Ciceronian oratory for contemporary politics,[5] Salutati exults in the achievements, the dignity of contemporary politics in the Ciceronian mode. The measure of this confidence is his pride in his office as Chancellor:

> For it is enough, and more than enough that God, the great governor and guide of all things, has in his goodness provided for me; God who has brought me, born in that very small, yet sunny town, to so famous a city, and who has assigned me, having gained beyond my merit the good will of so glorious a people, to the service, in association with my lords, of so honorable an office.[6]

Salutati has his commitments organized in a neat hierarchy: ". . . I am a Christian . . . and next Italian as to race, Florentine by fatherland, by nature and choice a Guelph" (*E.*, II, 254). If the rhetorical cast of mind emphasizes the will at the expense of intellect, so his rhetorical function helps to underline the preeminence of the public will, of patriotism:

> For no charity can be compared with the love of the fatherland. Parents, children, brothers, friends, relatives, neighbors, other necessary ties, taken individually or all together, are less than the relationship to the republic itself.[7]

We owe everything to the *patria*: "It has created us, it preserves us; from it, which is most important, we derive our descent. . ." (*E.*, I, 27).

[5] "De' consiglieri," *Rettorica*, p. 144f.

[6] "Satis enim superque satis omnium rerum gubernator et rector Deus sua michi benignitate providit, qui me parvissimo, tamen aprico, natum ex oppido, in tam celebrem transtulit civitatem et citra merita tam gloriosi populi benevolentiam assecutum me iuxta meos dominos in munere tam honorabilis officii collocavit." *E.*, II, 13; cf. *E.*, I, 203.

[7] "Nulla enim caritas est que sit cum caritate patrie comparanda. parentes, filii, fratres, amici, agnati, affines et cetere necessitudines quedam singula sunt et simul omnia collata minus habent ipsa republica." *E.*, I, 21.

Humanist arguments have more than their share of circularity; one facet of their patriotic fervor is rhetorical pride. To many Humanists Florence, particularly in this period of the first half of the fifteenth century, was peculiarly the home of eloquence: *"cui urbi propria et peculiaris atque innata eloquentia est."*[8] Even in the florid overstatement of Bruni's *Laudatio Florentinae urbis* the genuine pride in the gestation of a community of the articulate is recognizable:

> For what should I say of sweetness of speech and elegance of language, in which without any question it is supreme? For this city alone in all Italy is considered to employ the most pure and polished discourse. And thus all who wish to speak well and correctly take their model from this one city.[9]

And again Bruni uses his image of Camillus, the second founder of Rome; Florence, through its encouragement of eloquence, has become the second founder of the Latin language, ". . . it has restored to dignity and splendor what has long been lost and corrupt."[10] The excellent essay by F. Schalk on the public of the Humanists quotes the no less happily sincere praise of Filelfo:

> Florence pleases me much. For it is a city which lacks nothing, in regard either to magnificent and graceful architecture or the dignity and wealth of its citizens. Further, the whole city is wild about me. Everyone seeks me out, honors me. All praise me to the skies. My name is in every mouth. And not only the first citizens, but even the women

---

[8] Ludovico Carbone, "Oratio in funere Guarini Veronensis," in *Prosatori latini,* p. 388. See Santini, *Firenze e i suoi "oratori,"* p. 74f.

[9] "Nam quid ego de orationis suavitate et verborum elegantia loquor, in qua quidem re sine controversia superat. Sola enim haec in tota Italia civitas purissimo ac nitidissimo sermone uti existamatur. Itaque omnes qui bene atque emendate loqui volunt, ex hac una urbe sumunt exemplum." From the edition of T. Klette, *Beiträge zur Geschichte und Litteratur der italienischen Gelehrtenrenaissance,* Greifswald, 1889, Vol. 2, p. 104; cf. Andrea de Senis, "Oratio . . . in principio studii," *Reden und Briefe,* p. 108.

[10] "Oratio in funere Nannis Strozzae," *Baluzii Miscellanea,* p. 4.

of the highest rank, for the sake of honoring me give way to me when I go through the town, and so defer to me that their reverent attitude actually embarrasses me.[11]

It was equally obvious that the Florentine patriciate regarded the formal study of rhetoric as useful as well as ornamental, a conviction expressed over and over again in the statutes of the University of Florence:

> The priors with the colleges, considering that the art of rhetoric is not only the instrument of persuasion for all the sciences, but also the greatest ornament of public life, and since this faculty embraces the precepts for advocating or opposing anything we wish, and concerns itself with the sure methods of the notarial offices: lest so appropriate a pursuit for the Florentine Studium decay, and in order to keep it continuously flourishing, they, of their own will, hereby nominate, depute, and elect that man of inestimable eloquence and marvelous learning, Master John of Master James of Malpaghini of Ravenna, to the public reading and teaching of the art of rhetoric in the Florentine Studium.[12]

[11] "Florentia me plurimum delectat. Est enim urbs, cui nihil desit, neque ad aedificiorum magnificentiam atque venustatem, neque ad civium dignitatem et amplitudinem. Adde quod universa in me civitas conversa est. Omnes me diligunt, honorant. Omnes ac summis laudibus in caelum efferunt. Meum nomen in ore est omnibus. Nec primarii cives modo, cum per urbem incedo, sed ipse et iam nobilissimae feminae, honorandi mei gratia, locum cedunt tantumque mihi deferunt, ut me pudeat tanti cultus." From *Epistolae*, II (1506); cited in Schalk, *Das Publikum*, pp. 19-20.

[12] "Domini cum collegiis, considerantes quod ars Rhetorica non solum omnium scientiarum persuasiorium instrumentum est, sed rerum publicarum maximum ornamentum, quoniam hec facultas suadendi dissuadendique cuncta que volumus precepta complectitur, et circa dictandi ministerium certis rationibus occupatur; ne tantum decus in Studio Florentino deficiat, sed continuo reflorescat, proprio motu, virum inextimabilis eloquentie mirabilisque doctrine dominum Iohannem magistri Iacobi de Malpaghinis de Ravenna nominaverunt, deputaverunt et elegerunt ad legendum atque docendum publice in Studio Florentino artem Rhetorice. . ." (1397). From A. Gherardi, *Statuti della università e studio fiorentino dell'anno MCCCLXXXVII seguiti da un appendice di documenti dal MCCCXX al MCCCCLXXII*, Florence, 1881, p. 369.

Supposedly, among the citizens themselves the demand was strong; another statute appoints a professor of rhetoric "because in this city there are many young men who desire very strongly to study letters, and particularly the arts of oratory and poetry."[13]

At the same time, if Humanism represents a profound reorientation in language habits and attitudes, there must be change as well as continuity in Florentine political rhetoric. The contradictions within the *oeuvre* of Trecento figures are primary evidence of change. In the preface to his edition of Salutati's notarial protocol, A. Petrucci notes how Salutati himself is aware of the tension between the rigid formalism of his notarial training and his literary aspirations as a Humanist.[14] Perhaps the distinction of A. Gramsci between organic and traditional intellectual elites can illuminate this relationship. But where Gramsci sees the Humanists as a traditional elite devoted to a learned culture and detached from the reality of a social class programme, Humanists such as Salutati and Bruni more probably represent a fusion of the two types: in function they were descendants of notaries, bureaucrats with organic ties with the ruling class, while at the same time they had genuine enthusiasm for, and training in, the new and rigorous critical learning which is of the traditional type, of an autonomous "caste." Salutati and Bruni assimilate the separate traditional learning for the benefit of their organic political function: in so far as they are traditional intellectuals they have status according to their command of classical rhetoric; in so far as they have a class function, they are rhetoricians.[15]

---

[13] (1454), Gherardi, *Statuti*, p. 264.

[14] "Il S. avvertita, e con notevole disagio, il contrasto fra le sue aspirazioni umanistiche e la tradizione rigidamente formalistica cui era costretto a piegarsi nelle sue funzioni di notaio o di cancelliere." Petrucci refers to S.'s letter to Tommaso Vergiolesi, Oct. 24, 1370, *Il Protocollo Notarile*, p. 16. See also F. di Capua, *Insegnamenti retorici medievali e dottrine estetiche moderne nel "De vulgari eloquentia" di Dante*, Naples, 1944, p. 122f., who describes the strong contrasts of medieval and "modern" within the *oeuvre* of Dante; also R. Weiss, "Dante e l'umanesimo del suo tempo."

[15] A. Gramsci, *Gli intellettuali e l'organizzazione della cultura*, Turin, 1955, esp. p. 4f.

Moreover, for the Humanists it is literature, not communal politics, which furnishes the primary model for freedom. Thus Professor Gombrich points out that it is precisely the new freedom to criticize the literary heritage manifest in the "merely" grammatical activity of Niccolò Niccoli which is the vital new posture of Quattrocento culture; the fashionableness and self-confidence of the Humanists has its source in their rhetorical and grammatical skill, in the depth of their scholarly commitment. It is one thing to see rhetoric as a useful embellishment and to regard one's trade as rhetoric; it is another to confront all the linguistic *aporia* of the classical period using rhetorical terms and maxims as your fundamental categories.[16]

The change represented by Humanism is also a quantitative one; as the intellectual elite of the Italian city-states became more literary, their formative influence on the sociocultural ambiance becomes stronger; the firmer their literary identity, the more glamorous their public identity. If, on the one hand, there is a real difference between the tentative achievement of the early communal rhetoric and the mature culture of the Humanists, there is a real complementarity between Volgare and Latin expression, between the active and contemplative modes in the fully developed Humanism of the Quattrocento.[17] The alternative choices Bruni presents in the *Dialogi ad Petrum Paulum Histrum*—the culture of *disputatio*, of civil conversation of which he makes Salu-

[16] Professor Gombrich has a twofold response: on the one hand, he finds the Humanists' glamour, their superiority "based at first on precariously narrow foundations"; on the other, the Humanists' language skills are the paradigm for the new Renaissance freedom "to criticize the tradition and to reject anything that seems 'a crime and a sacrilege' in the eyes of ancient authority." "From the Revival of Letters to the Reform of the Arts; Niccolò Niccoli and Filippo Brunelleschi," *Essays in the History of Art Presented to Rudolph Wittkower*, ed. D. Fraser et al., London, 1967, pp. 71, 80.

[17] Baron, *Crisis*, chap. 15, "Florentine Humanism and the Volgare," p. 332f.; Auerbach, *Literary Language and Its Public*, p. 318; Apel, *Die Idee*, p. 201; R. Spongano, "La prosa letteraria del Quattrocento," *Due Saggi sull' Umanesimo*, [Florence, 1964]; F. Tateo, "La tradizione classica e le forme del dialogo umanistico," *Tradizione e realtà nell' Umanesimo italiano*, Bari, 1967, p. 245.

tati the exemplar, and the retired, bookish learning of Niccoli —are simply that, alternatives.

In the case of these Florentine rhetoricians, then, their interest in the creation of a separate sphere of literary activity merges with their political interest in the formation of another highly artificial sphere—the public space in which the conventions of political life rule. And just as the Sophists functioned as *"maestri di cultura"* in instructing the newly enlarged citizenry of Athens in the techniques of their public duties, so the Humanists self-consciously assume the role of pedagogues to the mobile classes of the powerful, the competent, and, hopefully, the engaged.[18] The goal of Humanist education is the achievement of an *impalcatura*, a scaffolding which will order and sustain a public character as well as a private virtue, for Bruni specifically makes the point that the *studia humanitatis* which Florence has restored to all of Italy are *"privatim et publice ad vitam necessaria."*[19]

The relation of Humanist pedagogy and political life is based on the strict relation of group to individual persuasion; as Gorgias as well as Salutati has pointed out, the means of moving a community are qualitatively the same as those which move an individual (*De verecundia*, 288).[20] There is no simple juxtaposition of expendable masses and scholarly caste; rather, the Humanists addressed themselves to a fair number of citizens inclined to sensible deliberation through predilection and education. Further, there is no simple opposition of rhetorical training as pertaining to *otium* and its political uses as *negotium*; Professor Goldthwaite has very rightly asserted that for the Florentine financial and commercial patriciate political involvement as well as literature was the product, not the antithesis, of leisure.[21] These Florentine Humanists recognized, then, that part of the strength of

[18] On the Sophists see R. Mondolfo, "Intorno alla storia della filosofia," *RCSF*, 12 (1957), p. 224; see also Galletti's long comparison of the Sophists and Humanists in *L'eloquenza*, p. 539f.

[19] "Oratio in funere Nannis Strozzae," p. 4.

[20] On Gorgias see Segal, "Gorgias and the Psychology of the Logos," p. 109.

[21] *Private Wealth in Renaissance Florence*, Princeton, 1968, pp. 49-50.

rhetoric lies in its character as a circulatory system; an audience trained in rhetoric is sensitive to rhetorical argument; the Humanist projected an appeal to an audience trained as Isocrates had trained the Greeks for listening to Demosthenes. The rationale of the increase in Humanist rhetorical training was a question of power, not of size; nor is it a question of esoteric knowledge but of a shared intellectual apparatus, the *topoi* of common sense; when a citizen spoke to a citizen the presupposition was that both possessed a certain competence, rationality, and education. They desired to advance not so much in originality as in intelligibility.[22]

The *studia humanitatis* as concerned with the *logos* became the basic structuring agent in the *città terrena*.[23] Specifically, in the *Dialogus* Bruni emphasizes in the person of Salutati the Humanist self-consciousness of intellectual community, of the efficacy of dialogue among free and equal men, of the nature of life as colloquium. Further, in the *Vita di Dante* Bruni relates that Dante regarded *"conversazioni urbane e civili"* as part of his education,

> . . . nella qual cosa mi giova reiprendere l'errore di molti ignoranti, i quali credono, niuno essere studiante se non quelli si nascondono in solitudine e in ozio, ed io no vidi mai niuno di questi camuffati e rimassi dalla conversazione delli uomini che sapesse tre lettere. Lo ingegno alto e grande non ha bisogno di tali tormenti. . . .[24]

To the early Quattrocento Humanists, Dante was outstanding in that he combined poetic, philosophical, religious, and civic commitment: "For there is no type of duty, either

---

[22] There is a wide-ranging body of erudition and opinion on this subject: see the works already cited of Galletti, Santini, Schalk, and Buck, *Italienische Dichtungslehre*, p. 58; also Schalk, "Il tema della 'vita activa' e della 'vita contemplativa' nell'Umanesimo italiano," in *Umanesimo e scienza politica*, ed. E. Castelli, Milan, 1951, pp. 559-66; A. Messer, "Quintilian als Didaktiker und sein Einfluss auf die didaktisch-pädagogische Theorie des Humanismus," *Neue Jahrbücher für Philologie und Pädagogik*, 156.2 (1897), pp. 161-204, 273-292; and A. Burk, *Die Pädagogik des Isokrates*, Part 3, pp. 199-224.

[23] Garin, "Discussioni sulla retorica," *Medioevo e rinascimento*, p. 124f; Schalk, "Il tema," p. 564.

[24] In *Le vite di Dante*, ed. Solerti, pp. 99-100.

public, domestic, forensic, civil, or military which Dante did not ably fulfill."[25] For the Humanists, like the Duecento and Trecento masters of rhetoric, functioned as rhetors both in the training of citizens for public life and as officials of the political community. Nor were the Humanist Chancellors mere clerks of the powerful Florentine oligarchy; their activity was not limited *"all'esecuzione formale di disegni progettati dai potenti, o alla modesta funzione di 'litterati' disposti a porre in un latino elegante, le decisioni della Signoria."* They were diplomats, propagandists with a *"straordinaria capacità nell'elaborare tutto un 'piano' ideologico utilitissimo per la Fiorentina."*[26]

This competence was a matter of principle: the point Bruni and other "civic Humanists" attempted to make was that there is a qualitative difference between public life and private life, for a public life involves a more strict sense of honor as well as the possibility of winning more honor. In his *History of Florence* he attributes to the Pisan Gambacorta the words:

> We will tolerate much in private men and we will be indulgent about inconstancy, avarice, and self-seeking, which are not to be tolerated at all in a state.[27]

The integrity of a city, and thus of its magistrates, is a more fragile thing than that of a private person: thus in Bruni's defense of himself from a charge of malfeasance he argues that when one becomes a public official "one ought to put aside one's private *persona* in assuming the public one." This status requires both greater probity and greater protection against slander, "for if in private life we become justly incensed at the slanders of those who think badly of us and judge us less than honest, how much more should we make

---

[25] G.M. Filelfo, "De clarissimi poetae Dantis Florentini vita e moribus," *Le vite di Dante*, p. 179.

[26] Vasoli, "Storia e politica," p. 125.

[27] ". . . multa in privatis hominibus toleramus, et inconstantiae avaritiaeque ac sordida questibus veniam impartimur, quae in civitate nullo modo forent toleranda" (p. 180). Bruni's *Historiarum Florentini populi libri XII* will be cited henceforth as *H.F.*, with page numbers.

of the aspersions cast upon us while acting in the public faith?"[28]

The core of Bruni's position is Aristotle's dictum that man is a political animal.[29] Private virtue is not enough; the public sphere contains possibilities for virtue and happiness which the private sphere does not. The primacy of the military life is the theme of Bruni's *De militia*, his oration to Niccolò da Tolentino, his funeral oration for Nanni Strozzi.[30] That soldiering is the most positive engagement to the *patria* is the ground of both Bruni's and Machiavelli's defense of a citizen militia; such commitment makes for energetic, not effete armies.

But the life spent in wise debate and counsel on public issues, in diplomacy, in writing and speaking in defense and praise of the commonwealth is also meritorious.[31] Plutarch in his *Life of Cato* used a metaphor which expresses the need for rhetoric exactly: Cato's discourse was "a second body, as it were, and, for the use of a man who would live neither obscurely nor idly, an instrument with which to perform not only necessary, but also high and noble services."[32] Bruni, whose father was of the middle class in Arezzo, attacks Niccoli's pride in his rank as a Florentine patrician, for ". . . nobility springs not so much from the fame of our ancestors as from our own virtue and excellencies . . . ," and he goes on to claim that he was ". . . in this a better citizen than you: as more useful to the *patria*, since I have never faltered in

---

[28] "Leonardo Florentini pro se ipso," in the appendix to Santini, *L.B.A. e i suoi "Historiarum . . . libri,"* p. 166.

[29] Aristotle, *Politics*, 1253a; compare Bruni, "Praemissio quaedam ad evidentiam novae translationis Politicorum Aristotelis," *Schriften*, pp. 73-74.

[30] There is an edition of the "De militia" in C.C. Bayley, *War and Society in Renaissance Florence*, Toronto, 1961, pp. 369-389; the "Oration to Niccolò Tolentino" was edited by O. Gamurrini, Florence, 1877.

[31] Thus Andrea de Senis makes eloquence the absolute condition for great deeds, *Reden und Briefe*, p. 111: "quin etiam reges ipsi ac principis sine eloquentiae studio numquam ad res praeclare gerendas accedere posse putaverunt, sed et permulti hac ipsa maximos magistratus, splendissimam gloriam summamque potentiam adepti sunt."

[32] *Marcus Cato, Vitae parallelae*, I, 4.

writing and acting for the glory of the Florentine people."[33]
And to put a more sordid construction on it, there is nothing,
as Matteo Palmieri said crisply, so pertinent to winning
glory as being good, and having one's goodness well-known.[34]

The Humanists tend to oppose the occult, the contemplative, the private, and that which pertains to the few, to
the useful, the active, the public, and that which concerns
the many:

> For many both of the Greeks and of the Egyptians have
> delighted in contemplation, for they have written much
> which refers to the knowledge of occult and marvelous
> things, all of which pertains to the few. But I praise and
> admire the Romans most of all, who, in writing about laws
> and morals, consult not private commodity and inward
> pleasure, but the common utility of men.[35]

In political fact, however, the "many" seems to refer to "the
many of the rich."[36] For certainly Bruni felt no contradiction
in the fact that he served as rhetorical functionary for the
few, for the oligarchic class which ruled Florence during his
Chancellorship; Bruni, in the *De Florentinorum republica*,
connects the public virtues with the class of *optimates* in his
period:

> Then truly the power of the city is seen to inhere, not in
> the multitude, but in the aristocratic and the rich, who

[33] "Oratio in nebulonem maledicum," in G. Zippel, *Niccolò Niccoli*,
Florence, 1890, pp. 81, 82.

[34] *Della vita civile*, ed. F. Battaglia, Bologna, 1944, p. 145: "Sopra
ogni cosa e attissimi alla gloria l'essere buono, e per buono consciuto:
molto poi giova l'essere eloquente e bello parlatore, e operarsi nel difendere la patria e gli amici . . ."

[35] "Delectati quidem multi cum ex Graecis tum ex Aegyptiis contemplatione sunt, multaque ad cognitionem rerum occultarum et admirabilium pertinentia conscripsere, quod quidem ad paucos pertinet. Sed
ego potissimum Romanos laudo et admiror, qui post habita commoditate, et voluptate animi, de legibus et moribus scribentes, communi
hominum utilitati semper consuluere." Platina, *De optimo cive*, ed.
F. Battaglia, Bologna, 1944, p. 180.

[36] This is an expression of Fra Paolino of Venice, cited in F.C. Lane,
"Political Ideas and the Venetian Constitution," *Venice and History*,
Baltimore, 1966, p. 300.

contribute money to the republic, and are skilled in counsel rather than military exercise.[37]

The views of Bruni and his patrician acquaintance seem to coincide perfectly on the formal as well as the political values of language; their public eloquence is not a private jargon, is not characterized by a precious classicism. The instructions of Bruni as Chancellor to the *oratores*, the members of the powerful Florentine families on diplomatic missions, attest a grasp of realistic rhetorical idiom similar to that of the early Sophists: one speaks to win, not to impress with irrelevant learning. Bruni even admonishes one Chancellery

> We would like you to omit all this philosophy, because it is neither appropriate to you or to the times, and particularly because its advice isn't even true.[38]

He chides another for its fraudulent appeal with "*coloratis verbis, ac ficta quadem simultatione.*"[39] The letters emanating from Bruni's Chancellery do not reek of the lamp. In the registers preserved of his state correspondence there are surprisingly few direct classical references; the devotion of Bruni is to rhetorical principle, not rhetorical copying. An explicit reference to the style proper for diplomatic usage is Bruni's attack on a letter addressed to the Council of Basel vilifying

[37] "Tunc vero urbis potentia, non in multitudine, sed in optimatibus et divitibus consistere visa est, qui pecuniam in Rempublicam conferrent et consilio magis, quam armis uterentur." Latin trans. B. Monetti, Florence, 1758, pp. 27-28.

[38] "omittite quesumus hanc philosophiam que nec vos decet, neque tempori congruit, praesertim cum non vera ea sit sed falsa sententia." *Sig. Miss. I Canc., Reg.* 32 f. 33r. Except for one volume (Bibl. Naz. Panciatichiano 148), the state correspondence extant of Bruni is in the Archivio della Repubblica in the Archivio di Stato in Florence: under the rubric *Signori. Legazioni e Commissioni. Elezioni e Istruzioni a oratori* are the instructions in Italian to Florentine commissaries, military leaders, and ambassadors (orators); under *Signori. Carteggio. Missive. I Cancelleria* is the Latin correspondence with foreign political bodies, heads of state, or foreign "*oratores.*"

[39] *Sig. Miss. I Canc., Reg.* 32, f. 83r. Bruni himself seems to have exercised another type of self-denial; there are surprisingly few references to Providence or appeals to the Deity in the correspondence.

Florence as a possible meeting place for the Council. This letter is a forgery, he claims; for

> I have shown, moreover, that the style and figures of speech are not those of letters of the Duke of Milan, since that lord is accustomed, and accustomed above all in important affairs, to write elegantly and accurately, while these letters published in the Council have a gross and unlearned, even rustic style, with ambitious, hasty, and inconsidered statements.[40]

His instructions bespeak a shared idiom of public discourse—crisp, sensitive, with the main principle that of aptness, of decorum, the suiting of the word to the occasion which is the goal of rhetorical training and practice. The injunctions as to form for the ambassadors are simple and brief; the very frequent use of the *clausola di confidenza* witnesses an easy understanding. They are told to use *"parole efficaci et convenienti et apte,"* or *"costumate et efficaci,"* or to speak *"con parole ample et grandi,"* or *"convenienti a honore del communità nostra."* "Voi," he tells Palla Strozzi and Filippo Pandolfini, *"sete prudentissimi uomini, et cognoscete optimamente le parole che vi bisogna usare a riducere le menti de Sanesi a questa credulità et effecto."* Bruni and the *oratores* are sensitive to mood and tone; at times he urges them to use words *"grandi et sonanti,"* at others, words that are *"humane et piacevoli,"* or *"dolci et de conforti e prieghi."* Once he advises Nerone de' Nigi *"et questa parte, che è d'importanza, tracterai con buona diligentia ingegnandoli levar via ogni diversità d'animi."* At times ambiguity is called for, at others clarity, when one should speak *"con parole fuora del generale."*[41]

---

[40] "Ostendi preterea stilus figuraque dicendi non esse illas domini ducis mediolani litteras, cum ille dominus eleganter et accurate presertim in rebus maioribus scribere suas litteras consueverit, hec autem littere in concilio publicate stilum haberunt grossum et incompositum ac pene rusticanum, sententias ambitiosas et inconsideratas." Panciatichiano 148, f. 68r.

[41] The quotations are from the *Sig. Leg. Elez. Istruz., Reg. 9* and 10, *passim*. The use of the *clausola di confidenza* is probably more

Sabbadini has said that *"il Rinascimento è il trionfo dell' eloquenza,"* but not as "mere" rhetoric, since *"eloquenza è perfino la politica."*[42] It is neither Cicero the amoral formalist, nor Cicero the sage removed from worldly affairs, but Cicero the orator who employs form to persuade on public issues who is the archetype, who "can just as properly be called the parent of our eloquence and letters as father of his country," and it is Cicero's *De officiis* which is the handbook of the "civic Humanism" of the Renaissance.[43]

2. POLITICAL DEBATE AND HISTORY

While the relation of aesthetic principles of rhetoric to historical consciousness was characterized by *reciprocity* or mutual influence of the notions of continuity and discontinuity, of limitation and liberty, Humanist political rhetoric has a peculiar *duality* of influence on Bruni's *History of Florence*.[44] And again, in order to understand the nature of this connection it is necessary to assign the rhetorical cluster of ideas to a deeper level of assumption and motive than has hitherto been the case, for the complex of ideas which guides the practice of political debate also acts as a

---

frequent in the Florentine *istruzioni* than in those of the Milanese, for example; see G. Rondinini, "Ambasciatori e ambascerie al tempo di F. Visconti (1412-1426)," *NRS*, 44 (1965), p. 341. On the nature of Bruni's political eloquence the negative view of Garin expressed in his "I cancellieri umanisti," p. 23, should be contrasted with the encomiastic summary of Santini in his *L.B.A. e i suoi "Historiarum . . . libri,"* p. 240.

[42] *Il metodo*, p. 65.

[43] Bruni, "Cicero novus," *Schriften*, p. 115. There are some interesting parallels between Bruni's discussion of Cicero's political eloquence and that of Michel, *Rhétorique et philosophie chez C.*, see esp. pp. 586, 607. On Cicero as the Humanists' model see also Seigel, *Rhetoric and Philosophy*, p. 246f.

[44] On the relationship of political eloquence and historiography in Italian Humanism see, besides the works cited in chap. 2, note 52—especially those of Baron, Santini, Ullman, Varese—, Vasoli's "Storia e politica," A. Renaudet, "Humanisme, histoire, et politique au Quattrocento," *Humanisme et Renaissance*, Geneva, 1958, pp. 99-113; F. Gilbert, *Machiavelli and Guicciardini; Politics and History in Sixteenth-Century Florence*, Princeton, 1965, chap. 5, "The Theory and Practice of History in the Fifteenth Century," pp. 203-235.

screen which permits certain historical insights and rejects others. For the Sophists, for Isocrates, for Cicero, for the Italian Humanists rhetoric was a coherent body of knowledge of human behavior with a special focus on the relation of discourse to action. For them rhetoric functioned as a psychology which stressed the sophisticated analysis of problems of will and choice, motivation and compulsion; which developed a concrete self-consciousness in the author of the relation of meaning to intention; and which placed a high value on a sense of *opportunità* (*kairos*), a grasp of the relation of choice to circumstance.

More specifically, a perusal of Bruni's state correspondence reveals his rhetorical commitment as not so much a matter of pedestrian imitation of empty classical formulas as of a truly viable rhetorical sensitivity exercised daily in his political role; the difference is that between a mental straitjacket of rhetorical tags and a pragmatic and lucid frame of mind. This rhetorical mental set has a dual nature: it is both self-conscious commitment and critical analysis. In turn, this dual nature manifests itself in two main areas of historical insight in Bruni's *History of Florence*: first, rhetorical values reinforce the specific political *values* which the Florentine historical process generates; second, concepts of rhetorical structure underline, make clear the *structure* of Florentine political history.

In the first place, Bruni appreciates the practice of rhetoric as a value in itself; the practice of eloquence is the practice of liberty; as Alamanno Rinuccini will maintain in his *De libertate*, no man can consider himself free unless he is free to speak openly in the forum just what he feels.[45] *Libertas*, then, is not merely the slogan of the Florentine commune and the Guelph party; history becomes the story of liberty; the de-

---

[45] "Nessuno chiamerà libero chi nel Senato o nel parlamento, o in qualunque assemblea giudicante non osi parlare ed agire apertamente come sente; per questo giustamente dirai esser la libertà parte del coraggio," from the *De libertate*, quoted in F. Adorno, "La crisi dell'Umanesimo civile," p. 25; Adorno has edited the *Dialogus de libertate* in the *Atti e Memorie dell'Accademia La Colombaria*, Vol. 22, pp. 265-303.

velopment or decline of public freedom is the strand of meaning on which all political history is made to depend. And
since Bruni's historical ideal or goal is the creation of a political community on the model of the Athenian polis or of
republican Rome, his professional and intellectual commitment to the principles of classical rhetoric allows him to
separate out favorable and untoward events in this process.

Just as there is a continuity between the political rhetoric
of the thirteenth-century masters of the *dictamen* and that of
the Humanists, so there is continuity in the historical insights
into the politics of choice from the Trecento Florentine
chronicles through the formal historiography of the Humanists. In Hermann Broch's sense that both myth and history
simply represent that part of humanity which endures, the
chroniclers as well as the Humanists preserve the public
myths of the Florentines.[46] A. del Monte has affirmed that
Giacotto Malespini (1282-1320) was

> il primo a intendere perspicuamente l'esigenza d'accor-
> dare in una sola opera storica il mito del passato e la realtà
> del presente per attuare nel futuro una realtà, degno di
> mito.[47]

Further, there is no conflict between their literary and historiographical identity, for literature for these Florentines
was as much public duty as personal recreation, was not only
a "personal myth-making activity but a species of public
myth, articulating not what is held to be true but what is held
to be creatively viable and relevant."[48] Indeed, there is a

---

[46] Broch, "L'héritage mythique de la littérature," *Création littéraire
et connaissance*, trans. A. Kohn, Paris, 1966, pp. 242-48.

[47] A. del Monte, "La storiografia fiorentina del secoli XII e XIII,"
Bull. Ist. Stor. Ital., 62 (1950), p. 190.

[48] "A work of literature is both part of an inheritance of literary
practice and a personal and often *ad hoc* methodology for interpreting
the world, or *a* world. But it is involved in all the public consequences
of the social nature of language and of its mediating function: within
itself it creates typologies and representative universals, and reaching
outward it coheres social groupings, forms a culture—in the literary
rather than the sociological sense," "Sociology and Literature," *TLS*,
April 4, 1968, p. 345.

gain in historical consciousness connected to the firmer literary identity of the Humanists. Where the early myths are tentative or dominated by religious hierarchies, there is a quality of explicitness about the first rhetorical history of Florence by Bruni which is missing in the chronicles: here is a clarity which stems from a congruence between the political fact of the thirteenth and fourteenth centuries, Bruni's historical insights, and his rhetorical values. Clarity or *perspicuitas* is related to critical control; the change in language is one of the keys to the change in historiography; the rhetorical commitment to persuasion intensifies the commitment to define the values and articulate the public myths held by the Florentines.[49]

For Bruni, then, the central motif of Florentine history is the formation of a public space; the purpose of the series of changes in government was "to establish and keep in existence a space where freedom as virtuosity can appear,"[50] the creation of a sphere of good faith where one can debate without fear of intimidation or constraint, in which men talk and act in real *libertas*. It is obvious that "public" had a more vital and specific meaning for Bruni than it has now. The different contexts of the many uses in the *History of Florence* of the antinomy public-private give the world "public" the connotations of open, frank, free, moral, altruistic, rational, political, etc.: adjectives which in Ciceronian treatises de-

---

[49] Cf. Dazzi, *Il Mussato preumanista*, p. 82; Vasoli, "Storia e politica," pp. 123-24. This rhetorical intensification may perhaps underline both continuity and change; thus Morghen, "La storiografia fiorentina," p. 84f., points out that while the real worlds of both the early Trecento Dino Compagni and Machiavelli are the same, are viewed from the same shrewd, pessimistic attitude, the ideal worlds, the "myths" are different: rhetoric can contribute to both disenchantment and secularization. E. Mehl, *Die Weltanschauung des Giovanni Villani*, Leipzig, 1927, pp. 10-36, stresses the discontinuity of medieval and Humanist historical styles; F. Chabod, "La 'concezione del mondo' di G. Villani," *NRS*, 13 (1929), pp. 336-39, sees the same "myths," the cult of personality, the passion for *virtù*, informing stylistic choices of both chronicler and Humanist.

[50] Arendt, *Between Past and Future*, p. 154; but it is exactly this intention which J. Habermas would deny the Humanists, *Strukturwandel der Öffentlichkeit*, Neuwied am Rhein and Berlin, 1965, pp. 11-22.

scribe the debate which is the goal of rhetorical training. Bruni uses the dichotomy public-private to delineate the tension which results from the reaction to the Florentine drive to "publicity"; through Machiavelli the Humanists regard Florentine history as the history of a struggle between private expediency and public utility, private faction and public interest, private constraint and public persuasion.[51]

Here again, however, the tendency of the rhetorical attitude is not only to set up a framework but to fill it with concrete content. The public-private tension is a chain of specific events related to the presence or absence of public debate; the rise of faction is as important to the nature of Florence as its Etruscan origins and the decline of Rome (*H.F.*, 27). While the rise of Florence as a new arena of public life, the new seat of freedom has an invigorating effect on its citizens, private faction over and over again appears as the source of all difficulties (*H.F.*, 115, 169, 180, 198-99). Bruni stresses in the *Vita di Dante* the deplorable tendency of the Black and White factions in the early fourteenth century to refuse public deliberation before resorting to private force; the whole point of the developing Florentine constitution was to get people to resort to public debate before or instead of taking up arms in private quarrels. When he discusses the political aftermath of the reign of the Duke of Athens in Florence he argues the impossibility of giving public power to people with great private power without injury to the community (*H.F.*, 168), for their public acts of vengeance are nothing but private injuries in public form— "*privatam iniuriam publica manu factam*" (*H.F.*, 102). The expulsion of Giano della Bella was an attempt by private power to get rid of the man who stood for public constraint (*H.F.*, 87).[52] Later in the fourteenth century the attainders

[51] On Machiavelli's sensitivity to this creative core of politics see H. Arendt, *Between Past and Future*, pp. 136-37.

[52] Cf. G. Villani, *Cronaca*, VIII, 8, in *Cronache di Giovanni, Matteo, e Filippo Villani*, Trieste, 1857, p. 173: Villani lays the blame for Giano's death in exile on Florence, "o massimamente al popolo, perocch'egli era il più leale e diritto popolano e amatore del bene comune che uomo di Firenze, e quegli che mettea in comune e non

by the Parte Guelfa became examples not of public discussion but private licence, an extra-public force exerted on the magistracy (*H.F.*, 268).

Repeatedly Bruni makes the point that the creation of a public space is the creation of a sphere of good faith; that both in domestic and foreign affairs a republic offers opportunities of open discussion and frank dealing impossible in a tyranny with its *"modi serpentini."*[53] Bruni feels that open deliberation in honesty and good faith will expose the path to greatness for the *civitas*; the opposite course is full of risk: "For it is not right for that which pertains to the many to be decided by the few, nor is it safe for the very ones who do the deciding" (*H.F.*, 176). He specifically ascribes the major blunders of the Florentines in the Viscontean war of the late fourteenth century to ruthless grasping at opportunity, to lack of cool deliberation (*H.F.*, 266-67). A city has its honor to lose; Bruni conceives of all Italy as the audience of this honesty or dissimulation, fraud or plain-dealing that went on during this, the greatest of Italian wars. Faith in public discourse is the mark of the civilized Italian, while one expects deceit from a German barbarian (*H.F.*, 251).

In his discussion of the constitutional change in Florence from election by vote to election by lot, Bruni brings up another aspect of the public life: that the seeking for public honor by the suffrage of one's peers is in itself a curb on private expediency (*H.F.*, 121-22). Here is also the classical sense that public honor can be conferred only by peers; it is not the accolade of a tyrant. In domestic affairs *consilia* is the source of honor, abroad, military *fortitudo*. The search for honor, fame, and glory is a passion to be in the public eye—either as a military or civic leader; history, which dispenses fame and glory, is the narrative of military *virtù* and the *virtù*

---

ne traeva." Landino also sees Dante as a champion of public constraint in his "Vita e costumi del poeta," *Le vite di Dante*, p. 189.
[53] *Sig. Elez. Istruz., Reg.* 9, f. 25r; *Sig. Cart. Miss. I Canc., Reg.* 35, f. 44v; Panciatichiano 148, f. 210v, 188v; and the "Difesa di Leonardo Bruni Aretino contro i reprensori del popolo di Firenze nella impresa di Lucca," ed. P. Guerra, Lucca, 1864, p. 24f.

of discourse. Bruni underscores the *virtù* of discourse, the impact of discourse on event when he dwells upon the role of Giovanni Ricci in the war with Milan in the 1380's and 90's. In the taut, spare narration of negotiation and battle Bruni takes time to portray Gian Galeazzo Visconti's bitterly angry reaction to Ricci's public accusation of Gian Galeazzo's lack of the public virtue of honest speaking; the reply of the Florentines protesting the openness and publicity of their words and actions, as opposed to those of tyrants; the public valuation of the insult in the enormous ransom demanded by Visconti for Ricci, captured on a mission to the French (1391) (*H.F.*, 241-46; 254-55; 261-64).[54]

For Bruni, then, rhetoric is both means and end: rhetoric is the means for achieving public honor and at the same time the free practice of rhetorical powers is the goal of political development, the proof of liberty. Moreover, Florence is but one instance of the coincidence of liberty and eloquence in the history of the world for the Humanists; and always liberty appears in this history as virtuosity rather than as a state of mind in which the will is in agreement with God's design for mankind, the Augustinian version of free will. History is properly the history of free choice within the public sphere, the conflict of *virtù* and *fortuna* in the search for community.[55]

The connection of eloquence with free civic life had often been made in classical rhetorical texts. Cicero in the *Brutus* (12, 45-49) saw oratory as peculiar to Athens, as only arising

[54] Bruni's insights find some corroboration in recent scholarship: for some contemporary discussions of the development of a public space and the importance of consultation and debate in Florence see both volumes of M. Becker's *Florence in Transition* and his article "The Republican City State in Florence; An Inquiry into Its Origins and Survival (1280-1434)," *Speculum*, 35 (1960), esp. pp. 46-49; G. Brucker, *Florentine Politics and Society*, 1343-78, Princeton, 1962, p. 72f. On the other hand, P. Villari had commented on the lack of genuine debate, and thus the absence of true eloquence in all the councils of early Trecento Florence, *I primi due secoli della storia di Firenze*, 3rd ed., Florence, n.d., p. 220; see also Galletti, *L'eloquenza*, p. 491f.

[55] Thus in the "Invectiva in Antonium Luschum," *Prosatori latini*, p. 32, Salutati posits a continuity of Roman and Guelph republicanism through their political freedom and activity.

out of well-established civic order, as becoming contaminated when it traveled outside of the Greek polis. Bruni repeats this idea in a Preface to his translation of the *Ethics* of Aristotle;[56] he also makes the point of the coincidence of liberty and eloquence in republican Rome, and that, with the fall of the republic and the rise of the empire, liberty, eloquence, and, indeed, the glory of Rome declined.[57] The parallel of rhetorical and historical worth is complete; the eloquent age is the illustrious age, according to Juliano:

> Formerly the Athenians and Romans took the greatest pains to produce extremely eloquent men, for they not only fulfilled the needs of the state in their own time, but illumined the future memory of the greatest deeds.[58]

Thus the Humanists' rhetorical commitment leads directly to a renewed apprehension of the historicality of freedom; their public experience as rhetors reinforced their quest in history for the values of justice and freedom. For example, Professor Ullmann has already noted the peculiar redundancy of language habits; in the late medieval period, and particularly in the communes of northern Italy, the use of the terms *cives* and *civitas* furthers the process by which citizenship becomes the accepted social goal and political activity becomes of prime importance; "the gulf between the earlier and largely neutral meaning and the later meaningful import of the citizen was bridged by linguistic familiarity with the

[56] *Schriften,* p. 73.
[57] "Vita di Petrarca," in *Le vite di Dante,* pp. 289-90. Compare Poggio's letter to Scipio of Ferrara, *Opera,* Basel, 1538, ph. rep. as Vol. 1 of *Opera omnia,* ed. R. Fubini, Turin, 1964, p. 365: "Caesar . . . non enim magis patriae quam latinae linguae et bonarum artium extitit parricida. Una enim cum libertate corruit eloquentia. . . ."
[58] "Fuit olim Atheniensibus ac Romanis summa cura in sua republica viros eloquentissimos facere, qui non modo suorum temporum commodis satisfacerent, sed maximarum rerum suarum memoriam futuram illustrarent," Andrea Juliano, "Oratio super principio orationum M. Tullii Ciceronis," *Reden und Briefe,* p. 117. And thus Toscanelli, in his "Oratio pro legendi initio Bononiae," *Reden und Briefe,* p. 196: "eloquentia enim in omni pacata ac libera civitate semper principatum obtinuit semperque dominata est."

term citizen."[59] In short, the thread of historical significance the Humanists traced was in part a thread spun by their predecessors, the rhetors and notaries of the early Italian city-states.

Arendt defines public happiness as the taste of public freedom; the essential antinomy is not between sacred and profane but public and private commitment; the republic is cherished as providing an opportunity for the exploiting of human potential to the full.[60] Similarly, "individualism" is not at all characteristic of this Humanist cluster of historical insights; here the vital core of liberty is not found within the individual, but only within society; history is the history of communities, not individuals.[61] In Bruni there is not the Petrarchan or Romantic connection of privacy and freedom, of an inner freedom where one escapes from the world and feels "free," but the Classical connection of "publicity" and freedom.[62] At the same time publicity is a necessary characteristic of the historical in the sense of providing a continuity of the manifest, the phenomenal; history deals with the virtuosity which impinges on decisions of wide import. His rhetorical attitude thus also underscores the Renaissance and Sophistic antinomy of *virtù* and *fortuna*; in a hastily conceived action that succeeded, Bruni argues that fortune, not prudence of counsel was responsible; in discussing a notable setback in Florentine policy, Bruni observes that the failure was due not to fortune but to poor advice (*H.F.*, 271, 267). The antinomy is used diagnostically; publicity forces criticism. Nor is public freedom a matter only of institutions:

[59] W. Ullmann, *Individual and Society in the Middle Ages*, Baltimore, 1966, p. 121.

[60] *Between Past and Future*, pp. 146, 214.

[61] Baron, *Crisis*, p. 414f.; "La rinascita dell'etica statale," p. 10; Curcio, *La politica italiana*, p. 14; Varese, *Storia e politica*, p. 146; Adorno, "La crisi," p. 25. See G. de Lagarde, *La naissance de l'esprit laïque*, Vol. 1, p. 118f., Vol. 2, p. 311f. on the anti-individualist nature of the Trecento commune Bruni describes.

[62] For R. Stadelmann, Quattrocento Florence offered the last opportunity for the fulfillment of this Classical ideal in the history of the West, "Persönlichkeit und Staat in der Renaissance," *Die Welt als Geschichte*, 5 (1939), pp. 137-55.

freedom, which Bruni has Giano della Bella say one should regard equally with life—*"cupere autem pariter ac vitam omnes debemus"*—depends more on the healthy participation of the citizenry than on the power of the magistracy (*H.F.*, 82, 83).[63]

In other words, in rhetorical historiography active gratification as well as passive scholarship is the source of historical intuitions; Bruni's rhetorical role is a pressure for control and involvement as well as observation and detachment.[64] The Humanists emphasize the existential dimension of the traditional political concepts of liberty and common good; they are aware that the pursuit of the common good requires the establishment of a sphere of public life in which men are required to be *"in agendo dicendoque in primis efficaces"* (*H.F.*, 211). Every political doctrine sets a requirement in human activity; the rhetorical historian concentrates on measuring its force and success. Bruni with his rhetorical flexibility towards words can either fill a cliché with new experience, or he may take a classical concept and drain it of its contemporary reference—as on occasion he deprives *libertas* of its Guelph associations—in order to isolate a recurrent

[63] On the diagnostic usage of the antinomy *fortuna-ragione* by Florentine merchants contemporary with Bruni see C. Bec, "Mentalité et vocabulaire des marchands Florentins," *Annales, E.S.C.*, 22² (1967), pp. 1206-26; rhetorical and "practical" usages obviously are reinforcing, since the same concepts of time and space and human ability obtain in both spheres. Similarly, the *volgare* historian Giovanni Cavalcanti, also Bruni's contemporary, writes of the folly of the war with Lucca, "non accusando tanto la mobilità della fortuna, quanto la immobilità delle diverse persone, e de' perversi uomini della nostra Repubblica. Al tutto dico, che questa pertinacia e questa stabilità della condizione de' nostri cittadini è stata la cagione delle tante sventure della nostra Repubblica (e non fu per mancamento di ricchezze; ma per la scarsità della ragione, mischiatamente colla detta perversità de' cittadini: al tutto vergogna acquistammo, e riputazione scemammo, e la impresa perdemmo)." *Istorie fiorentine*, Florence, 1838, Vol. 1, p. 292.

[64] Thus Curcio, *La politica italiana*, p. 73: "Com'è caratteristica di tutti i periodi di cultura razionalista, estetizzante, illuminista, e difficile dire dove finisca la letteratura e cominci la politica e vice versa."

historical value (*H.F.*, 48). Rhetorical sophistication invites comparative judgments.[65]

History thus becomes the history of publicly-shared experience on the one hand; on the other, historiography itself has a function of providing the materials for discussion of public issues. The practice of rhetoric is the practice of liberty; rhetorical historiography speaks to the points raised in the political dialogue begun by the Ancients, interrupted by the decline of the Empire and the barbarians, and started afresh in the city-states of Italy. Politics, history, and rhetoric had simultaneously lapsed and revived because their interconnection is logical and strict.

In the second place, the Humanists assume that the model for the structure of history is the structure of discourse. Both consciously and unconsciously they resume the Aristotelian position that man is a political animal by virtue of his capacity for discourse (*Politics*, 1253a); for the Humanists rhetoric is essentially conflict or dialogue (Salutati, *E.*, II, 295), politics is the dialogue of expressions of power, and history is the articulation of this power dialogue. In this respect, they see no tension between the historian's engagement as rhetorician and his commitment to truth, since the forms of rhetorical argument—definition, equation, analogy, parallelism, antithesis—inform the political life they wish to describe; both rhetorician and politician must master the same structure and method.

If the classical political *topoi* are "reproposed" or rejuvenated as intellectual themes or values, causing a reorientation

---

[65] It is the independence of this rhetorical judgment which is relevant to historical consciousness; for example, Varese discusses the survival of a cultural consciousness of liberty in Quattrocento Florence even when the political possibilities had disappeared, "Aspetti e limiti quattrocenteschi della 'Florentina libertas'," *Storia e politica*, p. 146. On the persistence of this cultural consciousness, even in Medicean politics, see the speeches reported in N. Rubinstein, *The Government of Florence under the Medici* (1434 to 1494), Oxford, 1966, pp. 93f., 141f.

of the subject matter of history, the Humanist attitude towards language also rehabilitates the *topoi* in their classical
rhetorical function as heuristic devices, causing a change in
historical method.[66] Cicero had defined a *topos* or *locus* as
"the region of an argument, and an argument as a course of
reasoning which firmly establishes a matter about which there
is some doubt" (*Topica*, 2, 8). For the Humanist also the
ars inveniendi, the art of "finding" arguments, associated
with rhetoric, not only has priority over the *ars iudicandi*,
the art of judging an argument's validity, associated with
logic, but entails a whole set of priorities. The priority of
invention is part of his insistence on the union of philosophy
and eloquence; to concentrate on the *loci* exhibits a distaste
for an abstract language which only judges other language,
shows a preference for the living concrete language which is
a continuous dialogue on general human questions.[67] In
Ciceronian and Humanist rhetoric a search for order takes
the form of a quest for a common humanity.[68] The priority
of invention reveals the Humanist's acceptance, his assump-

[66] Curtius has written on the *topoi* as intellectual themes, *European
Literature*, p. 70f. This discussion of the importance of the *topoi* in
Humanist hermeneutic is based on Apel, *Die Idee*, p. 138f., which in
turn derives some of its insights from the work of J. Lohmann; Apel
makes an important distinction between the *loci communes* and "commonplaces"—a post-eighteenth-century English and German usage con-
noting the trite, or even trivial (p. 140). The more exciting developments in the topics occur in the sixteenth century; see Ong, *Ramus:
Method, and the Decay of Dialogue*, p. 104f., and W. Risse, *Die Logik
der Neuzeit*. It is the new *ars inveniendi* of the High Renaissance
based on a direct experience of nature which Apel finds as the real
bond between the Sophistic Age and the Renaissance (p. 186).

[67] Michel, "Éclectisme philosophique et lieux communs; À propos
de la diatribe romaine," in *Hommages à Jean Bayet*, ed. M. Renard and
R. Schilling, Brussels, 1964, p. 494; cf. M. Lavency, "La technique
des lieux communs de la rhétorique grecque, *Les Études classiques*,
33 (1965), pp. 113-126.

[68] "Les *loci communes*. . . . ne sont plus du tout des idées reçues,
mais, ce qui est bien différent, des idées générales: cette généralité
constitue une garantie de vérité et de fécondité en même temps; en
effet l'argumentation repose sur des inférences logiques qui sont cer-
tains et, d'autre part, elle se dégage des details, des circonstances,
comme on dit, elle domine la question." Michel, "Éclectisme philosophique," p. 488; cf. pp. 490, 494.

tion of the equality of his audience, as well as his pedagogic bent.

Here rhetoric is predominantly pragmatics; that is, concerned with the relation of language to those who use it; "it is in relation to an audience that all argumentation is developed."[69] This rhetoric creates as well as addresses an audience competent in rhetoric as *scientia civilis* (*De inventione*, I, 5, 6), in making political distinctions and comparisons. It serves as the reader's method as well as the historian's: the *locus* merely "finds" and arranges material which is used in the subsequent operation of another mind; the *topos* allows the author to pass from discourse to dialogue.[70]

The *topoi*, then, are not mere storage bins but active organizing principles, familiar and efficacious points of departure. Bruni's *History of Florence* is a tissue of simple arguments of cause and comparison, enumeration and division; the *topoi* which prevail construct a narrative which is a web of relationships. The *koinoi topoi* or *loci communes* as general lines of argument lead naturally into discussion of lines of political force, into the *topoi* as intellectual themes. Thus, for example, Bruni uses the topic *comparatio* (*Topica*, 18, 68) to enable the reader to rehearse the priority of Florentine political values (*H.F.*, 154, 180, 209); and the topic *divisio* (*Topica*, 5, 27-28) induces the reader to eliminate extraneous factors, to distinguish class attitudes behind a class event (*H.F.*, 169).

While the use of *topoi* ostentatiously hands to the reader the means to reconstruct history as the discourse of the past, the special use of the speeches and debates in Humanist historiography is to expose the structure of history as that of debate and tension; the speeches are descriptive essays, the antilogy—a set of two opposing speeches—is an analytic

---

[69] Ch. Perelman, *The Idea of Justice and the Problem of Argument*, trans. J. Petrie, London, 1963, p. 138.

[70] Thus Michel, "Éclectisme philosophique," p. 490: the *topoi* "permettront, par un retour aux notions communes, de dépasser l'esprit de système, et de chercher, au delà des dogmes et des sectes, ce qui fait l'unité de la nature humaine. . . ."

tool.[71] The orations, as Pontano said later, are the soul of history;[72] in Bruni's history they are not empty rhetorical flourishes, but most rich in historical insights. The pattern of speeches is the pattern of Florentine history; at each vital juncture in Bruni's narrative they intervene to make clear the central issue, the crucial alternatives. Bruni uses speeches in a much more sophisticated manner than the Trecento chroniclers; sophistication betrays motive. Bruni's articulateness is a conscious innovation; by means of the speeches he attempts to bring out the political discordance which he feels gave shape to Trecento politics.

The speeches in the *History of Florence* serve as its intellectual armature: they point out that there are two parallel trends in Florentine history; one away from the disruption of civic affairs by private faction towards the creation of an internal sphere of public discussion in which the issue is liberty or license, and a second towards the creation of an external sphere of diplomacy in which the issues are security and expansion, a system of independence or a system of regal authority. The antilogy between the Pope and a Florentine Guelph of 1273 delineates the domestic confrontation between faction and public interest; the great speech of Giano della Bella of 1292 announces the program of public liberty and its responsibilities for Florence. In external affairs the speech of Pino della Tosa of 1329 sets forth the public utility of the expansionist policy of Florence; the antilogy of the Perugians and the Florentines (1336) which establishes the priority of actions over professions of trust in foreign affairs reinforces the priority of public trust over political promises set forth in the Florentine debate (1323) on the domestic problem of recalling factional exiles. The speech of Francesco Gambacorta (1351) and the speech of the Aretines against the recall of their exiles of 1354 assert that good faith in in-

---

[71] I use the word "antilogy" in Mme. de Romilly's sense of "discours antithétiques"; the following discussion is based on her chap. 3, "Discours antithétiques," *Histoire et raison chez Thucydide*, p. 180f.

[72] Pontanus, "Actius," in *Dialoghi*, ed. C. Previtera, Florence, 1934, p. 234.

ternal affairs and public trust in external affairs are inter-
dependent.

In the first antilogy, that of 1273 between the Pope and
the Guelph faction in Florence, one of the major issues of
Duecento politics is joined—the conflict between the external
uses and internal abuses of the factions aligned along the
Papal-Imperial axis (*H.F.*, 61-63). This antilogy conveniently
summarizes motives of previous debates and speeches (*H.F.*,
33-34, 41-42, 46-47). Regardless of the source of the speeches,
whether chronicles, archives, or Bruni's imagination, there
is no doubt of the structural purpose of these antilogies—
they carry the main burden of the historical argument, they
are there to explain causally and analyze rationally the historical events; the speakers in their own words, Villani's, or
Bruni's are masks for Bruni, they explicate what he wishes
to clarify. For the cultivated men of the Renaissance the
dialogue as civil conversation or literary form became a
means of moral perfection;[73] in Humanist historiography
dialogue or debate is hermeneutic.

First, we notice in the antilogy a kind of objectivity which
could be characterized as "prismatic" historicism. The purpose of the antilogy is to present the different views of the
historical protagonists as alternatives to be judged by the
reader; Mme. de Romilly, in her brilliant discussion of the
antilogies of Thucydides, thus defines the purpose of these
historical tools:

> Le discours isolé degagé des idées: les discours anti-
> thétiques, en les opposant, les serrent de plus près; ce
> sont eux qui permittent le mieux d'épuiser tous les aspects
> d'une situation.[74]

The principle of the antilogy demands that both theses are
not only presented, but defended and understood; the antilogy makes deliberation possible.[75] The core of the antilogic

[73] Tateo, "La tradizione classica," *Tradizione e realtà*, p. 234.
[74] *Histoire et raison chez Thucydide*, p. 180.
[75] *Histoire et raison chez Thucydide*, p. 220; H. Arendt claims that
Thucydidean objectivity is the product of this dialogue, *Between Past
and Future*, pp. 51-52.

method is to consider the same events from different points of view; the best antilogy derives from the slightest difference in presenting the givens of a situation, the greatest difference in conclusions.[76] Thus in the antilogy between the Pope and the Florentine Guelphs Bruni has both sides start with the same fact, the vengeful attitude of the triumphant Guelphs to the Ghibellines which was disturbing the peace of Florence, and both try to relate this fact to the structure of political and ethical assumptions which they share. The Pope makes a strong case for the injustice of the behavior of the Guelphs, pointing out that for a mere name they deprive a person of his civic rights:

> He is a Ghibelline, but also he is a Christian, a citizen, a neighbor, a relative. Do all these many and important names have to give way to "Ghibelline"? And will that one empty name (for what it signifies no one knows) more powerfully incite hate than all those worthy and solid names incite charity?[77]

The Guelphs, on the other hand, claim that the Pope's idea of justice is celestial, not terrestrial; they reverse the Pope's contrast of the real and the illusory with their own opposition of the idealistic and the realistic:

> Do not, I beg you, call us to this overscrupulous norm of living, for earth is ruled one way, heaven another.[78]

For the Guelphs as well as the Pope a source of difficulty lies in the deceptions of language:

> For much, indeed, too much, serves to keep the memory of injuries alive, nor will anyone not stupid deliver himself to the enemies he has injured, since the motives of men

---

[76] *Histoire et raison chez Thucydide,* pp. 202, 215.

[77] "Gebellinus est: at christianus, at civis, at proximus, at consanguineus. Ergo haec tot et tam valida coniunctionis nomina gebellino succumbent? et id unum atque inane nomen (quod quid significet nemo intelligit) plus valebit ad odium, quam ista omnia tam praeclara ac tam solida et expressa ad charitatem?" H.F., 61.

[78] "Noli, quaeso, nos ad hanc scrupolosam vivendi norman vocare: aliter enim coelum, aliter terra regitur." H.F., 62.

are kept hidden, and their words and appearance often deceive. And then, this is not so much a regard for what you call our vain arrogance as for our safety: we do not aim so much at honor from taking them back as security from their exile.[79]

Both employ the same argument—the problematic relation of names, illusions, professions to reality—to bolster opposite points of view; the reader, however, may draw a third conclusion: that the relation of language to reality is problematic. Bruni, like Thucydides, has a "precise and subtle technique" utilizing parallelism and antithesis in diction and argument to bring out his aperçus into cause and character. Further, just as Thucydides, Bruni conveys the exasperating lack of finality to all historical debate, as compared to the arguments of the schools; he seldom permits one side to monopolize the truth. It is difficult, Bruni remarks of the stalemate which this debate presages, to tell which was worse, the stubbornness of the Pope or the contumacy of the Guelphs—"*Nec facile dixerim, maior obstinatio in pontifice, an contumacia fuerit in civibus*" (H.F., 64). The provisory nature of the points made in set speeches is, according to Tateo, a technique introduced by Bruni which he derived from Cicero's *De oratore*; it serves a dialectical function in that it enables the reader to gain a more comprehensive view.[80]

The justification of the antilogy is that it permits the analysis of the situation in its totality;[81] the choices are presented to the reader within the framework of circumstance; these are not decisions which were made in the privacy of the study, nor were they simple choices between abstract evil and abstract good. The choice is between programs and partisan arguments, between two different views of justice, or between

---

[79] "Plerique enim plus quam oportet infensionis memoriam servant: nec quisquam inimico et laeso non stulte credit, quoniam hominum voluntates obscurae sunt, verba et frons persaepe mentiuntur. Itaque, non tam huius inanis, ut tu modo vocitabas, fastus nobis est cura, quam salutis nostrae: nec tam gloriam affectamus illorum ex reductione, quam ex reiectione securitatem." H.F., 63.

[80] Tateo, "La tradizione classica," *Tradizione e realtà*, p. 248.

[81] de Romilly, *Histoire et raison chez Thucydide*, p. 187.

a partisan view of justice and an impassioned defense of equity; the struggle also can be not only between two concepts of right but between two exponents of wrong. Thus the Papal-Guelph debate is a function of Bruni's interest in depicting two trains of political motivation as contrasted with Villani's partisan condemnation of the Papal side in straight narrative form.

The Sophist or rhetorician prefers the "impure," the probable, the dynamic to the pure, the certain, the stable; he perceives ideals, notions of value as they are imbedded in the matrix of debate. On the one hand, then, the Humanists' rhetorical commitment affirms and underscores the specific political values whose development they trace; on the other hand, rhetorical structure makes clear the connections between goal and motive, value and the clash of interests. True, the rhetorical argumentative method works from a limited vocabulary and imposes a simplistic structure on events and intentions. But the monotonous argumentative tone is a clear historicist gain: the only confrontations are those of human wills, only the products of human strength and weakness are historical subjects—in Vico's phrase, only the *factum est verum*.[82] In contrast, the Trecento chronicles display the euphonious trait of escalation in causation; Villani does not present the strife between the Black and White factions simply as a struggle between diverse groups; he directly links these events to final causes, presents them as results of a divine judgment upon moral corruption, and only a plethora of realistic detail saves them from appearing as shadows manipulated by transcendental principles.

The taste for eloquence directs the historical understanding. Mme. de Romilly illumines the rhetorical-historiographical temper when she claims that the "relativist" Protagoras furnished the presuppositions and force of Thucydides, and

---

[82] See Varese, "Aspetti e limiti della 'florentina libertas'," *Storia e politica*, p. 145; and Michel, *Rhétorique et philosophie*, pp. 579-80. On Vico's epistemology see V. Rüfner, *Die Geschichtsphilosophie G. Vicos*, Bonn, 1946; Rüfner tends to emphasize the *Logosmystik*, rather than the rhetorical, tradition as the source of this insight.

that the antilogic method of his history is more closely related to rhetoric than to dialectic in its dependence on what Plato termed the heart of rhetoric, a verbal facility which can make the strong argument seem weak or the weak strong.[83] The amoral techniques of rhetoric are used to express the amoral force of circumstance on principle; the rhetorical historian does not aim at superhuman objectivity, but at enlightenment and compassion. The Humanist's attraction to debate *in utramque partem* is a positive sign of a generosity and tolerance which rejects the arid disputations of the Scholastics as tautological.[84]

For Humanist rhetoric revives both facets of rhetoric distinguished by Rostagni: the epideictic "irrational" strand of Gorgias as well as the judicial or deliberative "rational" strand associated with Aristotle.[85] The original Gorgian figures, such as antithesis, derived, according to Rostagni, from the Pythagorean doctrine that only a recognition of multiplicity contributes to a sense of unity, that disharmony evokes harmony.[86] The figure of irony, for example, defines by contrast, by juxtaposition of illusion and reality, intention and event; the repetitious use of irony in rhetorical history evokes an emotional response as well as rational conviction. Like Sallust, Bruni contrasts the illusions set forth in a speech with the hard realities of the narrative; thus Bruni allows the reader to compare the professions and the actions of the Papacy in the unhappy period preceding the war with Florence (*H.F.*, 214f.).[87] Once again, the *dual* nature of rhetorical influence is obvious: irony is both structure and value; it is a

---

[83] *Sophist* 267A; see de Romilly, *Histoire et raison chez Thucydide*, pp. 181, 216.

[84] Tateo, "La tradizione classica," *Tradizione e realtà*, pp. 235-36: Humanist dialogue "non procede secondo il metodo dialettico di confutazione e ritorsione degli argomenti dell'avversario, che era divenuto per colpa degli scolastici il metodo odioso d'una arida cultura, ma segue il filo logico d'una eloquente e persuasiva chiarificazione, in cui gli animi eletti, discutendo, si ritrovano."

[85] Rostagni, "Un nuovo capitolo," pp. 57-58.

[86] Rostagni, "Un nuovo capitolo," pp. 16-17.

[87] Syme, *Sallust*, p. 198; *Tacitus*, Vol. 1, p. 192; cf. Thucydides, III, 83.3.

form of historical activity, a historiographical paradigm, and it describes a certain complexity which inheres in the data, the content of history.

Irony, however, depicts complexity in a manner which invites compassion; if the archetypal reaction to history is the tears of remembrance of Ulysses,[88] irony is an archetypal historical technique. The most prevalent ironic situation is unanticipated by the protagonists but expected by the reader. The reader knows, for example, the peace treaty of Florence, Milan, and Venice of 1435 to be beset by difficulties; he anticipates that "these things most solemnly concluded and full of the highest hopes will have but the briefest duration" (*Commentarius*, 453). Bruni self-consciously uses irony as he uses the antilogy—to make demands upon the reader, to invite him to participate in discovery. Humanist irony does not simply point to the continuous victories of cosmic fate over the human will, but attempts to involve the reader in the imaginative re-creation of difficult choice. At times both fortune and interest conspire against program, leaving the reader to speculate on the inadequacy of political foresight:

> For such is the instability of attitude and fortune, that he [Sigismund] went away most hostile to Filippo of Milan, by whose favor and subsidy he had come to Italy, and left most friendly to the Venetians, to whom he was an enemy when he arrived.[89]

Irony is also an example of the *reciprocity*, the mutual reinforcement of rhetorical and historical modes: historical ironies abound in societies committed to open rational debate and rhetorically expressed program; rhetorical ironies discover historical tensions.[90]

[88] Arendt, *Between Past and Future*, p. 45.

[89] "Et quidem tanta varietate vel animi vel fortunae, ut inimicissimus Philippo Mediolanensi abierit, cuius favore atque opibus intrasset, Venetorum autem, quibus maxime inimicus venerat, amicissimus recederet." *Rerum suo tempore gestarum commentarius, RIS*, Vol. 19³, ed. C. di Pierro, p. 451; cited here as *Commentarius*.

[90] See G. Wise's unpublished paper, "Making 'Irony' Operational; Niebuhr's *Irony of American History* Revisited."

Where antilogy and irony induce the reader to compare two attitudes or two protagonists, the isolated speeches use the epideictic as well as the deliberative vein to characterize individual moments of historical force. Here we must invoke the principle of overdetermination to understand how the aesthetic and political aspects of rhetoric interlock to reinforce Bruni's historical insights. The function of the speech does not vary from Herodotus to Machiavelli; the elaboration of character it provides contributes to the analysis of cause which is its aim. The extreme example of rhetorical overdetermination is Machiavelli's *History of Florence*; it is within the speeches that Machiavelli makes the most pungent observations on human nature and politics, and he does so very often by means of strict parallelism, most formally in a series of parallel members where the absurdity of successive propositions builds a proof of the sanity of the converse propositions. Machiavelli's wisdom is "Humanistic" rather than "scientific" in so far as it is not only rhetorically expressed but also geared to rhetorical concerns of persuasion and choice.[91] Epideictic techniques of praise and blame underline the crisp juxtapositions of antinomies—of necessity and will, *virtù* and *fortuna*—which are diagnostic forms employed to eliminate and select.[92] Bruni, Machiavelli, and Thucydides try to separate out from the web of history the "*données comparables*," equivalent factors to be weighed and assigned units of force.

Bruni most frequently uses speeches to present recurring types of civic virtue. Thus the speech of Giano della Bella is

[91] See Varese, *Storia e politica*, p. 148; also J. Condé, "La sagesse machiavellique; politique et rhétorique," in *Umanesimo e scienza politica*, pp. 89-90, and Gilbert, *Machiavelli and Guicciardini*, p. 203f.

[92] Thus for Bruni antithesis is the shortest way to pungency in his letter to the Duke of Milan, *Sig. Miss. I Canc.*, *Reg.* 35, f. 171: "Tenemus enim, . . . excellentissime domine, nonnullas huc usque turbationes et bella, ex suspicione potius ac formidine alterutrius potentie, quam ex libero proposito ac voluntate spontanea processisse. Quis enim non se armet, cum timeat? Aut quis expectare velit, ut is quem formidat, primam sibi plagam infligere possit? Atque ita fit, ut metu belli persaepe ruatur in bellum. . . ." Compare *Reg.* 32, f. 179r; *H.F.*, 114, 202, 211, 253, 278; *Commentarius*, 446, 451.

Bruni's explanation of the direction of Florentine political development; in it Giano della Bella unfolds his own personality as the type of good citizen concerned with repressing internal faction (*H.F.*, 81f.); the speech of Gambacorta presents him as the very type of public honor abroad. Gambacorta exemplifies what he describes: the free spirit, untrammelled by hate and motivated solely by a desire for the honor and utility of the state (*H.F.*, 180).[93] That the speech in Bruni's historiography is the vehicle of neither particulars nor universals but types is a reflection of Bruni's rhetorical realism. If the speeches are self-consciously constructed, not simply reported, and thus are dissociated from radical particularism, they also are remote from the commitment to universals implicit in personification. They eschew the allegorical principle of movement from more real human passions and virtues to less real abstract personages which had marked medieval taste and colored medieval historiography.

Like irony, the type is a "middle-range" concept;[94] taken in Georg Lukács' sense as an organic synthesis of general and particular, it is a literary solution to the philosophic problem posed by Plato of finding mediate terms between particular cases and the most general laws (*Philebus*, 17A).[95]

[93] "Numquam enim recte consulit qui odio consulit. Honor sane atque utilitas libero animo in consultantibus quaeri debent." *H.F.*, 180. To some extent, this use of types is an anticipation of a late Humanist development described by F. Gilbert: what in the medieval and early Humanist treatises on the prince was merely a catalog of virtues, in Pontano and his successors becomes a unified psychological sketch; see "The Humanist Concept of the Prince and *The Prince* of Machiavelli," *JMH*, 11 (1939), pp. 462-63.

[94] Wise, "Making 'Irony' Operational."

[95] Georg Lukács, *Studies in European Realism*, New York, 1964, p. 6: "The central category and criterion of realist literature is the type, a peculiar synthesis which organically binds together the general and the particular both in characters and situations. What makes a type a type is not its average quality, not its mere individual being, however profoundly conceived; what makes it a type is that in it all the humanly and socially essential determinants are present on their highest level of development. . . ." Panofsky describes the aesthetic implications of the *typenprägende Kraft* of classical and Italian Renais-

The concept of the type is also closely related to that of the rhetorical *topos* as a useful collection device for ordering a number of experiences through space and time.[96] And the type as a dimension of personal experience works against radical ethical solipsism, for a sense of historical continuity in choice: in Bruni's history as well as in art "in every case the notion of freedom signified the flowering of the personality into a typical example of a specific ideal of man, rather than the fulfillment of the individual soul in its uniqueness."[97]

Rhetorical argument calls upon the general to illuminate and order its specific purpose. The speech of Pino della Tosa of 1329 which urges Florence to take advantage of the opportunity to purchase Lucca from the Emperor establishes the unique significance of the proposal by recourse to the resonant general terms of Roman imperial policy, of *cura reipublicae et pietas in patriam* (H.F., 140).

> The Roman people, our forbears, never would have obtained world empire, if they had been content with the *status quo* and shunned new undertakings and responsibilities. A plan is completely different in its public and private aspects. For in public affairs magnificence is proper,

---

sance art as the investment of "all possible subjects with forms both universally valid and saturated with reality"; typification both takes in the multitude of phenomena and "was its insurmountable barrier. Typification necessarily implies moderation," "Albrecht Dürer and Classical Antiquity," *Meaning in the Visual Arts*, New York, 1957, pp. 267-68.

[96] Perelman and Olbrechts-Tyteca, *La nouvelle rhétorique*, Vol. 1, p. 112f.; and A. Michel, "Éclectisme philosophique," p. 488: "Les traités de rhétorique de Cicéron présentent en effet une conception très originale des *loci communes*: l'on peut dire, brèvement, que ces schémas d'argumentation permettent de rattacher les problèmes particuliers que posent les différentes causes à des questions générales que les rhéteurs nomment 'theses'. . . ."

[97] R. Klibansky, Panofsky, and F. Saxl, *Saturn and Melancholy: Studies in the History of Natural Philosophy, Religion, and Art*, London, 1964, pp. 242-43; see also Burckhardt, *Civilization of the Renaissance*, p. 200.

which consists in riches and glory; for private life, modesty and frugality are more appropriate.[98]

Bruni uses the classical *topoi* to establish the coordinates of the positions of the protagonists in the stream of historical events: the cautious and the frugal are the political innovators—

Those who dissuade us from undertaking these things, who condemn them and judge them as nothing, would revolutionize our way of life.[99]

In the context, then, Bruni's use of the classical political vocabulary underlines the difficulty, not the inevitability, of maintaining the classical posture of honor and utility in the face of specific contemporary situations. Bruni may also use the general descriptions of the speech to prepare the reader for a crucial event; for example, the speech of Giano della Bella analyzes and anticipates the later head-on collision between the magnates and Giano which resulted in his exile.

But if an individual speech isolates the "givens" of a particular event, the antilogies predicate history as movement, they lend a dynamic tension to the continuum of events. Free debate becomes the dominant metaphor for the representation of historical action; the rhetorical historian depicts the passage of time as confrontation, tension, successive choice, pressure and counter-pressure, conflict and resolution of program. Bruni seems to establish the rhythm of history by means of the rhythm of argument: thus the alternation between the periodic and the pointed style projects an alternation between the elaboration of political forces and their interruption by the unique, by the grasped opportunity and the failure of *virtù*. After the brilliant speech of Pino della

[98] "Populus romanus parens noster nunquam orbis imperium nactus esset, si suis rebus contentus nova coepta impensasque refugisset. Nec sane idem propositum est homini publice et privatim. Nam publice quidem magnificentia proposita est, quae in gloria amplitudineque consistit; privatim vero modestia et frugalitas." *H.F.*, 140.

[99] "Haec si illi qui suscipiendam nobis dissuadent contemnunt ac pro nihilo censent, novas porro vivendi normas in vitam adducunt." *H.F.*, 140.

Tosa, for example, the ominous decision of the Florentines to reject his advice occupies two brief, ironic sentences (*H.F.*, 141).

The rhetorical model is neither static nor progressive. It is difficult to extract from Bruni's history the classical cyclical metaphor which emphasizes the essentially unchanging nature of man and society. Rather, the debates allow the protagonists to find and express significant difference and irregular change. Nor does the rhetorical model permit a simplistic, providential view of Florentine history, where Florence as the chosen vessel of the Lord, moves in steady unilinear progress toward a transcendent goal.

The two great confrontations of the later Trecento, and the two highly-structured antilogies which enunciate the issues at stake in Italy, are those between the Papacy and the Florentines in 1376 (*H.F.*, 211f.) and between the Florentines and the Milanese in 1401 (*H.F.*, 284f.). In the antilogy between the Pope and the Florentine orators Bruni concentrates the gist of the previous antilogies with the Perugians and the exiles—that the reasons of equity can confront an ideology of justice, that the combination of justice and necessity can be faced by one of justice and equity.[100] The Pope accuses the verbal machinations of the Florentines which disguise the fact of rebellion against ordained authority; the Florentines point to their long history of Guelph partisanship so unjustly repaid by the ruthlessness of the Papal Legate's policy. If the rhetorical construction of the speeches does not allow personification, the devices of antilogy do not permit a psychomachy of idealized forces which takes place on a transcendental plane: over against the Pope's claim to supernatural obligations the Florentines depict the hardships inflicted by the Legate, not on slaves and barbarians, but on the faithful and the free. The values of history are immanent values; the notions of authority are not permitted to escape the description of their applications.

The concern for equity in this antilogy is a manifestation of the crepuscular tone common to both the historical and

[100] See *H.F.*, 119-21; 153-55.

rhetorical cast of mind; recall that Thucydides' Melian dialogue also had expressed that justice is a problem, not a solution, a significance, not a substance.[101] Further, just as Thucydides' debate established the arrogance of the Athenians toward the Melians, so Bruni depicts his debate as a conversation of the deaf. And where Bruni stresses conflict, not resolution, note the resonance of his method: here, just as in Protagoras and Thucydides, debate is heightened to an ontological presupposition; humanity is neither a matrix of constants nor an instrument of Providence, but the locus of conflicts of principle. Protagoras sought not a universal truth, but the "stronger side" of a particular struggle; a process of weighing and "measuring" ends in "mastery of experience"— which is the epistemological content of Protagoras' epithet "man the measure" (*metron anthropos*).[102] By repeating and "weighting" the claims and illusions of the Pope and the Florentines Bruni "masters" the event; the aim of the antilogy is to extend the possibility of mastery, and the simplicity of Bruni's restatements relates to his readers' effort of comparison. The critical impulse of rhetorical historiography is relativization rather than secularization. The end of history is not only compassion for the conflicting participants, but mastery of their rationalizations.

In the final confrontation, that between Milan and Florence, a series of speeches and antilogies afford Bruni an opportunity to summarize his views on the direction and force of historical change in the Trecento. The conflict between Florence as the proponent of Italian liberty and Milan as representing an attempt to impose a regal system on Italy is a conflict between the two types of government developed in the previous centuries of history and the previous chapters of Bruni's history, between the consolidation of political freedom and the public sphere and the domination of Italy by a single "private" interest. Thus the famous speech of

---

[101] Thucydides' Melian dialogue (V, 85-113) is discussed in relation to Sophistic political realism by Untersteiner, *The Sophists*, p. 321f.

[102] On *metron* as "mastery" see Ramnoux, "Nouvelle réhabilitation des Sophistes," pp. 4, 9.

1387 of Ricci warning Florence against Gian Galeazzo Visconti associates tyranny with privacy, with the lack of constraint provided by open public discussion. Florence should fear Milan because Gian Galeazzo "keeps his own counsel"; in the manner of a tyrant who has completely confused the interest of the state with his private interest, he is able to say one thing, mean another (*H.F.*, 242-43). Yet Bruni also recognizes that duplicity is the peculiar advantage as well as vice of tyranny, and the speech of Rinaldo Gianfigliazzi of 1399 elaborates on the difficulties as well as the strengths of the Florentine form of government; the lack of necessity to consult in a tyranny is efficiency, where "*tarditatem vitium est populorum.*"[103] Gianfigliazzi harangues the evils of divisiveness and jealousy, the necessity for speed and silence in negotiations with a tyrant. Too much licence in speech endangers the health and safety of the republic itself: "nor did anything contribute more to the power of Milan in Tuscany than our own dilatoriness and sloth" (*H.F.*, 277; cf. *H.F.*, 83).

In the final debate between Florence and Milan at Venice (1401), when both parties are striving for the crucial alliance of Venice, Bruni uses the Florentines to present his most fundamental axiom: the identity of goal and method, structure and purpose. The strength of their argument lies in their persuasion that the congruence between publicity and peace and freedom, and privacy or secrecy and violence is strict and necessary. Although Bruni allows the Milanese to make a good case for seeing the commercial activity of Florence as the cause of Italian troubles and the expansionist policy of the Florentines as motivated solely by "*inquietudinem animi et superfluitatem pecuniarum,*" the Florentines point out that what is good for Florence in this case is good for Italy, that the party of freedom contains the possibilities of justice (*H.F.*, 284-86).[104]

Bruni, then, prefers a technical rather than a substantive treatment of political values; for him the events of history

[103] *Sig. Miss. I Canc., Reg.* 32, f. 79r.
[104] See also Panciatichiano 148, f. 148, 210-11v; and the "Difesa . . . contro i riprensori del popolo di Firenze," *passim.*

predicate the coalescence of the values and methods of rhetoric. There can be debate on the ideas of justice, but there must be debate. Here he seems to have anticipated R. G. Collingwood's definition of "classical" politics: "Being civilized means living . . . dialectically, . . . in constant endeavor to convert every occasion of non-agreement into an occasion of agreement."[105] The creative act of virtuosity must be sought within the area of public discussion where the classical forms of dialogue obtain; to the extent that Gian Galeazzo functioned eristically, he threatened the Italian polity. Again note the circularity of assumptions about language; a commitment to political action has become a commitment to discourse; political rhetoric in turn "socializes"; it demands a posture of *disponibilità*, of openness to the possibilities of action.[106]

Thus the strong similarity of the arguments in Bruni's *History* and in his state correspondence reflects the fact that rhetorical and public exigencies impinge on both; to use Gramsci's terms, in the fusion of traditional and organic intellectual roles the Humanists use their rhetorical discipline to reinforce choices already made, to see old choices in a new light, to find new choices hitherto unappreciated in political experience. Like Thucydides, Bruni contemplates the springs of action from the vantage of categories he had tested as a participant. Moreover, there is an increase in the range of choice: minor choices achieve relevance; there is a whole intermediate field of public value ignored by the earlier theologically dominated culture; the Humanists' rhetorical taste for activity in the grey area of public responsibility rescues the individual from the countless false dilemmas imposed by too abstract categories of black and white, good and evil.

[105] *New Leviathan*, 39.15, Oxford, 1958, p. 327.
[106] K. Burke, *Permanence and Change*, Indianapolis, 1965, p. 262f.; and Merleau-Ponty, *Les aventures de la dialectique*, p. 30: "L'histoire ne s'offre en spectacle qu'à ceux qui ont déjà décidé de s'intéresser à toutes les solutions, qui s'établissent en face d'elles dans un état de disponibilité, elle fait donc contraste avec les passions étroites et profondes qu'elle contemple."

The field of rhetoric is the sphere of authentic alternative possibilities (Aristotle, *Rhet.*, 1357a); the historian's task is to place alternatives before the reader. The function of the historian is not merely to describe but to *initiate* dialogue. Bruni uses his rhetorical discipline to define and shape the political choices in history; he assumes the *riproponibilità*, the historicity of political debate; he acknowledges the public role of the historian, his responsibility to communicate public values by presenting the materials for a debate that is by definition a historical continuum. Where Salutati had recognized the debt of rhetoric to history—for what is rhetoric, he asks, *nisi quedam rerum gestarum aut gerendarum conflictatio atque pugna?* (*E.*, II, 295)—, Bruni tried to show the place of rhetoric at the core of history, and to illuminate history by exposing its rhetorical form.

FOUR

Rhetoric, Ethics, and History—
POGGIO BRACCIOLINI

1. Rhetorical Isolation and Ethical Identity

THE basic assumption of this study is that the new awareness of language of the Italian Humanists necessarily involves
a new awareness of history: that any investigation of the
workings of language is an investigation of meaning, the
central problem of historical study. In Poggio Bracciolini one
more strand of the rhetorical tradition is dominant, a strand
discovered by the triangulation of Poggio's rhetorical, ethical,
and historical interests; here the locus of rhetorical influence
is the identity of the rhetor-historian.[1] There are two factors

---

[1] On Humanist ethics see Seidlmayer, "Petrarca, das Urbild des
Humanisten"; R. Stadelmann, "Persönlichkeit und Staat"; F. Adorno,
"La crisi dell'Umanesimo civile fiorentino"; and K. Heitmann, *Fortuna und Virtus*, Cologne, 1957. Both Messer, in "Quintilian als
Didaktiker und sein Einfluss auf die didaktisch-pädagogische Theorie
des Humanismus," and Burk, in *Die Pädagogik des Isokrates als Grundlegung des humanistischen Bildungsideals*, discuss rhetorical training as
a vehicle of ethical theory.

On Poggio Bracciolini specifically, see Wm. Shepherd, *The Life of
Poggio Bracciolini*, Liverpool, 1837; E. Walser, *Poggius Florentinus:
Leben und Werke*, in *Beiträge zur Kulturgeschichte des Mittelalters
und der Renaissance*, Vol. 14, Leipzig, 1914; C.S. Gutkind, "Poggio
Bracciolini's geistige Entwicklung," *DVLG*, 10 (1932), pp. 548-96;
R. Roedel, "Poggio Bracciolini nel quintocentenario della morte,"
Rinascimento, 11 (1960), pp. 51-67; C. Nisard, *Les gladiateurs de la
République des Lettres au XVe, XVIe, et XVIIe siècles*, Vol. 1, Paris,
1860; F. Tateo, "Il dialogo 'realistico' di Poggio Bracciolini," *Tradi-
zione e realtà*, pp. 251-77.

Poggio's works have recently been collected, edited, and reproduced
under the guidance of R. Fubini, in the *Opera omnia*, Turin, 1964:
the *Opera*, Basel, 1538 will be henceforth cited as *Opera*, I, with page
number; the *Epistolae*, ed. T. Tonelli, Florence, 1832f., ph. rep. as

in the rhetorical tradition which make major contributions
to the structure of Humanist identity: the rhetorical doctrine
of *imitatio*, with its many pronouncements on the relation of
the author's "self" to the continuing stream of past literary
expression, of "otherness"; and rhetorical detachment, the
sense of distance, the subjunctive mental mode which has its
source in the fact that rhetoric focuses on language and expression, rather than on a specific subject matter.

The first self-conscious attempt to regain the power, as
well as the content, of the classical rhetorical theories of
imitatio, and probably the most inclusive expression of Humanist theory of imitation is that of Petrarch.[2] Petrarch
anticipates Salutati's rejection of cookbook rhetoric, the
pedestrian, almost slavish reproduction of handbook formu-
lae which he attributed to his contemporaries without Humanist orientation, to the "Scholastics." The notion of
imitation developed at length in Petrarch's correspondence
is similar to, and in part derived from, the much freer concept

---

Vol. 3, will henceforth be cited as *Epistolae*, with Tonelli's volume
and page number; the *Opera miscellanea edita et inedita*, Vol. 2 of
the *Opera*, will henceforth be cited as *Opera*, II, with Fubini's page
numbers. See also the *inedita* in Walser, *Leben und Werke*, pp. 325-460;
the edition of the letter to Bruni on Jerome of Prague, along with
letters to Niccoli and Guarino Veronese (Tonelli, I, i, ii, and v), and
the *De avaricia* in *Prosatori latini*, pp. 218-301; and the letters and
other documents in A. Willmanns, "Über die Briefsammlungen des
Poggio Bracciolini," *Centralblatt für Bibliothekswesen*, 30 (1913),
pp. 289-463. I have used the Muratori *Historia Florentini populi*,
RIS, Vol. 20; henceforth cited as *H.F.* with column numbers.

[2] The most important study on the idea of imitation on the Renais-
sance is H. Gmelin, *Das Prinzip der Imitatio*; but see also F. Ulivi,
L'imitazione nella poetica del Rinascimento, Milan, 1959; P. de Nolhac,
Pétrarque et l'humanisme, Vol. 2; Messer, "Quintilian als Didaktiker";
Vossler, *Poetische Theorien*; Borinski, *Die Antike in Poetik*, Vol. 1;
Spongano, "La prosa letteraria del Quattrocento," in *Due saggi*; E.
Battisti's "Il concetto d'imitazione nel Cinquecento italiano," *Rinascimento e Barocco*, Turin, 1960, pp. 175-215, deals with artistic imitation but is still useful. Representative Humanist discussions of imitation
are *Le epistole "De imitatione" di Giovan Francesco Pico della Miran-
dola e di Pietro Bembo*, ed. G. Santangelo, Florence, 1954; and the
work "De imitatione" attributed to Gasparino Barzizza in the British
Museum Harleian 5238, f. 108v-112v; there is also a partial version
in Riccardiana 779, f. 182r-184r.

of imitation of Quintilian (*I.O.*, X, 1-2) and Seneca (*Letter to Lucilius*, 12).[3] Thus on the margins of his partial manuscript of Quintilian Petrarch annotated the section on imitation heavily: he copies over the dictum *"nihil crescit sola imitatione"* (*I.O.*, X, 2, 9); opposite "But imitation (for I must repeat this point again and again) should not be confined merely to words" (*I.O.*, X, 2, 27) he notes "Read, Silvanus [Petrarch], and remember"; and adjacent to "we must realize . . . that imitation alone is not sufficient, if only for the reason that a sluggish nature is only too ready to rest content with the inventions of others" (*I.O.*, X, 2, 4), Petrarch writes "This applies to the Scholastic discipline."[4]

In Quintilian the crossing of two generative maxims of the rhetorical tradition, the principles of decorum and of imitation, produce a concept of the author who must construct his own literary personality:

> The next step is for each student to consult his own powers when he shoulders his burden. For there are some things which, though capable of imitation, may be beyond the capacity of any given individual, either because his natural gifts are insufficient or of a different character.[5]

This dictum finds its Humanist analogue in the famous rejoinder of Politian to Cortesi:

> You do not write, says one, like Cicero. What then? For I am not Cicero, therefore it seems to me that I should express myself.[6]

[3] See the following letters in *Le familiari*: I, 7, 8; XX, 2; XXI, 15; XXIII, 19.

[4] Both Messer, "Q. als Didaktiker," p. 274, and de Nolhac, *Pétrarque et l'humanisme*, Vol. 2, p. 89f., refer to this manuscript, Codex Parisinus 7720.

[5] "Tum in suscipiendo onere consulat suas vires. Nam quaedam sunt imitabilia, quibus aut infirmitas naturae non sufficiat aut diversitas repugnet." *I.O.*, 2, 19.

[6] "Non exprimis, inquit aliquis, Ciceronem. Quid tum? Non enim sum Cicero; me tamen, ut opinor, exprimo." This is quoted in Ulivi, *L'imitazione*, p. 17; see *Prosatori latini*, pp. 902-910 for the full text of Politian's and Cortesi's letters. Compare Salutati, *Epistolario*, IV, 148: "sed aliud est referre, aliud imitari." Sabbadini discusses the

Petrarch uses a succession of metaphors, some of them derived from Seneca, to express the same insight. For example, the writer must take care to strive not for identity, but for similitude:

> For the likeness should not be as that of a portrait to its subject, where the closer the resemblance the greater the praise given the artist, but as a son to his father, where often there is a great difference in build, but a certain semblance or what our painters call "air," most easily discerned in the face and eyes, creates that kind of likeness that the sight of the son at once brings to mind the father.[7]

But Petrarch also emphasizes that freedom consists not only in being true to one's own identity, but in the wide range of choices available to the literary personality, that we must consider *"quicquid ab ullo bene dictum est non alienum esse sed nostrum"* (*Fam.*, I, 8, 4).[8] Here also Petrarch borrows Seneca's image as he enjoins that

> . . . we write as bees make honey, not conserving the individual flowers, but converting them at the honeycomb, so that from many and various things one thing is produced, and that different and better.[9]

---

relation of imitation and decorum in his *Storia del Ciceronianismo e di altre questioni letterarie nell'età della Rinascenza*, Turin, 1885, p. 8.

[7] "non qualis est imaginis ad eum cuius imago est, que quo similior eo magis laus artificis, sed qualis filii ad patrem. In quibus cum magna sepe diversitas sit membrorum, umbra quedam et quem pictores nostri aerem vocant, qui in vultu inque oculis maxime cernitur, similitudinem illam facit, que statum viso filio, patris in memoriam nos reducat. . . ." *Fam.*, XXIII, 19, 11-12.

[8] Seneca, *Ad Lucil.*, 16, 7. Compare Barzizza, "De imitatione," Ricc. 779, f. 182v on the use of decorum to enhance freedom.

[9] "ut scribamus scilicet sicut apes mellificant, non servatis floribus sed in favos versis, ut ex multis et variis unum fiat, idque aliud et melius." *Fam.*, XXIII, 19, 13. See "De imitatione," Ricc. 779, f. 183v f. for an almost scholastic discussion of imitation as change; a discussion which employs many of Petrarch's images. Paolo Cortesi, *De hominibus doctis dialogus*, Florence, 1734, pp. 122-23, claims that the very copiousness which makes Cicero so desirable as a model also makes him almost inimitable; compare Bembo, "Ad Joanni Francesco Pico," in *Le epistole "De imitatione,"* p. 57; Poggio, *Invectiva in Vallam I, Opera*, I, 189.

This last statement contains two major points: it imparts a sense of the pluralism of choices from the past; and it expresses the importance of "surpassing," that, as Nietzsche will say later, creating something different and better is the justification of imitation.[10]

But if there is a continuity between Petrarchan and classical ideas of imitation, there is also a connection between Petrarch and Poggio in their sense of free literary identity. Most scholarly discussions of imitation in Poggio are devoted to his practice rather than his theory; when F. Ulivi discusses Poggio's style he equates the freedom of Poggio's imitation with "realism."[11] For Sabbadini, Poggio's self-consciousness, his awareness of his own identity, is such that it raises a dead language from the grave; Poggio may acknowledge his great indebtedness to Cicero,

> Ma in realtà poi se imito Cicerone, non lo imito ne nelle parole, ne nella frase, ne nella costruzione, ma nel colorito, nella vivacità dello scrivere, nella genialità dello stile; perche lo stile di Poggio è tutto suo proprio, ne egli poteva imitarlo da altri, ne altri potevano imitarlo da lui. È stile originale. . . .[12]

Poggio himself applies the notion of freedom not only to stylistic imitation but to translation as well; in the preface to his translation of Xenophon's *Cyropaedia* he points out that

[10] Nietzsche's fragment #35 in W. Arrowsmith, "Nietzsche on Classics and Classicists," *Arion*, 2² (1963), p. 23. See also Palmieri's citation of Zeuxis' procedure of combining the traits of many ladies to produce one beautiful figure as a model for Humanistic political eclecticism, in *Della vita civile*, pp. 77-78, referred to in F. Gilbert, *Machiavelli and Guicciardini*, pp. 93-94. See also Gmelin, *Das Prinzip*, p. 121: "So finden wir bei Quintilian schon die Grundgedanken von Petrarcas Imitationstheorie beisammen: die Unzulänglichkeit der blossen Nachahmung, ihren Mangel an lebendiger Fülle, den Rat eklektischer Nachahmung, die Warnung vor wörtlicher Nachahmung und die Ermutigung zu neuer 'Inventio'." Compare Ricc. 779, f. 182r.

[11] *L'imitazione*, p. 10.

[12] *Storia del Ciceronianismo*, p. 19; Poggio refers to Cicero as his archetype in, among other places, *Epistolae*, II, 86-87, 278; III, 176-77. See also Weise, *L'ideale eroico del Rinascimento*, Vol. 1, p. 29, for an assessment of Poggio's style as vital, realistic, and personal; also Walser, *Leben und Werke*, p. 272.

I have not, however, expressed every single word, every little comment, every chatty aside, which indeed frequently appear, . . . but I have followed the history, and have sometimes omitted that which does not detract from the truth or which is difficult to express decently in Latin.[13]

Moreover, in a late fifteenth-century appraisal Paolo Cortesi claims that Poggio's imitation of Cicero is commendable because he does it with his whole soul (*toto animo*), i.e., not slavishly, but with a strong sense of his own personality. The result, according to Cortesi, is that the outstanding trait of Poggio's style is not correctness but ingenuity, "*facundia et mirifica facilitas ingenii.*"[14] If, then, the end of oratorical training for Isocrates was the harmonious patterning of the self-determined personality, for the Humanists "*imitare,*" according to Vasoli, was the same as "*ad evocare nostra natura.*"[15] Originality becomes a matter of intention, of integrity, not of novelty, while successful imitation rests upon active choice, not a passive state of proximity: Theophrastus, Poggio observes, was more like Aristotle than Aristotle's son Nicomachus.[16]

Thus there are two facets to Poggio's view of the essential core of the personality which are derived, in part at least, from his notions of literary identity: the unity or totality of the personality, and its critical, rational nature. One of the main themes which runs through all of Poggio's writings was

[13] "Non autem verba singula, non sententiolas omnes, non collocutiones, quae quidem frequentius inferuntur, expressi, . . . sed historiam sum sequutus, ea quandoque omittens, quae neque veritati rerum detraherent, et concinne dici latine vix posse viderentur." Bandini, *Catalogus Codicum Latinorum Bibliothecae Laurentianae*, Florence, 1775, Vol. 2, c. 352.

[14] *De hominibus doctis dialogus*, p. 22.

[15] "L'estetica," p. 347; see Burk, *Die Pädagogik*, p. 217, for a description of Isocratean ideals; also Argan, "The Architecture of Brunelleschi," p. 99; Bonora, *Stile e tradizione*, p. 17, on the Humanists' novel understanding of rhetoric in their profound renovation of pedagogy; Battisti, "Il concetto d'imitazione," on the independence of artistic imitation from external necessity in Raphael, p. 183.

[16] "Quare plus Aristotelice nobilitatis iudicio participasse Theophrastum, qui illi in schola et doctrina successit, quam Nicomachum filium, qui longe illo doctrina fuit." *De nobilitate, Opera*, I, 82.

a notion of the wholeness, the indivisibility of the personality which closely resembles the appraisals of Poggio's own literary identity; he has Niccoli in the dialogue on nobility claim that nobility can only be explained as a concerted effort of spirit (*animus*) (*Opera*, I, 65). Further, true piety was a matter solely of interior life: the edifying qualities of Jerome of Prague are those of a firm and undivided identity; in his letter to Bruni on the trial of Jerome, Poggio marveled most at the self-contained, coherent deliberateness of his actions; the overwhelming impression that Poggio conveys is that in a most admirable fashion Jerome "chose" his identity and his fate.[17] In the same way Poggio juxtaposes rational rhetorical methods over against the arbitrary vagaries of allegorizing. He despises the attempts at allegorical interpretation of texts, at poetic evocations of occult meanings, because they lack critical standards, any consciousness of the relation of the text to intention or genre; he describes Salutati's attempts in the *De laboribus Herculis* as intellectual waste, a personal loss.[18] In the second part of the *Historia tripartita* Poggio develops arguments which do not allow even the methods of law and medicine as much probity as he attributes to his rhetorical-critical studies of sources in his polemic on the relative merits of Scipio and Caesar. Similarly, Cortesi will be careful to point out that imitation is not a matter of nature or of chance, but of the self-conscious use of reason.[19] Thus under the rubric of imitation the Humanist forms a notion of identity; nor is this a theoretical discussion only: if freedom is the foundation of his achievement, his rhetorical-critical activity fills this concept of freedom with concrete activity, and exercises his convictions in quotidian employment. *Imitatio* is a source of freedom, the creation of a style is a prime expression of freedom of choice; and since the concept of

[17] See Poggio's letter to Bruni, *Prosatori latini*, p. 228f. Poggio discusses religion as a matter of interior life in the *De miseria humanae conditionis*, *Opera*, I, 100.

[18] See the long quotation from the *De avaricia* of the Florence B.N. Conv., I, 1, 16, f. 201v-202r in *Prosatori latini*, pp. 1129-30.

[19] *De hominibus doctis dialogus*, pp. 10-11; cf. Cicero, *De oratore* II, 22, 90-91; cf. Bembo in *Le epistole "De imitatione,"* pp. 52-53.

freedom involves a sense of responsibility, the connection between the formal and the responsible is strict.

But freedom in historical consciousness is exactly the point: there is a brilliant statement in *Saturn and Melancholy* to the effect that a major contribution of the Renaissance and Reformation was to allow man to find *direct* access to his own cultural past instead of relying upon the current of traditional opinion.[20] And for Petrarch the idea of imitation becomes the source of this directness, the model for the freedom and self-limitation of the historian.[21] It is precisely in imitating the great classical historians that Petrarch finds the principles of historical activity which include the same notions of identity as those of all other literary activity. In the Preface to the *De viris illustribus* Petrarch makes a distinction between the absolute authority of a timeless *pacificator* of historians or the passivity of chronicling or cataloging and true historical activity.[22] The historian must balance the exigencies of his freedom of creation with the exigencies of the evidence which is available; the choice must be both entirely his own and entirely coherent. The important point here is that rhetorical imitation, as it is developed by Humanists such as Petrarch and Poggio, leads to literary activity which is not a matter of passive conformity to mechanical rules externally imposed, but an autonomous function, with norms internally produced, which recognizes the necessities to respond to contemporary as well as past realities.

But the rhetorical doctrine of *imitatio* has a second major implication for the historiography of Renaissance Humanism;

[20] Klibansky, Panofsky, and Saxl, *Saturn and Melancholy*, p. 242.

[21] Thus Gmelin speaks of Petrarch's historical works: "In dem er nun dasselbe Prinzip der freien, wählenden Nachahmung, das er in seinem Stil befolgte, auch auf die Behandlung des stofflichen Materials anwandte, hat er in diesen Biographien [*De viris illustribus*] zugleich den Grund zur modernen kritischen Geschichtsdarstellung gelegt. . ." (*Das Prinzip*, p. 130).

[22] "Ego neque pacificator historicorum, neque collector omnium, sed eorum imitator sum, quibus vel similitudo vel autoritas maior, ut eis potissimum stetur, impetrat. . . ," ed. de Nolhac, *Le "De viris"* . . . *Notices sur les manuscrits*, pp. 55-56; see de Nolhac's discussion in *Pétrarque et l'humanisme*, Vol. 2, p. 14.

beyond positing the author-historian as a free personality, it focuses on man's symbolic heritage as the peculiarly human past. For the Humanist as imitator the vital confrontation is not with a transcendental or magical nature but with the continuum of past expressions and representations man has created. In rhetorical imitation the symbolic past is an inexhaustible treasury of expression to be drawn upon at will; thus Poggio alleges that Valla's false idea of imitation—the slavish copying of a single model, in his case Quintilian—leads to intellectual isolation, and his arrogant rejection of the best that has been thought and said to permanent immaturity.[23] Poggio takes pains to confute Valla's claim that Cicero was the first and therefore the weakest Roman orator; both argue, then, that the best possible historical position is at the end of a rich and varied historical development.[24] The Humanist rhetorician's aggressive anti-primitivism is directly opposed to the magical ahistoricism of the adherents of the Hermetic tradition of the later Renaissance, who see themselves as engaged in sorting out later expressions of a pure and perfect first revelation. F. Gundolf points out that for Petrarch fame is no longer dependent on a poetic-allegorical, arcane intervention of the author, but on his knowledge of deeds: the past—in particular the past as preserved in symbols—is all we have.[25]

According to Ulivi, Poggio's and Petrarch's doctrine of imitation places them between two antihistorical moments in artistic theory—the Scholastic traditionalism of the Middle

[23] *Invectiva in Vallam I, Opera*, I, 189f.; *Invectiva in Vallam II, Opera*, I, 203, 229.

[24] *Invectiva in Vallam III, Opera*, I, 241; cf. Bembo, in *Le epistole "De imitatione*," p. 56.

[25] "Hier hat zum erstenmal ein leidenschaftlicher Heldenverehrer Cäsars Taten, Cäsars Eigenschaften, und Cäsars Anekdoten gereinigt von den Zutaten des magischen Wahns und schweifenden Phantasie, aus den echten Quellen wieder vollständig zusammengestellt und als Ausfluss einer geschichtlichen Einheit, einer menschlichen Person zusammengesehen," *Caesar, Geschichte seines Ruhms*, p. 114. But contrast A. Chastel and R. Klein, "Humanism, Historical Consciousness, and National Sentiment," *Diogenes*, 44 (1963), pp. 1-18, esp. p. 13f.: they see the aggressive primitivism and the sense of occult intervention of the late fifteenth-century Humanists as a manifestation, not a negation, of historical consciousness.

Ages with its metaphysical notions of language, and the subjectivism of later Florentine Platonic theory which is so
closely allied to magical-occult ideas of language. Their
notion of the author as one who uses free, i.e. historical
judgment, but who is tied to his symbolic past—who is both
bound and bound to choose by the past, to use it as the
seedbed of all meaningful achievement—Ulivi sees as a mean
between the two extremes of necessitous traditionalism and
artistic expressionism.[26] Quintilian offers a paradigm for both
rhetorical and historical activity for the Humanists: his first
step in imitation, the organization of past experience on the
principle of appropriateness (*I.O.*, X, 1, 5f.), parallels the
historical critique of sources; the injunction to recognize the
author's own personality and purpose (X, 1, 8) is equivalent
to the self-conscious development of strands of contemporary
political and ethical choice; and the moral-aesthetic, humanistic goals so often reiterated in Quintilian find their analogue
in the commitment to life, the devotion to vitality which is
both a historical and an aesthetic value in Petrarch and
Poggio.

The essence of Humanistic method is a relationship between freedom and constraint which can be either an easy
reciprocity or a difficult ambiguity. It often appears as a
pessimistic sense of freedom, and a liberation which isolates.
And both the ambiguity and the brilliance are rooted in the
Humanist perception that freedom must be treated as rigid a
necessity as the constraints of expression and event; that, as
Nietzsche says, only by creativity can one seize historical
Antiquity.[27] The rhetorical doctrine of *imitatio* postulates the
importance of the temporal dimension of the author's ethical
identity, the radical nature of his historical consciousness.
The Humanist looks for the timely, not the timeless, verities,
and the effort to establish the great ethical themes in their
exact temporal dimension is the basis of the type of historical
criticism which de Nolhac noted in the marginal commentaries by Petrarch on Livy's historical treatment of Scipio

---

[26] *L'imitazione*, pp. 16-17; here Ulivi seems to draw heavily from
Chastel, *Marsile Ficin et l'arte*, Geneva, 1954.
[27] Fragment #36, in Arrowsmith, "Nietzsche on Classics," p. 23.

Africanus.[28] For Petrarch, an ahistorical view of Scipio lacks the vital dimension of meaning.

Petrarch also furnishes the model for Poggio's exploitation of the second major contribution of rhetoric to Humanist notions of identity: a posture of detachment or disjunction. Perhaps because of a repetition of circumstance as well as of predilection, Poggio, like Petrarch, harbored negative or at least ambiguous feelings about his public role. E. Walser is careful to point out in his biography that Poggio's education had taken place in the Florentine intellectual milieu of Salutati's maturity and Bruni's youth; Poggio certainly shared Salutati's conviction that eloquence was power, and Bruni's belief in the coincidence of public, specifically political, opportunity and true eloquence.[29] Yet when Bruni accepted the Chancellorship of Florence in 1427 Poggio admonished him that "no reward ought to move a learned man to subject his liberty to public servitude."[30] While Salutati and Bruni held the truly responsible position of Chancellor for many years of their adult lives, Poggio came to the Chancellery only in old age, albeit vigorous old age. In the anecdotes of Vespasiano da Bisticci, Bruni appears as a man of recognized political importance to the commune.[31] But of Poggio, D. Marzi remarks slightingly that he was undoubtedly hired more as

> . . . un dettatore elegante, dotto conoscitore delle formule esterne e dello stile cancelleresco, che un esperto conoscitore dell'arte della politica.[32]

[28] See *Pétrarque et l'humanisme*, Vol. 2, p. 31f., for an analysis of Petrarch's careful reading of Livy; cf. Gmelin, *Das Prinzip*, p. 130f.; Garin, "La prosa latina del Quattrocento," *Medioevo e Rinascimento*, pp. 121-23.

[29] See Poggio's letter to Scipio of Ferrara, *Opera*, I, p. 365; and the *Defensiuncula, Opera*, I, 371-72.

[30] "Etsi enim nullum est pretium, quo homo doctus moveri debeat ad subjiciendam libertatem suam publicae servituti. . . ," *Epistolae*, I, 215.

[31] See the anecdotes used in chap. 7 of Marzi's *La cancelleria della Repubblica fiorentina*.

[32] Marzi, *La cancelleria*, p. 222; see also Garin, "I cancellieri umanisti," *La cultura filosofica*, p. 23.

It is a matter of discerning the primary allegiance, and Poggio and Petrarch come very close to being "stateless" personages; neither the Roman papacy nor the republic of Rienzi was able to provide them the kind of political consciousness and ideological role which Florence provided Salutati and Bruni.[33] Poggio spent most of his life as Apostolic Secretary attached to the Curia, a role which gave rise to some confusion and ambiguity; he was fond of claiming that he had two fatherlands, one by birth (natural), one by office (civil); in his old age he bitterly remarked that he had two fatherlands, both in difficulties, and "I seem to be in an alien land, and among strangers."[34]

But if the events of Poggio's life, as those of Petrarch's, underlined the disappointing aspects of public life, so also did his rhetorical discipline and commitment. Rhetorical interest in discourse can exist outside of any political framework, and Petrarch and Poggio very plainly share the Humanist trait that interest in language is on a deeper level than interest in politics. The strand of the rhetorical tradition in question here comes very heavily under attack by the philosophers: this is the idea of rhetoric as "mere" rhetoric, as discourse about discourse, mannered attitude toward manner. Rhetoric in this aspect appears as a permanent subjunctive mental mode; an inability to apprehend the world except as mediated by expressions of thinking, feeling, wishing, willing; a forced concentration on how the literary protagonist, the audience, or the author thinks, feels, wills, believes in relation to the content of the discourse. If the classical rhetorical doctrine of *imitatio* as expressed by Quintilian contributes to the author's sense of identity as a freely choosing being, rhetorical detachment or disjunction results in a sense of the layered and indirect quality of experience and thus to the isolation of the personality; if *imitatio* emphasizes the whole historical world

[33] Vasoli, "Storia e politica nel primo umanesimo fiorentina," p. 133.
[34] "Ideo conturbor mente, cum mihi tanquam in aliena patria esse videar, et apud externos. . . ," (letter to Cardinal Firmano), *Epistolae*, III, 255; on his notion of the two fatherlands, see also *Epistolae*, II, 54; III, 57, 72, 220.

of symbols as the proper field of human endeavor, the subjunctive mode emphasizes the "real" world as entirely mediated, indeed, distorted, by symbol. In other words, rhetorical theory and practice can engender a pessimism, a sense of limitation to the concepts of both subject and object. Yet the subjunctive entails definition as well as detachment; Roland Barthes describes the subjunctive as an admirable instrument of demystification.[35] Where in Bruni rhetoric reinforced political engagement, in Poggio rhetoric guides specific insights into the fragility and evanescence of the human condition (*humana conditio*) in general, and Italian Renaissance politics in particular.

Thomas Hobbes, then, is alluding to the rhetorical source of this pessimism and sense of limitation in his epitome of Aristotle's *Rhetoric* when he paraphrases the definition of rhetoric as "that faculty by which we understand what will serve our turn, concerning any subject to win belief in the hearer."[36] In emphasizing the persuasive purpose of rhetoric, Hobbes is pointing out that the essential trait of rhetoric is its *tangential* nature: rhetoric, like logic, is a universal discipline and has no specific subject matter (1354a; 1355b; 1359b); unlike logic, rhetoric posits no universal, that is, necessary, supporting framework. Moreover, while the close association of rhetoric and ethics is a *topos* from Sophistic times through the Renaissance,[37] in some periods there is more self-consciousness and uneasiness than others; then the relation appears as dynamic, not static, reciprocal, not unilateral. For as Aristotle pointed out, you can find not only ethical men employing rhetoric, but rhetoricians using ethical arguments for strictly persuasive purposes (1356a; 1366a; 1377b). In the body of rhetorical doctrine this results in the development of an interlocking network of maxims of a pessi-

---

[35] *Mythologies*, Paris, 1957, p. 244, note 13.
[36] He refers to 1355b, in A *Brief of the Art of Rhetorik*, in Aristotle's *Treatise on Rhetoric*, London, 1854, p. 276.
[37] Burk, *Die Pädagogik*, p. 199; F. Gilbert, *Machiavelli and Guicciardini*, p. 89.

mistic, "realistic" in the sense of disillusioned, tone. Sabbadini maintains that the Humanists had a strong sense of their own personalities;[38] at the same time, the aliment of these personalities was in part these maxims which express cynicism about the persuasive powers of the author, as well as about the self-concern and pliability of the receiving audience.

If words have become political counters or commodities with a definite market value,[39] there is an obverse side to the Humanist coins: eloquence may be politics, but "eloquence is the language of wise men in a world which disbelieves in wisdom."[40] On the one hand the Humanists discover language as an absolute milieu, they rediscover its sovereignty, its revolutionary force;[41] on the other hand their own position of detachment and autonomous power is related to their insights into what Hegel called the *negativity* of language. Poggio's strictures on the perversity of language recall the Gorgian metaphor which describes language as acting sometimes as a helpful, sometimes a harmful drug (DK 82 B11.14). The fluidity and evanescence of language which Poggio confronts recalls the problematic relationship of words and things of Gorgian rhetoric. When H. Lefebvre characterizes this negativity he claims "the words replace the thing in its absence, in a strange absence-presence at the same time alienation, evocation, and power." The relation of words and things is not atemporal but takes place in a tem-

---

[38] *Il metodo degli umanisti*, p. 56.

[39] H. Lefebvre, *Le langage et la société*; see chap. 7, "La forme marchandise et discours," p. 336f. While Valla employs an extended metaphor of language as coinage, "Oratio in principio studii," *Opera omnia*, II, pp. 283-84, the image connotes "currency" rather than the Marxist "alienation" which Lefebvre discusses; it connotes "artificiality" also, but an artificiality humanistically understood as both goal and achievement.

[40] Michel, *Rhétorique et philosophie*, p. 99.

[41] "The aim will then be to restore to language its normally active, and therefore revolutionary power. Language is not an instrument, it is an absolute milieu; it makes us and we make it." *TLS*, Dec. 5, 1968, p. 1354. This is probably the sense of Valla's other great metaphor: "Magnum ergo latini sermonis sacramentum est." *Elegantiae, Praefatio* I, *Opera*, I, p. 65.

poral continuum; this does not make language "unreal," but
defines its reality as specific, formal.[42]

Rhetorical attitudes provide a linguistic "realism" of a
different character also: while most discussions of historical
method take place under the rubric of the false dilemma
subjective–objective, rhetorical self-examination results neither in pure subjectivity or pure objectivity as genuine possibilities.[43] Rhetorical concentration on the mediated nature
of reality is also a focus on a middle range of experience.
There is a distaste for dealing with the products of pure
introspection as abstractions probably ineffable, as exigencies which reduce the author to gesture. Similarly, disenchantment or even deception marks the rhetorical use of the
universals which are the products of logical demonstration.
Recall the quarrels of the Trecento Humanists with the
dialecticians; according to Salutati, where the "Britannici"
were interested in mere *verba* the Humanists were interested
in *res*: here of course the Humanists use *verba* as an abstract
structure separated from *res* as valid and valuable insight and
behavior. The *res* to which Salutati refers in his antinomy is
a spectrum of human feeling and event; the concentration
on the culture of the spirit, the health of the soul is not an expression of a post-Cartesian subjectivity; to search in one's
own experience is not qualitatively different from the explorations of history.[44] In modern terms, logic can lead to logical
positivism, to the predication of the existence of only one

[42] Lefebvre, *Le langage et la société*, p. 84f.

[43] See Lohmann, "Das Verhältnis des abendländischen Menschen zur
Sprache," p. 10f.; the use of the subjective–objective antinomy to describe Humanist linguistic or historical consciousness would be anachro-
nistic, because the precise antithesis is only a possibility after the
complete separation of language from thought, a process which begins
with Occamism and is only completed after Descartes, when the ego
becomes the starting point of all thought, and language becomes a
"thing" like other things.

[44] Vasoli, " 'Antichi' contro 'moderni'," *La dialettica e la retorica*,
p. 9f. See D. Aguzzi-Barbagli, "Dante e la poetica di Coluccio Salutati,"
Italica, 52 (1965), p. 110f.: "Imitare significa. . . indagare nella psiche
stessa," at the same time that the poet is considered predominantly
as the interpreter of the human world.

ideal system of notation which it is the purpose of the logician to disclose; the logician becomes a crab, capable of only sideways, horizontal motion. Rhetoric recognizes that there are a great number of modes of discourse, and that no amount of its ordering effort can make these differences chimerical: rhetorical treatises eagerly grasp at the vertical exploration of different language situations and usages. Any rhetorically organized discussion of the truth is both a narrowing and a refining of identity.

An illustration of this rhetorical embracing of difference is the fact that rhetorical ideas of genre penetrate very deeply indeed: in Aristotle's *Rhetoric*, for instance, we find that different types of discourse not only employ different styles and arguments but have entirely disparate purposes—utility, justice, and honor are contemplated as separate, if not actually opposing, ends (1358b). The tendency of rhetorical treatises is to present the series of problems of persuasion as a series of language "games," that is, self-contained areas of communication set aside by their own well-defined rules and particular purposes. Rhetoric, in proposing the existence of a multiplicity of these games, in effect engages in exploring the possibilities of connectedness and dependence, isolation and opposition, ambiguity and paradox in the whole sphere of discourse.

Thus in Italian Humanism the relative importance of any one kind of discourse or explanation decreases; for example, theological language becomes one of many kinds of explanation. Indeed, Poggio interrupts his discussion of cause or motive many times to specifically deny himself the use of this language; there is an obvious lack of concern with the working of cosmic forces in the sense of occult powers which are unaccountable and inexpressible. Since a rhetorician deals only with the subjects on which decisions can be made (1359a), it is beside the point to speak of extra-verbal forces completely beyond our ken, and thus out of control.[45]

[45] Compare Bartolomeo della Fonte's letter to Pietro Cennini in *Epistolarum Libri III*, ed. L. Juhász, Budapest, 1931, pp. 17-18.

But to state that a simple feeling of hostility, a rejection of the arcane and magical, accompanies rhetorical ideas of language is an insufficient description. It is a structural attribute: starting from the interrelated assumptions of imitation, decorum, disjunction, it is extremely difficult for a concept of occult artistic power, or the existence of occult entities and metaphysical forces, to gain hegemony. Thus

Attraverso la continua analisi ed il confronto retorico di forme linguistiche e sintattiche, di forme e di modi e di situazioni letterarie, s'iniziava a concepire l'opera poetica come la pura espressione di un'attività umana autonoma, ottenuta con lo studio e la conoscenza dei classici.[46]

Unlike the identity of a *poeta-theologus* such as Dante, the rhetorical identity, even where there is a sense of completion in function or role, remains morally and epistemologically "unfinished" or open-ended. That is, modest. Considering the number of moral-historical treatises Poggio wrote, it is remarkable how few times Poggio felt able to state any but negative or permissive ethical rules.

To apply the term "negativity" to Humanist language and thought is not a judgment, however; the Humanist culture as "decadent" admits plurality, is extraordinarily receptive.[47] Humanist dialogue is the vehicle of pluralism; the fifteenth century, in Tateo's words, had developed a taste for polemic and confrontation of opinions and the capacity for illuminating fundamental contrasts of existence, without the decisive will to resolve these contrasts.[48] Poggio, like

---

[46] Vasoli, "L'estetica," p. 338.

[47] Georg Simmel, "The Ruin," in *Georg Simmel, 1858-1918; A Collection of Essays, with Translations and a Bibliography*, ed. K. H. Wolff, Columbus, Ohio, 1959, p. 266: "Perhaps this is the reason for our general fascination with decay and decadence, a fascination which goes beyond what is merely negative and degrading. The rich and many-sided culture, the unlimited *impressionability*, and the understanding open to everything, which are characteristic of decadent epochs, do signify this coming together of all contradictory strivings."

[48] Tateo, "Il dialogo 'realistico'," *Tradizione e realtà*, pp. 224-25, 273; "i dialoghi del nostro Poggio rivelano tutto un gusto per lo scontro delle opinioni senza conclusione univoca o prevalente," p. 265.

Bruni, returns to the Sophistic and Ciceronian maxim that truth may be elicited from either side in a debate: *"Disceptando enim in utramque partem veritas elici consuevit"* (*Epistolae*, II, 267). And, more frequently than Bruni, Poggio seems merely to question, not define, the truth. His hesitation forces the reader to hesitate.

Further, the rhetorical habit of dealing with subject-matter at one remove, with word and expression rather than with reified object, results in a concentration by professional rhetoricians on the rules of the language games, on the actual playing as a goal in itself. This of course affects their sense of identity, but also, on a deeper level, relates to a notion of free critical inquiry, of historical distance. Rhetorical playfulness for Poggio is not a source of ephemeral objectivity but of consciousness of bias and pattern; thus Poggio contrasts his obvious distortion of the merits of Scipio and the faults of Caesar in the pursuit of his polemical game with the naive, unselfconscious puffery of Guarino, who performs, he claims, like "a folk singer who extols the deeds of Roland for an audience of rustics" (*Defensiuncula contra Guarinum, Opera*, I, 380). There is a sense of power and mobility to be derived from literary employment, but this time from detachment, not engagement; *libertas* for the literati becomes *otium cum dignitate*, a kind of peace with honor, a leisure which is the result, not the antithesis, of urbanity.[49] The skeptical, critical stance of the Humanist, what R. Roedel calls Poggio's *"franca capacità di superare gli schema e i formalismi pui radicati,"* is in part a function of this rhetorically engineered urbanity.[50]

But since a characteristic of both rhetoric and logic is the capacity to draw opposite conclusions, to state alternative solutions (Aristotle, *Rhetoric*, 1355a, 1357a), rhetoric also contributes to the destructive self-consciousness, to the *Le-*

---

[49] "In hac vero florentissima urbe, que me ultro ad se vocavit, otium cum dignitate, que duo precipue civibus optanda sunt, fuerim consecutus," from his letter to Pietro Tommasi, *Inedita* 85, in Walser, *Leben und Werke*, p. 533.
[50] "Poggio Bracciolini," p. 56.

bensunsicherheit of the fifteenth century.[51] In so far as rhetoric sharpens, makes pointed the difficulties of choice, it enriches the critique of historical choice. If rhetorical style and imitation provide a model for free choice by the unified personality, rhetorical analytic methods tend to underscore ambiguity and paradox, to resolve personality into the separate aspects of its behavior. Perhaps Poggio's letter to Cosimo de' Medici is a reflection of this; in attempting to console Cosimo for his exile from Florence Poggio maintains that the only truly stable things are still left to him, that is, his good intentions and his memory of the good intentions which had colored the past events of his life; his identity becomes the product of will and memory, wholeness a product of continuity in behavior, in "appearances" (*Epistolae,* II, 37f.).[52] Rhetorical activity itself provides a model of the fragmented personality in the frequent separation of virtuosity from virtue; *virtù* becomes mere personal potential, *virtus* a personal possession, a *habitus animi*.[53] The Humanists are left with a world of mental processes, where the necessary form of an ethical event is provided not by an infused static quality but by the operation of the will, a will by nature mutable.

In sum, a study of Humanist rhetoric illustrates the aptness of M. Seidlmayer's dictum that the history of Italian Humanism is a chapter in *Seelengeschichte* rather than *Geistesgeschichte*;[54] rhetorical functions insure that the notions of identity are not just intellectual abstractions, but have an existential, rounded quality. Rhetorical theory and practice become one of the major sources for attitudes toward all important aspects of identity—the notion of autonomy, the relation of meaning and will, freedom and re-

[51] Seidlmayer, "Nikolaus von Cues und der Humanismus," p. 99: "Das Stigma, das das ganze 15. Jahrhundert an der Stirn trägt; die *Lebensunsicherheit*, fehlt auch dem Humanismus nicht."
[52] Similarly, Cusanus uses the figure of Trajan's column to illustrate his point that the will is the source of the existence of wisdom and power, *De non aliud, Opera Omnia*, Vol. 13, ed. L. Baur and P. Wilpert, Leipzig, 1944, chap. 9, p. 20.
[53] Heitmann, *Fortuna und Virtus*, p. 249f.
[54] "Petrarca, das Urbild des Humanisten," pp. 171-72.

sponsibility, freedom and necessity. Finally, both the rhetorical doctrine of imitation and the rhetorically-rooted detachment add force to a historicist conviction that the exploration of the past is an ethical imperative, and that the temporal is the most important, if not the only, dimension of mind.

2. RHETORICAL IDENTITY AND HISTORICAL CONSCIOUSNESS

For the Humanists, rhetorical principles and function affect the whole subject–object relationship in discourse, and thus transform the problem of historical knowledge: first, by providing an armature for ethical identity, and second, by enforcing a strict concentration on the temporal dimension, where the interest in symbol is always related to the problem of time. All genres, all facets of Poggio's literary accomplishment reflect this dual influence. If Poggio's style is an example of his self-consciously free relation to the symbols of the past, his efforts to reform the script of his period reflects a most basic concern with symbol, where clarity of physical contour as well as of style is regarded as transcendence, as a defeat of time.[55] His correspondence indicates that his aggressive efforts to recover ancient manuscripts are the result of a sense of mission in rescuing them from the ravages of time.[56] His ideas of translation reveal almost an ethics of style, a sense of aesthetic imperatives which is for him necessarily a part of historical consciousness. Finally, even the titles of his ethical treatises—*De infelicitate principum, De varietate fortunae, Contra hypocritas, In fidei delatores*—evoke his peculiar focus on time, change, and symbol.

But Poggio's rhetorical concerns also affect his specific historical insights as well as his general attitudes. These insights are, on the whole, negative in tone: where Bruni was the apologist for "civic Humanism," Poggio is the diagnostician of failure and isolation. One of the major factors con-

[55] B.L. Ullman, *The Origin and Development of Humanistic Script*, Rome, 1960, pp. 21-57.
[56] See particularly the letters to Niccoli and Guarino Veronese in *Epistolae*, I.

tributing to the crepuscular tone of Poggio's works is his preoccupation with the volatility of social forms, with the unhappy changes manifest in contemporary politics. While the key antinomy in Bruni's conceptual structure was private vs. public, it is the contrast of *labilis–stabilis* in Poggio.[57] He returns to the original Sophistic preoccupation with flux and change, but here rhetorical language potential relates less to public happiness than to the achievement of stability, the transcending of fragility.

On the most superficial level, Poggio seems to resort to the principle of decorum to explain the process of change, as well as to provide the core of his prudential maxims. Thus of the gifts of fortune Poggio remarks that *"nihil ab se perpetuo donari, sed commodari ad certum tempus"* (*De varietate Fortunae, Opera*, II, 586; cf. H.F., c. 303-04). Conversely, the prudent man who wishes to be considered wise also observes the same decorum and bows to the times: *"prudentis viri esse parere tempore"* (H.F., c. 344).[58] Of the presupposition of decorum is the radical contingency of world process, Poggio seems to conclude that there are no general challenges, only particular ones, to doubt whether any gift of nature is of permanent use, and to affirm that the conditions of fate demand flexibility and fluidity of response.[59]

But more fundamentally, there is a structural necessity to the relation of rhetorical to historical insight: just as for

[57] To cite only a few examples, this contrast appears in *Epistolae*, I, 110, 121, 357; II, 50, 65, 309, 357, 365; III, 8, 13, 58, 249, 258.

[58] "Quo magis sapientis esse videtur, accomodata singulis negotiis discretione, et praesentibus rebus consulere, et prospicere futuris, neque una quadam in sententia esse ita fixum ac perseverantem. . . ," *Epistolae*, II, 132.

[59] In rhetoric, of course, *kairos*, a sense of opportunity, is the fundamental concept, the "fulcrum of its system" (Rostagni, "Un nuovo capitolo," p. 11); but the search for the appropriate, the emphasis on decorum, is a general characteristic of fourteenth- and fifteenth-century ethics; recall A. Harnack's discussion of Nominalism in his *History of Dogma*, trans. W. M'Gilchrist, London, 1899, Vol. 6, p. 168: "But not only did this work [the revision of existing dogma] now acquire an entirely external, formalistic character, but there were also introduced into everything the principle of an arbitrary morality, of the *'conveniens'* too, the expedient and the relative."

Gorgias reality was the human psyche and its malleability and susceptibility to linguistic coruscation,[60] so the volatility and evanescence of Italian politics are connected by Poggio to the deception, hypocrisy, and artifice which dominate communication. A progression could be established from the high-point of Salutati's happy observation of the harmony of public and private interests in his official correspondence to obtain the release of his friend Giovanni Ricci from the power of Milan (*Epistolario*, II, 375), through Bruni's comments on the possible dangers of freedom in the sphere of public eloquence in his strictures against the *"libertas reprehendi nimia"* of the Parte Guelfa as harmful to the city-state (*H.F.*, 268), to the violent pamphlet of Poggio's last years, the *In fidei delatores*, which bitterly laments the complete collapse of good faith in public communication, and thus of the possibility of good policy.[61]

Poggio develops a sensitivity to the presence of lawless discourse, a feeling which becomes both acute and painful. In both the *In fidei delatores* and the *Contra hypocritas* Poggio attacks deception and hypocrisy as general social ills: he describes the *simulatio* of the hypocrites not so much as sinful as against nature,

> for Cicero testifies this to be more against nature than death, than pain, than the other ills which can befall the body or our possessions externally.[62]

[60] Segal, "Gorgias and the Psychology of the Logos," p. 110.

[61] On Bruni's doubts concerning political eloquence see, besides Gianfigliazzi's speech on the dangers of consultation and debate in *H.F.*, 277, his Preface to Angelo Acciaioli, *Commentariorum rerum graecarum Liber* (1439), *Schriften*, p. 146, where he speaks of failure of citizenship, failures exemplified in Athens at the time of the Peloponnesian War.

[62] "magis contra naturam testatur esse Cicero, quam mortem, quam dolorem, quam cetera, quae possunt corpori accidere, aut rebus externis." *Opera*, II, 50. Compare Poggio's declaration on legal and civil deception in the *In fidei delatores*, *Opera*, II, 901: "Nihil enim minus est hominis quam mentiri, nihil magis adversum rationi, nihil veritati contrarius." At the end of his life he remarks, "I speak only with the dead, who do not lie . . ." (*Epistolae*, III, 216). See Tateo, "Il dialogo 'realistico'," pp. 261-62.

The peculiar affliction of public life seems to be fraudulent discourse; in the *Contra hypocritas* Poggio not only describes the hypocritical Mendicants swarming at the Curia, but unhappily notes their success (*Opera*, II, 62f.). If hypocrisy and deceit are against nature, and bad in themselves, they are so much the worse when they appear in public officials and affect public policy (*In fidei delatores, Opera*, II, 891, 896-97). "When I survey the other courts as well as the Roman Curia," Poggio complains, "I see nothing pure, nothing sincere, nothing simple" (*Epistolae*, I, 142). If Poggio, as one committed to classical republican values, was deeply concerned by the increase in power and number of tyrannies, as a historian, he analyzes the growth of tyranny in terms of the decline in communication: the most essential and dangerous trait of a tyrant, the one which gives rise to his power, is faithlessness (*De infelicitate, Opera*, I, 396; *In fidei delatores, Opera*, II, 901-02). But loss of faith is characteristic even of republican Florence, and the loss of faith between polities is a mark of Italian decline (*In fidei delatores, Opera*, II, 899-900). The presence or absence of faith in communication becomes the key to the possibilities of politics and thus of political history; "without faith" there is "no society, no assembly of men, no city-state, no republic" (*In fidei delatores, Opera*, II, 892).

The structure of the *Historia populi florentini* is a simple one: Poggio intended to relate no more than the hundred years' war, with the approximate dates 1350-1450, between the free city of Florence and the succession of Italian, mainly Milanese, tyrants. The key point of Ricci's attack on Gian Galeazzo Visconti reported in Bruni's history in the speech "*Hic homo multa signa facit*" becomes the characteristic of the tyrant through Poggio's entire narrative. Florence was confronted by a series of tyrants—Giovanni Visconti, Bishop of Milan; Gian Galeazzo Visconti; Ladislas of Naples; Filippo Visconti—who share an efficacious hypocrisy, the ability to usefully deceive. Recalling Bruni's version of Ricci's speech, Poggio's description of Gian Galeazzo's approach to the Florentines is that of one who "*persuadet . . . se otium cupere, et quietum, sed unum volvebat lingua, alterum pectore versabat*" (*H.F.*, c. 248; cf. c. 278, 251-53). Similarly he assails Ladislas as nothing better than a pirate in breaking faith by impounding some merchants' goods (*H.F.*, c. 316), while he remarks that Filippo Visconti was

> the duke who spoke one thing, and carried out another which was hidden in his soul; who publicly claimed to be of peaceful intent, while war lurked within, since not peace, but desire to rule was in his heart.[63]

Poggio connects the failure of communication with the failure of community; he uses the isolating effect of certain types of discourse as a model for the description of political difficulty. For Poggio, the deceit and hypocrisy which afflict contemporary society, and the social failure and isolation which result, are intensified at the upper levels of society: the condition of isolation applies to princes of good intentions as well as to the tyrants of deliberate faithlessness. The prince by virtue of his power and office is surrounded by flatterers who make it their business to segregate the prince from reality: for

> there is no crime so horrible, no regal vice so nefarious, that the flatterers can't hide with the veil of some virtue.[64]

The lives of princes are lacerated by suspicion and fear, a situation which stems in part from their propensity to choose associates who are "*veri dicendi hostes*" (*De infelicitate, Opera*, I, 407). Indeed, it is very dangerous to tell the truth or give good advice to princes; after narrating the Archbishop of Milan's murder of a Brescian noble for giving advice to end the war with Florence, Poggio comments that it was

[63] "Ducem aliud ore loqui, aliud occultum animo gerere; pacem ab eo ostentati, bellum intus latere; cum nulla pax sed cupiditas regnandi cordi esset." *H.F.*, c. 321; cf. *H.F.*, c. 326-27, 333-34, 337.

[64] "Nullum est tam tetrum facinus, nullum tam nepharium in regibus vitium, quod non adulatores alicuius virtutis detegant velamento." *De infelicitate, Opera*, I, 407.

... a thing of bad example, more than tyrannical, for it teaches how a good man condemns himself, it instructs with how much danger wise advice is given to tyrants and princes.[65]

In contrast, Filelfo in his *Commentationes Florentinae de exilio* attributes to Poggio the opinion that Cosimo de' Medici is an exception in that he deals with solid realities rather than empty or deceitful words, that he was a *"vir gravis et callidus rem longe malit quam verba considerare."*[66]

The ethical and historical implications are obvious; there is a gross impairment of the possibilities for significant action. The princes by virtue of their condition, their isolation in a sea of hypocrisy and deceit, a condition generated by their own will as well as that of others, are deprived of *libertas vivendi*:

> This thing alone they lack, though other goods seem to be abundant, and those who think that they rule, are in reality the servants of all, which is certainly very little distant from unhappiness.[67]

When Poggio attempts to console Cosimo de' Medici for his exile from power in Florence he congratulates him on his restoration to true liberty, his escape from the slavery of public service (*Epistolae*, II, 42). Similarly, when Poggio congratulates Cosimo on his recall to Florence, his letter is more a eulogy of Cosimo's character, a courtly discussion of the honor already conferred, than an anticipation of public happiness (*Epistolae*, II, 64f.).

Beyond isolation, then, there is a peculiar emphasis on limitation; for Poggio the effect of the necessary mediation of language is to enhance the difficulty of human affairs; his histories and moral treatises emphasize the problematic na-

---

[65] ". . . mali exempla res, et plus quam tyrannica: docuit suo damno vir bonus, quanto cum periculo dentur tyrannis, ac principibus sana consilia." *H.F.*, c. 207.

[66] Florence, B.N., II, ii, 70, f. 92r; quoted in Garin, *L'Umanesimo italiano*, Bari, 1958, p. 52.

[67] "Hac equidem re sola carent, cum cetera bona circumfluere videantur, et qui se dominari putant, sunt omnium servi, quaeres parum distat ab infelicitate." *De infelicitate*, *Opera*, I, 415.

ture of society, and his primary intuition of limitation is of limitation of discourse. Where the rhetorical concentration on persuasion to decision reinforced Petrarch's definition of the task of history as the depiction of the maneuvers of power, rather than of the accidents of fortune,[68] it underlined Poggio's focus on the restrictions of choice rather than the potential of the will. Both are essentially moral investigations in so far as they concern themselves with the responsibility or irresponsibility of the will, and both are conducted in the area not so much of past experience, as of the expressions of past experience which exhibit a certain rhetorical form, clarity, and maturity.

Moreover, Poggio merely echoes Petrarch when he claims that to escape the harmful and isolating confines of public life, one must flee to the true liberty of solely private experience.[69] In contrast, Bruni had regarded the forum as the place for establishing one's full identity, as a place for deeds as opposed to behavior—deeds whose significance illumines the meaning of historical time.[70] Where Bruni asserted the higher standards demanded of the public *persona*, Poggio's tone is skeptical:

> Very often many private men judge more correctly of political affairs than those who rule. For not all whom we have seen ordained to dominion or office have been wise; and yet their opinions, no matter how pernicious and rash, are accepted as valid.[71]

[68] *Prefatio, De viris illustribus,* in de Nolhac, *Le "De viris illustribus,"* p. 56.

[69] Poggio was capable of several rhetorical stances on this issue: early in his career he refers to his secretarial post at the Curia as a life of slavery in letters to Niccoli (*Epistolae,* I, 72; cf. I, 46-47, 49, 59). In Florence at the end of his life, however, we find his new environment at fault, and he regrets leaving the Curia (*Epistolae,* III, 252, 257).

[70] See also Alberti, *I primi tre libri della famiglia,* ed. F. Pellegrini, Florence, 1946, p. 11. There is a perceptive discussion of the difference between the Classical goal of development of character and the Mannerist purpose of developing personality in Hocke, *Die Welt als Labyrinth,* p. 221.

[71] "Multi privati viri persaepe rectius sentiunt de republica quam qui illi praesunt. Non enim omnes, quos in magistratu aut dominio vidimus constitutos, sapientes fuerunt: et tamen eorum sententiae, quamvis pernitiosae atque inconsultae, ratae habentur." *Epistolae,* II, 24.

For Bruni as for the Greeks the organization of the polis is a kind of organized remembrance, and thus in the writing of history the natural categories of meaning were the political units, the city-states.[72] But Poggio advises Cosimo to fall back upon his private memories of his former good intentions as the only source of stability and tranquillity of mind (*Epistolae*, II, 39f.); the failure of Italian politics, of the dialogue of excellence, reduces Cosimo to the enjoyment of a *monologue intérieur*.

"The public" is both subject-matter and audience to Bruni and Poggio; yet the two authors address virtually the same audience as if it existed in two very different kinds of public space. They share and dispense the same classical models of political and military virtue, but for Poggio in the contemporary context the Florentines' military expertise is laughable, and their counsel of ill-effect—so that "when the accumulated wisdom of many is gathered into one it becomes the highest folly." Whatever their individual astuteness in business affairs (*in domesticis rebus*), in the public sphere it is either confounded or forgotten (*Epistolae*, I, 335-36).[73] For Poggio politics was the sphere of compulsion, not completion; in public life, he tells Cosimo, there had been a necessity of indulging in much "*propter voluntatem, ne dicam aequitatem, plura simulanda ac dissimulanda*" (*Epistolae*, II, 42). Freedom of choice actually ceases when one commits oneself to public debate and public action; he advises caution to the Cardinal St. Angelo in his difficult negotiations at the Council of Basle—

> For the beginnings of public affairs are within our power, since up to this point the faculty of deliberating and consulting remains ours; but truly, after the affair

[72] Arendt, *Between Past and Future*, p. 71f.

[73] "Saepius admiratus sum, non mecum solum, sed aliis cum plurimis, unde id contigat, cum multi prudentes, docti, ac perspicaces in nostra Civitate versentur, quorum singulatim lauderes ingenii acumen, et consilii gravitatem, tamen tam male rempublicam administrari, et sententias deteriores praeponi utilioribus, ut multorum accumulata in unum sapientia, in summam stultitiam convertatur." The letter to Niccoli attacks the war on Lucca (1430).

has once been put in motion, Fortune, the ruler of human affairs, adjudicates the coming and going, and Fortune proceeds, according to Sallust, more according to will than reason. For when you have not yet started to move forward, it is still in your power to stop where you will. We are able to discuss how we may save the ship, as long as we remain in port; when, however, you commit yourself to the winds, then it is necessary to submit unwillingly to their turbulent strength. Thus they oblige the captain either to wreck his ship or go submissively wherever they will.[74]

The voluntarist cast of mind of rhetoric reinforces the voluntarist emphasis of Poggio's historical insights; his harsh experience of deceit, hypocrisy, and faithlessness give constant examples of reason confounded by the will, of the feebleness of the intellect except in private experience. In politics force and violence is of more weight than rationality and legality: "For all that is brilliant and memorable originates in injury and injustice, in defiance of the laws" (*Historia tripartita II, Opera,* I, 49).[75] Power corrupts: "like the fire which burns or consumes whatever it touches, *imperium,* whatever it seizes, it renders evil, or at any rate less good" (*De infelicitate, Opera,* I, 398). Like Sallust, Poggio is fascinated by the "psychology of ambition and violence," and like Sallust, he is intrigued by the "mixed character," by the intertwining of virtue and vice.[76]

[74] "Nam principia rerum agendarum in nostro arbitrio sita sunt, cum adhuc re integra deliberandi et consulendi facultas datur; ubi vero negotium coeptum est, rerum humanarum imperatrix fortuna eventum exitumque dijudicat, ac metitur magis ex libidine, ut inquit Sallustius, quam ex ratione, neque enim cum prolabi coeperis, non in tua est potestate ubi velis consistere. Nostrum est discutere in portu consistentes, an navem solvamus; cum autem te ventis commiseris, etiam invito, est eorum turbini ac viribus obtemperandum, ut vel naufragium facere gubernator, quamvis optimus, cogatur, vel quo venti ducant non repugnantem proficisci." *Epistolae,* II, 53.

[75] Cited in Garin's *Italian Humanism,* p. 34; compare Walser, *Leben und Werke,* notes 3 and 4, p. 256; p. 258.

[76] Syme, *Sallust,* p. 269. Poggio speaks of vice hidden by a veil of virtue, by a net of lying praise (*Epistolae,* II, 132, 366); however, to

A cynicism relative to legal deliberation similar to that displayed in Aristotle's *Rhetoric,* with its anatomy of *Realpolitik,* qualifies rationalist idealism; in his comparison of medicine and law, law as a substantial reality opposes law as an empty form manipulated in power struggles; law as idealist statement, one argument runs, is an impediment to empire (*Opera,* I, 49). Areas optimistically assumed to be areas of free choice turn out to be grossly limited by the nature of men and their governments; tyrants are those "with whom will rather than reason, force rather than law prevails" (*H.F.,* c. 279); *cupiditas dominandi* is behind all the unhappy effects of political relations with tyrants (*H.F.,* c. 252; cf. *Epistolae,* II, 179f.). According to Tateo, it is exactly this sense of the incapacity for political dialectic, the uselessness of law which adumbrates Poggio's "brilliant, materialistic vision of history."[77] The failure of contemporary Florentine politics Poggio connects directly with a failure in will, in *caritas patriae;* he contrasts the different temper which motivated Florence in the struggle with Gian Galeazzo, when enormous imposts were readily granted, with the deficient patriotism and deficient policy of current events (*H.F.,* c. 282; cf. *Epistolae,* I, 334f.).

Poggio's rhetorically schooled sensitivity to limitation of will and choice seems to underline an emphasis on dilemma, on difficult choice. But the peculiarly historical choice is the difficult choice; that in so far as truth is immersed in the ceaseless flow of circumstance and expression it becomes obscure and hard to discern, is the historicist insight which

---

join the chorus is not wrong: "quibus in rebus si modum excessi, morem tamen priscorum virorum eloquentium sum secutus, neque in eo, ut videor, culpam recognosco" (*Epistolae,* II, 367). Recall Syme's description: "Sallust falls into place in a recognizable tradition of historiography, linking Thucydides and Tacitus. He belongs to the company of searching and subversive writers, preoccupied with power and the play of chance in human affairs, finding their delectation in disillusionment" (p. 256).

[77] "Il dialogo 'realistico'," p. 270.

most impinges on ethics.[78] The single most illustrious decision of Cosimo's career for Poggio was his decision to obey the Florentine Magistrates peacefully, patently unjust as their action was (*Epistolae*, II, 45-46). In his letter to Gian Francesco Gonzaga concerning the proper punishment of his rebellious son he rather sanctimoniously discusses the difficulty of regulating conduct to contingent circumstance (*Epistolae*, II, 131f.).

Even the form of Poggio's Florentine history reflects this negative tone; for Poggio the model which dominates political process was pejorative eristic, not creative dialectic. Where Bruni attempted to express the dialectical movement of Italian politics in his great antilogies, Poggio almost without exception forsook the antilogy for the single partisan speech. And even in the few antilogies he retained, as well as in the single speeches, Poggio displays his conviction of the atrophy of debate in reducing the arguments to generalities and ignoring the positions of genuine confrontation specified by Bruni.

Consider Poggio's and Bruni's versions of the speech by the Florentine legates to Gregory XI regarding the crisis in Florentine-papal relations of 1375 (*RIS* XX, c. 229-33; XIX, iii, 211-14). Both are very long speeches, indicating the importance of the debate for both Poggio and Bruni; but where Bruni typically makes his account into a confrontation, where the Florentine's speech is but one part of an antilogy with the Pope, Poggio contents himself with an eloquent defense of the republican political principles to be found elsewhere in his canon. Both Poggio and Bruni discuss the Florentine grievances—that Florence, beset by famine, asked the papal legate for grain, and the legate not only rejected their request, but sent Hawkwood's mercenaries to lay waste the new crops, a blow that was only parried by a

---

[78] Gallie describes very well one of Poggio's major emphases when he states that "it is quite a common situation in history for a succession of events to be followable only as a succession of misunderstandings or errors," *Philosophy and the Historical Understanding*, p. 86.

large ransom—but where Bruni discusses these events as ingredients of two conflicting political policies, Poggio launches directly into a denunciation of churchmen who would behave so unmercifully to Christians. Where Bruni begins the speech by plunging abruptly into the Florentine version of the basic political situation, into a description of the ambitious and avaricious attempts at tyranny on the part of the legates as the cause of the rebelliousness of the cities of the Papal States, Poggio devotes the first quarter of his speech to a discussion of the nature of the political liberty which was the core of Florentine motivation. Both make the point that Florence was defending itself against the pride and *cupiditas dominandi* of the legates, and that Florence did not wish to attack the papacy, or the church, or religion. But where Bruni grasps the opportunity to give a long and detailed résumé of Florence's loyal Guelph policy, Poggio simply mentions it in a brief sentence. Strangely Poggio gives the impression of prolixity, Bruni of pungent condensation; the republican principles of Bruni and Poggio may be the same, but Bruni deftly relates them always to concrete policy, his statements of principle narrate events, while Poggio treats them as detached propositions, occasions for words.[79]

If the model for political interaction is eristic rather than fruitful dialogue, then in reaction political stability becomes the goal. The antinomies are rhetorically expressed as black and white, the choices become absolute choices, with all the persuasive force exerted to reject the dynamism which had been a most engaging trait of Bruni's civic Humanism. If Bruni can see faction only as an evil influence in the generally positive process which constructed the Florentine state, and if Machiavelli can apprehend party as a healthy factor which engenders a truly dynamic political situation, Poggio turns finally to Venice as the model of a static, and therefore desirable, body politic which contrasts favorably with turbulent Florence (*Epistolae*, III, 261, 271). Toward the close of his life, Poggio considered removing to Venice

[79] See Santini, *L.B.A. e i suoi "Historiarum . . . libri,"* chap. 7.

to write the standard Humanist history of the Venetians;
the charm and attraction of Venice for him, according to
the encomium dated 1459, lay in its stable, perfect harmony;
in Venice

> There is no discord among those who administer public
> affairs, no dissension; no civil contentions, no factions, no
> jealous contests, no open hatred; individuals all think alike
> and all concur in spirit in regard to the public safety. . . .
> Thus diversity of opinion is brought back to concord, and
> not prolonged by compact or civil conspiracy. For by this
> agreement you could say all are made one in mind, will,
> spirit, and counsel.[80]

In contrast to the deplorable motility of the neighboring
states, the ideal Venetian order is not dynamic *libertas* but
static *justitia*:

> . . . and this is to be praised most, that their laws are
> firm and stable and the public utility has underwritten
> them to a great age. For neither are they abrogated by the
> desire of a private citizen nor do they vary from day to
> day, but they are preserved as by a perpetual sanction.[81]

In sum, Poggio takes pains to develop a negative concept
of *libertas* both in politics and discourse: the state becomes
merely the outward condition for internal peace, *"ut in libertate nostra cum ocio et in dignitate vivamus"* (*Epistolae*, II,

---

[80] "Nullae inter ipsos administranda re publica discordiae, nulla dis-
sensio, nullae civium contentiones, nullae factiones, nullae simultates,
nulla aperta odia: idem sentiunt singuli unoque omnes animo ad rei
publicae salutatem concurrunt . . . ita diversitas opinionum in con-
cordiam redacta, nulla pactione aut conspiratione civium retractatur.
Hoc pacto unam omnium mentem, unam voluntatem, unum animum,
unicum consilium diceres extitisse." *In laudem rei publicae Venetorum*,
Opera, III, 928, 933.

[81] "Id praecipue maxime laude extollendum, quod eorum leges firmae
sunt, stabiles longaevaeque, quoad rei publicae utilitas ferat, neque
pro voluntate cuiusquam abrogantur neque variantur in diem, sed per-
petua sanctione custodiuntur." *In laudem rei publicae Venetorum*,
Opera, III, 931; cf. *Opera*, II, 929, 933, 936-37.

186);[82] at the same time, the phrase *libertas dicendi* often distinguishes not the intellectual freedom of Athens or republican Rome, but dishonorable license (*Epistolae*, I, 181, 359; II, 53).

If Poggio's specific insights into historical experience are negative and pessimistic in tone, his general posture and mode of attack have some positive aspects; there is a kind of sophistication in the sense of a type of awareness, of acknowledgment of divergence and disparity and conflict which, in so far as it helps to define the truly operational spheres of human will and consent, leads to historical realism, not cynicism. This sophistication is intimately related to the flexibility of rhetorical methods; the use of the categories of "games" and *topoi* contributes to two modes of apprehension: a sensitivity to ambiguity and a modesty; these in turn permit or encourage the perception and expression of ethical–historical conflicts.

Poggio uses the words *ludus* and *theatrum* continually to express his sense of the coexistence of separate but internally coherent areas of human discourse and action. And his notions of these games is in great measure founded on the rhetorical-linguistic principles which acknowledge a large number of types of discourse, insist upon the decorum or coherence of the rules of each type of discourse, and predicate the relative validity of the functions of these kinds of discourse.[83] His rhetorical presuppositions allow him, in other words, to fill a time-worn image with critically ascertained experience; thus, for example, the faithlessness of tyrants

[82] See *De varietate*, *Opera*, II, 587-88; cf. Weise, *L'ideale eroico del Rinascimento*, Vol. 1, p. 31; Varese, *Storia e politica*, p. 147.

[83] A similar connection of rhetoric and the game *topos* seems to be involved in the discussions of the relation of rhetorical moments to Baroque style. For example, Huizinga sees the devotion to games at the center of the highly rhetorical Baroque style; he also sees game-playing as an outstanding characteristic of the highly rhetorical literature of the fifteenth century. See Huizinga, *Waning of the Middle Ages*, pp. 134, 238, 329; *Homo Ludens*, Boston, 1962, p. 182f.: J. Rousset, *La littérature de l'âge baroque en France*; *Circé et le Paon*, Paris, 1954; and the Italian symposium *Retorica e Barocco*, ed. E. Castelli, Rome, 1955.

becomes a definite type of discourse with rules, coherence, purpose of its own. In the Florentine history Poggio has Ricci attack Gian Galeazzo by asking his audience

> Why do we think we need further experience of his faith, since none is to be found in his letters, or words, or ambassadors? For his game is now to deceive us by fraud and perfidy.[84]

Later he has the Florentine Valori attack Filippo Visconti as one

> . . . who has been engaged in this game since adolescence and who has learned nothing but the rules for deceiving; not what he says, but what he does, not what he speaks, but what he has in view, not what he brings forward, but what he guards, is to be regarded.[85]

This contrived disparity between deeds and words, between public persuasion and private intent, is the condition of decadent politics and the assumption of historical analysis (*De varietate, Opera,* III, 597; *H.F.,* c. 205).

Poggio thus evolves the concept of politics as a difficult and dangerous game: public life becomes the *ludus fortunae* (*De varietate, Opera,* III, 504, 580, 605), the *fortunae theatrum* (*De varietate, Opera,* III, 504, 580, 587, 602). Descending into the theater of fortune is like entering a battle; one must abide by its rules; submission to its conditions is the only course.[86] If private interest compels the ty-

[84] "Quid fidem ejus amplius experiundam ducimus, quae nulla neque litteris, neque verbis, neque Oratoribus est habenda? Ludus iam est ei dolis, et perfidia nos fallere." *H.F.,* c. 253.

[85] ". . . qui in eo ludo ab adolescentia versatus nullas, nisi decipiendi leges didicerit: non quid dicat, sed quid agat, non quid loquatur, sed quo spectet, non quid offerat, sed quid observet, est animo advertendum." *H.F.,* c. 326.

[86] Thus Poggio points out in the *De varietate, Opera,* II, 587, that Sallust's advice should lead one to recognize that "maximam esse hominum dementiam, qui cum ipsis fere manibus comprehendant, in hoc tam celebri fortunae theatro, tam frequentes ejus mutationes, tam varios rerum casus, tamen proni caecique, et veluti inermes ad hoc tam durum certamen descendunt, relictis veris animi bonis, in quibus nullum possidet ius fortuna."

rant to dissemble, interests of state compel the magistrate
into lawlessness; in either political situation one commits
oneself to a venture in which the fortuitous and irrational
prevail. Kings cannot be wise men, and therefore happy men,
because they are nothing but dressed-up actors playing out
their particular game (*De infelicitate, Opera,* I, 404); they
take parts, moreover, in a tragedy rather than a comedy:

> For the life of a prince can be thought of as a kind of
> tragedy full of calamity, which can be broken up into
> many acts in order to represent as in a theater their in-
> felicity.[87]

In contrast, the forced exile of Cosimo de' Medici from the
theatrum fortunae offers him a *palaestra fortuita* in which
to display his true virtue: the *studia humanitatis* proffer a
game which one can actually win:

> Since, therefore, you would have a certain and impreg-
> nable seat in which your mind can find rest, a type of
> spacious theater of virtue and good conscience. . . .[88]

The emphasis is always on the artificiality and self-contain-
ment of these separate games. Just as Aristotle had warned
long before that one must recognize that politics has to do
with expediency, not justice, and the law with justice, not
honor, so Valla warns in the *De voluptate* not to depend
on the virtue *honestas* as the basis of politics, since the root
of *honestas* is *honor,* and the desire for public fame or honor
is generically a private goal, and, therefore, the game which
can be derived from it is a private, not a public, game
(*Opera,* I, 946). Poggio has a dismayed consciousness that
our words rarely escape their particular games or spheres;
at the same time, he hesitates to pass moral judgments on
certain manipulations of words simply because they do not

---

[87] "Constat enim vitam principum tragoediam quamdam esse cala-
mitatum plenam, ex qua multi actus confici possent, ad repraesentandam
tanquam in theatro eorum infelicitatem." *De infelicitate, Opera,* I, 416.

[88] "Cum igitur habeas veluti certam atque inconcussam sedem in
qua tua mens possit consistere, ingens videlicet virtutis et conscientiae
theatrum . . . ," *De infelicitate, Opera,* I, 314; cf. *Epistolae,* II, 41.

correspond to empirical reality. In the *Contra hypocritas* he echoes the Sophists' positive statements about deception (*apate*) when he allows his protagonist to maintain that not all simulation or figure is bad, but only that which relates to fraudulent deception (*Opera*, II, 52).[89] Recall that in the dispute with Guarino over the relative merits of Caesar and Scipio, he both chides Guarino for being so naive as not to recognize the encomiastic game being played in Cicero's praise of Caesar, and excuses Cicero for his exaggerations. Guarino's rhetorical training should have taught him what pertains to the rhetorical genre of epideictic, what is due to the compulsion of time and place. All verbal expressions have a time dimension, then; rhetorical criticism should discover it, should answer the question, what did the decorum of the situation demand? All questions of meaning, intention, originality relate to the problem of placing the statement in time. Cicero had to praise Caesar, *"non protulit veritas, sed temporum necessitas extorsit"* (*Ad Scipioni Ferrariensi, Opera*, I, 360).[90]

Rhetorical decorum functioning as the historical canon of internal coherence thus has an ethical as well as an aesthetic dimension; the discovery of two or more meanings to a text engenders a certain sophistication about levels of meaning in discourse. Historical criticism is not only a matter of grammatical accuracy, but of knowing what, under the circumstances, the author intended at the moment of writing, and how this contradicted or agreed with the general tenor of his life. The basic imperative is that distinctions must be carefully drawn: Poggio uses Themistocles as an example of an historical figure in whom one must distinguish between the pressures of society and of the private needs of the individual, or between the force of principle and the pressure of custom (*De nobilitate, Opera*, I, 77). Rhetorical analysis

[89] Compare Segal, "Gorgias and the Psychology of the Logos," p. 114.

[90] Similarly, in the "Oratio ad summum pontificem Nicolaum V" Poggio refers first to a dictum from Aristotle's *Rhetoric* that to praise the living is the work of adulation, and then to Cicero's praise of Caesar as an exception, since, "non hominis, sed causae et temporum fuit oratio." *Opera*, I, 288; cf. *Epistolae*, II, 365.

describes the complex activity of the "I" of the author of the text; here not the unity of the ego but the conflicts within the ego are the point. Some of Aristotle's writings show him compelled to express common opinion, rather than independently arrived-at truth; one of his definitions, Poggio has Niccoli claim, does not stem *"ex animi iudicio, sed ex communi opinione"* (*De nobilitate, Opera*, I, 74; cf. 77).

Further, the ethical dimension of decorum has another aspect; rhetorical emphasis on language is on the social use of language, on the relation of text to contemporaneous ambiance and previous tradition, an ambiance and tradition by definition shared. Poggio almost paraphrases the dictum from that rhetorical hotbed, Horace's *Ars poetica*, already quoted by Petrarch: *"Usus arbitrium est et ius et norma loquendi."*

> The propriety, strength, meaning of Latin words are construed not so much from rules as from the authority of former writers. Take this away and the foundation of the Latin language is undermined. For use alone was always master in Latin discourse, and usage is to be found only in the books and other writings of early authors.[91]

From decorum proceeds a functional view of language which allows the Humanist to make new kinds of distinctions. Just as the Humanist concept of *imitatio* stresses imitation of prior human expression, rather than of an object-nature, so in the Humanist concept of usage truth is social veracity, a truth which is opposed to lie, rather than to objective wrongness as in mathematics or logic. Any historical decision and thus any historiographical decision is an ethical decision, which accounts in part for the bitter personal nature of the Humanists' philological invectives.

---

[91] "Latinorum verborum proprietas, vis, significatio, constructio non tantum ratione, quantum veterum scriptorum autoritate constant. Qua sublata latinae linguae fundamentum et sustentaculum pereat necesse est. Latine loquendi usus semper fuit magister, qui solum autorum priscorum libris et scriptis continetur." *Invectiva in Vallam I, Opera*, I, 203. The passage from the *Ars poetica*, 70-72, is quoted by Petrarch in the *Invective contra medicum*, III, *Prose*, p. 656.

Yet, if they wish, the Humanists may coolly effect a disjunction of personalities and arguments (*Epistolae*, II, 75). The literary process of writing history then becomes itself a complex game; historiography is a game which can be played only by trained linguists who understand, for example, in the case of Roman history the rules of the Latin genres, and who also realize that the rules of the historiographical game bar fiction.[92] Poggio makes clear at the beginning of his letter to Francesco Barbaro that the black-white invective against Caesar addressed to Scipio of Ferrara was a game *"exercendi ingenii causa"* (*Opera*, I, 365; cf. *Epistolae*, II, 9f.). Yet he also makes clear that within the rules of each game one can win or lose. Challenged to discuss the historical Scipio and Caesar, he proceeds to qualify his oversimplified polemic, and to acknowledge the complexity of the subject once it is broadened to a historical project. But if once a definition is arrived at, if glory is conceded to consist only in the good report of good men, the facts are all on his side, and it is necessary to distort language to rule otherwise (*Opera*, I, 367f.).

In order to find out what the real significance of a document is, one must, through one's knowledge of the rhetorical rules and canons employed, reconstruct the process of writing. Poggio returns to an old argument of the Humanist treatises on law when he points out that comprehension is a matter of critical acumen, not of uncritical reading of masses of books as in the usual practice of law where

> There is no perspicuity, where the things to be learned do not require any acumen of mind, but only memory of texts and interminable reading of commentaries, which indeed are so contradictory that they seem not so much the opinions of counsel, as the idle words of dreamers.[93]

---

[92] Thus Poggio condemns Panormita for playing the wrong game: you, he accuses, who have taken the noble Brutus and "eum levem et lusorium in quadam vili scena inter actores ponas et mimos," *Epistolae*, I, 182.

[93] "Nulla perspicuitas, ad quae perdiscenda non ingenii acumen aliquod requiritur, sed scriptarum rerum memoria, et inextricabilis com-

The Humanist thus can actively entertain either the co-existence or historical succession of different games, as well as the completeness and coherence of each single game in itself. This produces a "bracketing" faculty which allows, for example, Poggio to accept Gian Galeazzo's virtuosity in two separate areas of discourse—the expedient deceitfulness of tyrants and the intelligent literary patronage of monarchs.

It was blameable in him that, allegedly, he kept faith and promises for expedient reasons, a vice he holds in common with many outstanding military leaders; yet the virtue of his more worthy of praise than all the rest was that he summoned to his court those men distinguished in all the arts and sciences, so that he made it a haven for outstanding men, whom he held in the highest honor.[94]

It is this predication of simultaneous detachment and co-existence which is essential to a historicist toleration of historical ambiguity. Through rhetorical-philological disciplines the Humanist can critically establish the vertical and horizontal discontinuity of human experience: the same person or age can indulge in radically different games and successive ages can employ typical languages, names for deeds. At times a certain constellation of events seems to demand a specific genre: it is difficult, Poggio writes in his old age, not to write satire in so great a perturbation of affairs (*Epistolae*, III, 216); later he remarks that only tragedy could encompass the occasion (*Epistolae*, III, 268). Like Quattrocento paint-

---

mentariorum lectio, quae sibi invicem ita aliquando repugnat in suis sententiis, ut non responsa prudentum, sed somniantium voces esse videantur." *Historia tripartita II, Opera*, I, 43. Where Poggio fails in perspicuity, however, is in apprehending certain aspects of the effect these games or spheres of discourse exert on the social-political ambiance; thus he totally fails to understand Valla's connection between Roman language and *Romanitas* (*Invectiva in Vallam I, Opera*, I, 195).

[94] "Id eo culpatur, quod fidem, et promissa ex utilitate traditus servasse, quod vitium commune cum multis egregiis bello ducibus fuit, sed ea laudanda prae ceteris est virtus, quod omnium doctrinarum, artiumque viros eximios, ad se, tamque egregiorum hominum receptaculum vocavit, summoque in honore habuit." *H.F.*, c. 290-91.

ing, Humanist rhetoric employs a plurality of perspectives; for the fifteenth century objectivity is a matter of illuminating, not eliminating perspectives.[95] The tendency in Poggio is away from a naive and notional grasp of ethics; the idea of spheres and jurisdictions of meaning implies a complex and fluid relationship between one kind of choice and another, and thus limitation of choice. Poggio's admiration of Cosimo de' Medici is in part an appreciation of one who understands the partial, alternating, overlapping hegemonies of ethical and political choice.

Historical method does not predicate a slave will, but detects the limitations of free will. In rhetoric, it is always a combination of attitudes which produces technique; thus the principles of detachment and decorum combine in the technique which evaluates the difficult freedom of a plenitude of meanings and games, and in the strict limitation of fortunate choice to what is appropriate, decorous. A focus on games is a focus on internally generated meanings, on meanings derived from the particular structures of interrelationships.[96] Rhetorical detection of linguistic complexity becomes a continuous discovery of the "victorious resistance of the real" in situations of choice, and liberates in so far as it confronts the real.[97] Poggio's emphasis is on the facticity and continuity of unhappy choice; in the defense of avarice which he attributes to Antonio Luschi the conflict of private and public interest is *"ab ipsius orbis ortu factitatum"*

[95] See P. Francastel, *Peinture et société; Naissance et destruction d'un espace plastique*, Lyon, 1951; Francastel demonstrates that there is no one dominant notion of perspective, that many systems of representation of space can be found in the *oeuvre* of fifteenth-century artists. Recall Ramnoux's point that a major insight of the Sophists was that the world not only alters, but has as many perspectives as there are centers of vision ("Nouvelle réhabilitation," p. 8).

[96] "L'entendement historien . . . forme une vérité 'objective' dans la mesure où il construit et où l'objet n'est qu'un élément dans une représentation cohérente, que peut être indéfiniment rectifiée, precisée, mais ne se confond jamais avec la chose même." Merleau-Ponty, *Les aventures de la dialectique*, p. 16.

[97] The phrase is from E. Auerbach's "Hôtel de la Mole," *Mimesis*, New York, 1957, p. 412.

(*Opera,* I, 16). There are injunctions to Stoic withdrawal scattered through a wide range of classical, medieval, and Renaissance literature, but there are different conditions under which Stoic formulas are expressed; Poggio's moral-historical treatises possess an awareness of attempt and failure missing in less sophisticated didactic literature.

But if identity is the negation of inadequate existence,[98] inclusiveness, even pessimistic inclusiveness, is a characteristic of liberal study. And Poggio's pessimism is inclusive; it does not have the ascetic narrowness and fearfulness of the bourgeois didactic literature common in the fourteenth and fifteenth centuries.[99] The ethical pessimism of the *De avaritia* is based on an appreciation of the naturalness and fullness of historical life; Poggio is arguing for the recognition of this fullness when he has Luschi claim that *"vita mortalium non est exigenda nobis ad stateram philosophiae"* (*Opera,* I, 16).[100] The Humanists' rhetorical interests, then, conduce to a richer, more inclusive, more heavily-textured sense of ethical choice in history; sophistication is a dependable awareness of conflict through analytic habits. As ethics is related to a grasp of conflict and ambiguity, so history is related to a grasp of the sanctions and possibilities of time. Rhetoric, however, necessarily underscores a grasp of conflict in time. Rhetoric presupposes a dialogue or debate which is a continuity; through its peculiar focus on the techniques of victory it defines the spatio-temporal boundaries of liberty, and through its continuous measuring and comparing, it refines a sense of relativity.

Once again, the philosophy of Nicholas of Cusa may perhaps order and clarify Renaissance Humanist experience. For

[98] Marcuse, "The Actuality of Dialectic," *Diogenes,* 31 (1960), p. 82.
[99] A brief description of this literature is in Seidlmayer, *Currents of Medieval Thought,* trans. D. Barker, Oxford, 1960, chap. 4. Humanists such as Poggio seem to elude both the late medieval and the modern categories of "bourgeois public" defined by Habermas, *Strukturwandel der Öffentlichkeit,* p. 11f.
[100] Tateo maintains that it is exactly Poggio's pessimism, skepticism which becomes a motive and a preparation for his scrutiny and description of the world in all its variety ("Il dialogo 'realistico,'" p. 275).

Cusanus thinking is a form of symbolic measurement; the mind (*mens*) comes from measuring (*mensurando*), and the mind "*mensurat etiam symbolice, comparationis modo.*"[101] Consider the use of rhetorical *inventio*: the *topoi* which prevail in Humanist works are those of comparison and contrast, they function as a flexible armature, not as a simple *aide-mémoire*. The Renaissance *episteme* which M. Foucault describes is dominated by the modes of "representing"—by analogy, sympathy, emulation, *convenientia*; it is a way of knowing informed by a sensitivity to relationship.[102] Cusanus' metaphor of man the map-maker is most illuminating of Renaissance attitudes: while God is the creator of the world, man is the cosmographer; man may share certain physical attributes with other living creatures, but only man can map the contours and the relationships of these attributes.[103] Further, the Cusan emphasis on the mind as a *living* measure is significant;[104] here Cusa points to a fundamental characteristic shared by linguistic changes of Northern philosophy as well as Humanist rhetoric of the fourteenth and fifteenth centuries; if the universal is an activity of the mind, not an entity, the *topos* always remains a choice, a heuristic tool. On the other hand, rhetoric encourages an idiosyncratic development in Italian culture. Where in

[101] *De mente*, ed. L. Baur, *Opera omnia*, Vol. 5, Leipzig, 1937, chap. 1, p. 48; chap. 9, p. 90.

[102] Foucault, "La prose du monde," *Les mots et les choses*, Paris, 1966, chap. 2, p. 32f. Compare Francastel, *Peinture et société*, p. 18f., who describes Brunelleschi as changing architecture from the manipulation of masses to the development of a system of relations of proportion and number.

[103] *Compendium*, ed. B. Decker, C. Bormann, *Opera omnia*, Vol. 11³, Hamburg, 1964, chap. 8, pp. 18-19. Here again this epistemological priority of relationships presents an analogue with modern Structuralism: G. Lantéri-Laura, in "Histoire et structure dans la connaissance de l'homme," *Annales, ESC*, 22² (1967), p. 792f., points out that an essential structuralist hypothesis is that the autonomy of the fabric of reciprocal relationships from any given substratum, any substantive base is a priority.

[104] *De mente*, chap. 9, p. 89; see also chap. 5, p. 65: "unde, cum omnium exemplar in mente ut veritas in imagine reluceat, in se habet ad quod respicit, secundum quod iudicium de exterioribus facit; ac si lex scripta foret viva, illa, quia viva, in se iudicandi legeret."

Northern Renaissance art details, the "busy little things,"[105] are really passive vessels charged with a metaphysical pathos, the rhetorical *topoi* organize details argumentatively, with the ulterior purpose of serving the rhetor's turn. The *exemplum* in medieval literature had not the humble status of fact, but, as Panofsky tells us, a quasi-religious prescriptive status as traditional material.[106] Still, both Northern Conceptualist and Italian Humanist reject such confusion where both words and things are magic names and concentrate on mapping the distortions of language; both assume the self-imposed task of adjusting two infinities to each other: the possibilities of language and the possibilities of behavior. An awareness of the difficulty of this task, and the aggressive artificiality of Humanist rhetorical linguistic actually permits the development of autonomous critical methods and refines, if it does not strengthen, the ethical posture of the historian.

One of the sources of critical autonomy, then, is the *comparative* nature of rhetorical method. Aristotle in his *Rhetoric* devotes a great deal of space to establishing notions of relative goodness and badness within the wide range of subjects covered by the three genres of oratory (1359a; 1363b f.). If the rhetorician's technique is a facility in making the strong seem weak and the weak strong, a sense of relativity must be the basis of choice. In the deliberative and judicial vein the rhetorician constantly compares the long and short range views, principle and decorum, nature and custom. Take, for example, the structure of the argument of Poggio's dialogue *De nobilitate*: he puts forward a large number of contemporary and classical views of nobility of many different states and societies, barbarian as well as civilized. His protagonist Niccoli looks everywhere for an immutable principle, but concludes that no such principle can be found in these socially conditioned ideas of nobility:

> But these species of nobility which I have explicated just now so vary among themselves, are so contrary and

---

[105] Panofsky, "Albrecht Dürer and Classical Antiquity," p. 244.
[106] Panofsky, "Dürer," p. 277.

diverse, that they seem to manifest no certain root, no obvious genus which relies in any way on reason, but they seem on the contrary to be produced by opinion alone, or by a certain arbitrariness, of which no true cause is able to be discerned.[107]

The relativity becomes the point: a comparative historical view reveals the non-existence of universal social values:

> This variety is so great and so widespread that it persuades me that this nobility of yours, beyond being a certain pomp and empty pride, is nothing but a fabrication of the folly and diversity of men.[108]

But Poggio also tempers his audience's acceptance of Niccoli's own principle of nobility by making them conscious that such a principle has never been and will never be accepted widely in reality; at the same time he makes clear that the type of social consensus which masquerades as a universal is nothing but an illegitimate generalization from particular experience; he literally, or rhetorically, forces his modesty on his readers.

There is still another facet of this modesty: rhetoric and history share not only the obvious purpose of relating particular deeds to general patterns of behavior, but also the lack of rigor with which they employ patterns and models.[109] Poggio's *topoi* are hollow carapaces which can be shifted at will to cover new areas of experience, for the characteristic of the rhetorical *locus communis* is that it is open-ended,

---

[107] "At istae quas modo explicavi nobilium species ita inter se variantur contrariae ac diversae, ut nullam certam stirpem, nullum certum genus praeferant quod ratione aliqua nitatur, sed a sola opinione institutoque quodam voluntario, cuius nulla vera causa reddi possit videntur prodire." *Opera*, I, 70; cf. 66.

[108] "Haec igitur tanta tamque pervagata rerum varietas mihi persuadet, nihil hanc vestram nobilitatem esse praeter pompam quandam ac inanem fastum ab stulticia hominum et vanitate confictum." *Opera*, I, 72.

[109] Thus in Cortesi's *De hominibus doctis*, p. 23, the lack of rigor appears as a lack of rules: Antonio has called history the most difficult of tasks, Alessandro marvels that history, with all its complexity, owns no set of precepts, no traditional "art" by which it can be taught.

it can be made to refer to an indefinite and fluctuating extent of experience.[110] Consider the use of "faith" by Poggio; he rarely employs the circumscribed religious and theological notions of faith; "good faith" includes all the instances of good intentions in the world of discourse and action. At the same time Fortune becomes a name for the inordinate complexity of the events which impinge on the human will; Fortune is not a cosmic necessity but a transparent shell focusing attention on the incoherence of the phenomena themselves, a mask for the existential. Just as N. Chomsky emphasizes the infinite potential of a finite grammar,[111] so the Humanist rhetoricians stressed that flexibility and creativity can also stem from the rules themselves, not just an attitude toward rules. The structure of rhetorical *topoi*, like the more advanced generation of computers, functions on the principle of random access: the rhetorician acknowledges that there are more reasons for using information or insights than for storing them in the first place. The purpose of rhetorical argumentative technique is to make fertile connections; it is knowledge *per comparatione*, but through a comparison of unstable units; it attempts to deal with disparate facets of intention and effect in continually changing relationships.

In Poggio's modest demeanor flexible structure and lack of rigor is in turn related to the conscious artificiality of rhetorical categories; to use rhetorical categories, which are manufactured, not pre-existing, is to deny certain metaphysical assumptions, to refuse epistemological metaphors such as positing a *deeper* layer, a truth *behind* phenomena, and at the same time to make ethical choice more real and immediate.[112] It is a matter of determining on what level one's categories

[110] Lausberg, *Handbuch der literarischen Rhetorik*, Section 407, note 1, points out that *communis* defining *locus* means "infinite."

[111] Chomsky, *Cartesian Linguistics*, p. 3f.

[112] P. Rossi, "La celebrazione della retorica e la polemica antimetafisica nel 'De principiis' di Mario Nizolio," in *La crisi dell'uso dogmatico della ragione*, ed. A. Banfi, Milan, 1953, pp. 99-121, discusses the self-conscious attack on metaphysical pretension by the sixteenth-century Ciceronian.

originate, at what level necessity occurs—before phenomena, in the phenomena themselves, or as freely attributed to the phenomena. Thus Poggio's rhetorical preoccupation with choice becomes a concern for the ethical rather than the ontological dimension of freedom and necessity; in historical terms, where the characteristic of truth is that it is endlessly *riproponibile*, it is not necessarily reproposed, it is always a product of ethical decision.[113] Rhetorical linguistic brings out the corporeal, rather than the abstract, nature of these restatements, and the imperative of apprehending these truths anew with each restatement; in the *De varietate fortunae* there is no feeling for the definitive event, the theological epitome which makes repetition of action or expression either ritualistic or unnecessary; truth must be created over and over again. Poggio's assessment of Jerome of Prague's historical significance is a case in point: through Poggio's isolation from logical and theological notions of truth as permanent essence he is able to "bracket off" Jerome's doctrinal vagaries; by means of rhetorical analysis of discourse he predicates the existence of insights in Jerome which the theological categories would deny. There is no ordained relationship between orthodoxy and eloquence; Poggio can accept the church's charge of heresy without letting it affect his judgment that Jerome expresses genuine religious feeling, and that such an expression has great meaning for his contemporaries.

Not from their more or less conventional religious lives, but primarily from their new intellectual allegiance, new language habits, comes the Humanists' ability to select humanistic causes, strain out theological imperatives. Their rhetorical modesty becomes historical modesty; in their relation of behavior to verbal rationalization they observe only a rhetorical

[113] Recall the passage from J. S. Mill's *On Liberty* where he argues "It is a piece of idle sentimentality that truth, merely as truth, has any inherent power denied to error, of prevailing against the dungeon and the stake. . . . The real advantage which truth has, consists in this: that when an opinion is true, it may be extinguished once, twice or many times, but in the course of ages there will generally be found persons to rediscover it . . . ," in the *Essential Works of J. S. Mill*, New York, 1961, p. 280.

decorum. The eclecticism built into rhetorical argumentative techniques results in some surprising connections: a heretic "worthy of eternal memory," a condemned enemy of the church who dies "like another Cato."[114] Rhetoric undermines the view of history which predicates hypostatized spiritual forces; it demands, rather, a sensitivity to the direction of force—to the *sens*, function of phenomena.[115]

Finally, from another member of the "set" of games, from the phenomenon of literary wit which is only indirectly connected with rhetoric, Humanists such as Poggio derive a kind of freedom which also has implications for historical consciousness. The sense of detachment which is so essential a part of the rhetorical mental mode, the lack of rigor and the conscious artificiality which characterize the use of rhetorical techniques combine to form a sort of negative capability, a playfulness which permits the entertainment of a new range of subject matter and of governing metaphor in the confrontation of past as well as of contemporaneous experience; here the focus is on the author as creator of the game, rather than on the content of the games.

For the rhetorician, qua rhetorician, has no necessary or secure position within a single ideology; in the Humanist rhetor we see the intellectual as hired hand, or at best, self-employed. Rhetorical vocation militates against the taking on of large metaphysical responsibilities. This social aimlessness, the shift to social opportunism is an element of the new social ideal developed most fully at the end of the fifteenth century in Giovanni Pontano's *De sermone*. This ideal, anticipated in Poggio's correspondence with Panormita, is not one of civic-mindedness, but of urbanity. But one of the chief ingredients of this urbanity is wit, and for a characterization of wit the humanists turn to a distinction derived ultimately from Cicero's *De officiis* between the urbane and illiberal wit:

[114] Letter to Bruni, in *Prosatori latini*, p. 238.
[115] Merleau-Ponty, *Les aventures de la dialectique*, p. 36.

For there are two genres of humor in all: the one illiberal, petulant, shameful, obscene; the other elegant, urbane, ingenious, facetious.[116]

This dictum Poggio paraphrases in his letter to Panormita defending his *Facetiae*: "*Diversae sunt genera iocandi, aliud liberum hominem, aliud servum decet, aliud facetum, aliud scurram*" (*Opera*, I, 355; cf. Valla, *Opera*, I, 236). And he counters Valla's attack on his work by claiming that the collection could not possibly please a man like Valla—"*inhumanus, rusticanus, barbarus*" (*Invectiva in Vallam* II, *Opera, I, 219*). And in the preface to the *Facetiae* he apologizes in advance for the contents by maintaining on the one hand that his collecting these jokes was merely a game, merely an exercise in eloquence and ingenuity, and on the other hand that to engage in such play in order to amuse, to raise people's spirits was honorable, "*honestum.*"[117]

It is the combination of the completely artificial with the artificially useful, the lack of any intrinsic merit whatsoever which is exhilarating. It is possible, of course, simply to note the realism of the *Facetiae* in so far as it deals with the lower classes and with everyday material, to see the anecdotes as expressing a kind of social candidness they share with the *novellae* of the fourteenth and fifteenth centuries and, indeed, with the satirical realism in general of the Italian vernacular associated with the development of the urban communities. For Walser the new subject matter marks a great literary advance; because it is seamy, it is realistic.[118] But in some ways Walser's approach is more indicative of twentieth-century tastes and contemporary historical consciousness,

---

[116] "Duplex omnino est jocandi genus. Unum illiberale petulans: flagitiosum: obscoenum; alterum elegans: urbanum: ingeniosum; facetum." I, 19, 104. On Renaissance theory of wit see Walser, *Die Theorie des Witzes und der Novelle nach dem "De sermone" des Jovianus Pontanus: Ein gesellschaftliches Ideal vom Ende des XV. Jahrhunderts*, Strassburg, 1908.

[117] *Opera*, I, 420; note also his equation of the facetious and the humane.

[118] *Die Theorie des Witzes*, p. 112.

than of fifteenth-century historical consciousness. For Poggio seaminess in itself is not edifying, but the ability to distinguish, and to make evident the distinction between social veracity and social lie is. This is urbanity and this is a matter of self-consciousness in literary identity; wit is not a vague matter of taste but a product of conscious orientation, of sharply-defined role. The detection of flummery in the *Facetiae* is of a piece with the constant marking out and inveighing against loss of faith in politics in Poggio's history, as well as with the kind of attack he mounts in his moral treatises against hypocrisy and delusion. And this ethical skill, the faculty of the truly urbane man to make the distinction between hypocrisy and truth wherever they originate, in any level of society, depends not on his scientific capacity as *collector omnium* but on his linguistic virtuosity; the *homo facetus* is marked by a formal capacity which has ethical as well as aesthetic implications.[119] The development of the free skeptical spirit with its surgical skill in separating out the established hypocrisies of society is here directly related to the development of literary humor and the disengagement and detachment it requires to transcend traditional categories and attitudes. This connection of liberality and formal competence is a vital ingredient in the development of the critical, as opposed to the dogmatic, use of reason.[120] Where Panofsky extolls the Italian Renaissance historical achievement as the reintegration of classical form with classical content, the rhetor-historians themselves, as they become

[119] Thus Vasoli points out that a review of Humanist pedagogical treatises demonstrates the prevalence of the expectations of control and mastery to be derived from rhetorical training, *L'estetíca*, p. 336; cf. Walser, *Die Theorie des Witzes*, p. 129.

[120] Banfi, "Osservazioni sull'uso critico della ragione," in *La crisi dell'uso dogmatico della ragione*, pp. 7-32. Francastel also ties formal competence to ethical sophistication: "Le grand effort du Quattrocento a été un effort de distinction. Il est évident que les peintres l'ont grandement aidé chaque fois qu'ils ont matérialisé une observation qui établissait l'existence matérielle ou morale soit d'un objet, soit d'une relation entre les choses, soit d'un événement anecdotique ou significatif emprunté au spectacle de la vie quotidienne," *Peinture et société*, p. 102.

more conscious of their mechanical separation of form and content, become more aware that their joining is also mechanical, that integration is simply a personal accomplishment.[121] The freely-choosing literary identity, adumbrated by Petrarch, defended by Salutati, delimits an area of critical responsibility. There is no need to assume the posture of an authority standing outside of time, since the transcendental significance they seek is always a product of their own temporal will.[122]

To summarize the positive values of this rhetorical sophistication: the problem of history is a problem of meaning; the purpose of historical criticism is to determine the temporal processes which create meaning. Since the assumption of the rhetorical concept of language is that all meaning is attributed, the explorations of rhetorical technique are investigations of historical process. Further, the essential prerequisite for criticism is a critic; rhetoric contributes to the destruction of the naive *persona* of the historian by requiring a certain level of consciousness of self-created meaning.

Then, rhetoric can also add a vital temporal dimension. First, the notion of continuity in change is central to historical consciousness: rhetorical *imitatio*, with its concept of virtuosity as both a command of past techniques which possess continuous sanctions and a sensitivity to the unique demands of the present situation, provides a model of continuity in change. In the Humanists' literary experience the relation of one mode of time to another becomes the model for the relationship of self to self,[123] and historical awareness

---

[121] This is an archetypally rhetorical attitude, according to Vossler: "In dem Begriff *Convenientia*, das Passende, steckt als Voraussetzung der Gedanke an eine mechanische Tätigkeit des geschickten Zusammenfügens mechanisch getrennter Teile," *Poetische Theorien*, pp. 80-81.

[122] F. Flora, *Orfismo della parola*, Rocca San Casciano, 1953, p. 93; Grassi, *Verteidigung des individuellen Lebens*, p. 165.

[123] Thus Merleau-Ponty, *Phenomenology of Perception*, p. 426: "It is of the essence of time to be not only actual time, or time which

an intrinsic part of self-awareness; in *imitatio* the past is never totally efficacious, but the stress is always on the *relationship* to the past,—there is a tacit demand for reciprocity. Second, it is the function of eloquence to endow events with fame, and it is their rhetorical function of creating fame that gives the Humanists their insight that attribution of meaning is dynamic, not static—that an event is only completed and fulfilled in the assessment of a congeries of future histories; that for each meaningful event its history is both a surrogate and its only existence. At the end of the *De infelicitate principum* Poggio remarks in standard fashion on the immortality of great deeds in literature and, reversing the Augustinian judgment, he claims that the men who despise this immortality, "*qui hanc vitam veluti peregrinantes transeunt, contemnamus*" (*Opera*, I, 419).[124] And later, in Machiavelli's discussion of Agathocles in the *Prince* it becomes clear that the only dimension of virtue is a temporal one; its only reality is in glory; virtue is not a timeless substance, but a historical meaning.[125]

There are, of course, qualifications of this view of rhetorical influence. Poggio demonstrates the complexity of the relation of rhetoric and historical consciousness: in some ways rhetorical ideas of language contribute to a truly creative realism and a free creative spirit; in other ways rhetoric and history resemble each other in their limitations. If modesty is the virtue of their epistemology, rhetorical and historical virtues are often modest ones—urbanity, *Weltklugheit*, a shrewdness in assessing experience, rather than a science of exact causal relationship, which results in proverbial maxims

---

flows, but also time which is aware of itself, for the explosion or dehiscence of the present towards a future is the archetype of the relationship of *self to self*, and it shows up an interiority or ipseity."

[124] See Guarino, "Epistola ad Poggium," *Prosatori latini*, p. 332: "Vitam enim esse non hanc qua morimur in dies, sed gloriam qua immortalitas propagatur sapientissimi diffiniunt, quam qui auferre conantur longe magis furti tenentur, quam qui pistillum aut sarculum interceperit."

[125] See Seidlmayer, "Petrarca, das Urbild des Humanisten," pp. 158-161; Gundolf, *Caesar: Geschichte seines Ruhms*, pp. 123-24.

rather than objective rules.[126] Further, there is a kind of irresolution, of fatal hesitation which characterizes many of their insights. Some classical rhetors classified history as of the epideictic mode, and Aristotle pointed out that this mode has for an audience an observer, *theoros*, who makes no decisions (*Rhetoric*, 1358a, 1391b). Sophistication as the constituent of rhetorical identity can be a negative capacity, an incomplete mental reaction. The exaggerated motility of the rhetorical cast of mind is not necessarily creative; Humanist modesty is often cynical, their critical function merely destructive, their wit truly mordant.[127]

Albertini properly remarks that there is no genuinely pragmatic historiography in Italian Humanism till Machiavelli:[128] just as Gorgias made the foundation of his pedagogy the belief that it is impossible to teach virtue, so Antonio Luschi warns Poggio in the dialogue *De varietate fortunae* that "*Omittamus . . . principum vitia, quae magis reprehendi, quam corrigi possunt*" (*Opera*, II, 569).[129] This pessimism is one facet of what A. Buck calls the crisis of Humanism, the shift from the *studia humanitatis*, from a theory of education as the building of a harmonious character to a preoccupation with superficialities, to a *Lebenskunst* in the pejorative sense. The weakness of the introspective moment, the emphasis on shrewdness in manipulating external factors in rhetorically oriented Humanism is an obvious factor in the disappearance of self-awareness as the basis of ethic, of

---

[126] Cf. Syme on the changes in Roman historiography, *Tacitus*, p. 196: "Sententiousness was inherent in the genre, but the tone changed. . . . It was a hard and bitter doctrine, using for texts the moral precepts turned upside down and converted into maxims of statecraft."

[127] Rhetoric thus contributes not only to a sensitivity to evanescence in the Renaissance, but to the evanescence itself; Cassirer, for instance, remarks that in Renaissance thought "Developments are quick and lively; no sooner is a point reached, a system established, than it is abandoned" (*Individual and the Cosmos*, p. 59).

[128] *Das florentinische Staatsbewusstsein*, Bern, 1955, pp. 304-06.

[129] Untersteiner, *The Sophists*, p. 182. See *Epistolae*, II, 195; III, 117, 212, for statements by Poggio on the lack of correlation between increased knowledge and increased virtue in many instances.

the change from a "responsible sense of relativity" to a cynical relativism.[130] In Poggio this at times appears as a failure of the inclusive identity which is the secret of successful political history as well as of successful politics; Poggio's apprehension of complexity seems to outrun his ability to integrate it, without distortion, into a meaningful whole; an example of this failure is his praise of Venice.

Further, when W. Welliver claims that ambiguity and obscurity are among the most prominent Florentine traits, he is trying to describe in this instance not useful flexibility but pejorative hesitation.[131] For the ambiguity of the rhetorical mental set is very fundamental indeed; rhetoric in its lack of rigor permits illogicality, inconsistency. Borinski sees Cicero as serving as the model for Italian Humanists of eccentric, not balanced, ambiguity, of the deeply divided personality.[132] In Petrarch, for example, the experience of personal force, of autarchy, subsists side by side with the experience of meaninglessness, of the staleness of existing categories accepted by his peers. The presence of this stale ontology simply enhances the isolation of the ego, and rhetoric, with its monumental unconcern for ontology, is unable to criticize it; gains in self-consciousness which are in part the result of rhetorical function are, on the other hand, all weapons which can be turned against the self, which increase vulnerability. A spent metaphysic acts as a limit on the intellect; anthropocentricism becomes eccentricity; autarchy becomes isolation. If paranoia is the occupational hazard of millenarianism, schizophrenia is the disease of Humanists. Seidlmayer describes Petrarch as oscillating between the two poles of solitude and the forum: a solitude where the self becomes the bounds of experience, and a forum where one must devote oneself to some detached, overarching ideal

---

[130] Buck, "Die Krise des humanistischen Menschenbildes bei Machiavelli," *Archiv f. Stud.*, 189 (1953), pp. 304-17. The phrase "responsible sense of relativity" comes from Erikson's "The Legend of Hitler's Childhood," *Childhood and Society*, New York, 1950, p. 355.

[131] *L'impero fiorentino*, Florence, 1957, p. 16.

[132] *Die Antike in Poetik*, pp. 107-08.

such as Rienzi's state.[133] R. Stadelmann sees the modern dilemma of the false extremes of absolute personality and absolute state, a dilemma which has inhibited the growth of creative politics, as beginning in the Renaissance; for him the Florentine city-state of the early fifteenth century was the last chance of constructing a healthy political situation, the last expression of the reciprocal unity of citizen and state, where the personality only reaches completion acting as citizen.[134] Poggio would appear to be a Machiavelli *manqué*: the rigidity of his harsh alternatives of rigid order or anomial turbulence contrasting with the fruitful paradoxes of Machiavelli, since Machiavelli is often most helpful where he is most ironic, most penetrating when he states his insights as problems.

Rhetorical ambiguity, then, can encourage disabling polarity, and it is obvious that Poggio is a pivotal figure in the history of Humanism, in that when he reiterates the ambiguities of Petrarch, he anticipates the tensions of the late fifteenth century. But perhaps here Poggio merely exemplifies the formal, ahistorical pattern of intellectualism in which intellectuals, merely by virtue of being an elite and thus "separate," tend to practice a cycle of withdrawal and return which has little relation either to real spiritual recruitment or genuine efficacy. Italian Humanist self-consciousness is not genuinely secure; the invectives demonstrate a care for the opinion of others that is both excessive and insatiable, and public eloquence often resolves itself into merely a search for private egoistic satisfaction. Their isolation is so forcefully experienced that obscenity becomes a kind of serious game. Poggio's lack of a solid political role during most of his life reinforced this rhetorical isolation, of course. But the dominance of the rhetorical subjunctive mode also involves a lack of an indicative mood, a too acute sense of the ephemeral and transitory, an inadequate sense of the present which

---

[133] "Petrarca, das Urbild des Humanisten," p. 152.
[134] Stadelmann also points out that the crisis in the Florentine state parallels that of the Sophistic Age ("Persönlichkeit und Staat in der Renaissance," p. 152).

at times can be one of the flaws of the Renaissance appreciation of the past. At the same time, the tangential nature of rhetoric is confusing, and the preoccupation with language tends to encourage a concern for the texts rather than for the phenomena as seen through the lattice of the text; this is related to the "learned" quality of Humanist culture which at times allows the past to dominate the present, and reduces the classics to erudition, and history to philology.

But if Poggio's rhetorical and historical virtues seem to be those of a voyeur, rather than of a hero, perhaps it is because Poggio wishes to invoke compassion, rather than action, with his moral-historical treatises. Vulnerability is an external sign of internal understanding. It is a historical half-truth to appreciate only the positive lessons of the past; it is necessary also to be dissatisfied, to recognize the present's difficulties as historical failures. History has a permissive, not a dogmatic, tone; according to Max Weber, it is able to teach us only what not to do,—it cannot find your truth but it teaches to avoid error. The lucidity which is the aim of the rhetorical-historical temper is an ethical vigilance, not a system.[135] History as the interrogation of the past is an achievement only of "an age which has eaten of the tree of knowledge";[136] there is a shared pessimism of rhetoric and history: both posit the universality of the human predicament without positing any extra-verbal referend—any permanence or truth—capable of extricating man completely from this fragility.

The tangential nature of rhetoric can provide a model for the simultaneous detachment and commitment of the historian, the peculiar double focus which is both disturbing and functional. And even rhetorical solipsism could furnish a reason why historians so often provide the most coherent and therefore the best expressions of the style and tone of their own age; rhetorical self-reliance recognizes the paradoxical coexistence of free choice and limitation, and thus frees the author from the dogmatic presence of tradition.

[135] Ricoeur, *Histoire et vérité*, p. 173.
[136] Merleau-Ponty, *Les aventures de la dialectique*, p. 31.

But all three dialectical modes in the rhetorical *impalcatura* —reciprocity of aesthetic method, duality of political insight, ethical ambiguity—contribute to a very basic appreciation of movement: to the notion of historical activity as both bond and free, and of historiographical activity as the definition of the significant interaction of past and present.

INDEX

Index

cursus, 49, 81
Curtius, E. R., 23n, 126n
Cusa, Nicholas of, *see* Cusanus
Cusanus, Nicolaus, 45 and n, 51, 90 and n, 92n, 93, 162n, 184-85 and n
cyclicism, 98, 139

Dal Pra, M., 45n
Dante, 45 and n, 55n, 57, 89n, 95 and n, 102n, 109-110, 119, 120n, 160
Dazzi, M., 80n, 118n
debate, 7, 18, 64, 111, 161; historical structure and rhetorical, 131-33, 138f, 173-76, 184
De Bruyne, E., 49n, 71n
deception, history and linguistic, 32, 47, 165f, 171, 177f, 182. *See also apate*
decorum, 27-30, 67f, 79, 82 and n, 96, 97, 100, 114, 160, 164 and n, 176, 179-80, 183, 186
deliberative rhetoric, 133, 135
Demosthenes, 109
Dempf, A., 36n
Descartes, R., 158 and n
detachment, ethics and rhetorical, 20, 38, 145, 155f, 182-83, 192f
dialectic: historical (Hegelian), 7, 131, 173, 199; and aesthetics in Gorgias, 15; and eristic in Plato, 20; and rhetoric in Cicero, 29-30; Scholastic, 34-35, 57; and rhetoric, 60, 69 and n, 133 and n, 158-59; political, 172; *See also* logic
dialogue, 64, 109, 170; as historical method, 19, 125f, 129 and n, 142-43, 174-76, 184; and dialectic in Plato, 20; in Cicero, 30. *See also* debate
dictamen, 117. *See also ars dictaminis*
Diels-Kranz, *Die Fragmente der Vorsokratiker*, 11n
Dionysius of Halicarnassus, 16n
disponibilità, 90 and n, 142 and n
Dominici, Giovanni, 52n, 57
doxa, 13

duality, of rhetorical influence, 115, 133, 199
Dürer, Albrecht, 186n
Dupréel, E., 10n, 14n

Eco, U., 49n, 71n
eikos, 6, 12
elegantia, 54, 82 and n, 114
elites, intellectual, 106-07, 142, 197
eloquence: and wisdom in Cicero, 30, 54 and n; in Salutati, 53f; and amorality, 55f; infinite range of, 56-57; and voluntarism, 58-59; and power, 58f, 72-73; and history, 61f; and immortality, 86; form and content in Humanist, 98-99; Florentine, 104f; public, 113; and liberty, 116f; and philosophy, 126-27; and wit, 191
emphasis, 25 and n
enargeia, 25 and n, 76
Ephorus (Hellenistic historian), 25n
epideictic, 25, 133f, 179, 195
epieikeia, 14. *See also* equity
epistemology: and rhetoric, 5-6, 9f, 10f, 29, 33-34, 37-39, 44f, 87f, 157f, 188f, 194; and aesthetics, 9, 11f; and history, 26, 37-39, 86f, 136, 156f, 185f
equity: in Thucydides, 17f; in Bruni, 139-40. *See also epieikeia*
Erasmus, 74
Erikson, E., 60 and n, 92 and n, 196n
eristic, 20, 142, 173-76
eruditio, 72n
ethics: and form, 55f, 74f, 78f, 82, 85; and historical judgments, 129f; typology of, 135f; and ambiguity, 153f; history and ambiguity in, 176f, 183; and urbanity, 192; and Humanist pessimism, 194f
exemplum, 76, 186

Fabius (Hellenistic historian), 27n
fabula, 75

Index